Picture BIBLE™ Devotions

Edited by Jeannie Harmon

Chariot Victor Publishing
A Division of Cook Communications

Chariot Victor Publishing
A division of Cook Communications, Colorado Springs, Colorado 80918
Cook Communications, Paris, Ontario
Kingsway Communications, Eastbourne, England

PICTURE BIBLE DEVOTIONS
© 1991, 1998 by David C. Cook Publishing Co.

Edited by Jeannie Harmon
Art Directed by Andrea Boven
Cover design by Paz Design Group
Internal design/production by Paul Mouw and Associates, Glen Ellyn, IL

Scriptures quoted from the *International Children's Bible*, New Century Version, copyright ©
1983, 1986, 1988 by Word Publishing, Dallas, Texas 75039. Used by permission.

Illustrations from *The Picture Bible* © 1978 by David C. Cook Publishing Co.

Previously published as *Awesome Real-Life Bible Devotions for Kids*

First printing, 1991
Printed in the United States of America
02 01 00 99 98   5 4 3 2 1

What's in This Book?!

Devotions from the Old Testament

What's in This Book?!

Devotions from the New Testament

SPENDING time with God is a totally awesome addition to any day. Most of us, though, don't know how to have devotions or pray or understand the Bible. It's all so confusing.

Awesome Real-Life Devotions for Kids is the answer to the problem. Everything you need is right here. We'll take you through the Old and New Testaments in a fun way, breaking them into bite-size pieces so that you'll understand God's Word, get some direction on how He wants you to live, and get some good ideas on how to put all this into practice.

Each devotion is two or three pages long and chock full of exciting things to look at and read. Look for these special features:

• **Character Value Box:** The key idea for each devotion is shown in a black box. This tells you what the main theme will be for that devotion. It's a principle from God's Word to help you strengthen your relationship with God, others, and yourself.

Confidence

• **Bible Stories:** All Bible stories are taken from the *International Children's Bible,* an easy-to-understand version of God's Word for kids like you. Look for the large bold type and you'll know that the story begins here.

THEN the Lord God took dust from the ground and formed man from it. The Lord breathed the breath of life into the man's nose. And the man became a living person. . . .

¹⁵The Lord God put the man in the garden of Eden to care for it and work it. . . .

¹⁸Then the Lord God said, "It is not good for the man to be alone. I will make a helper who is right for him."

¹⁹From the ground God formed every wild animal and every bird

• **Pictures:** Each devotion will come alive with colorful illustrations taken from *The Picture Bible.* A story is always easier to understand if you have pictures to give you a feel for what is going on.

• **Key Verse:** Each devotion has a key verse that will help you develop the character trait given in that day's devotion. You will want to learn these verses by memory so that when you need help, God's Words will be in your mind to help you through the situation.

Remain in me o
follow my teach
you do this, th
can ask for anything
and it will be given

• **Something To Think About:** These questions and ideas will help you to think about situations in your own life that might be similar to those in the Bible story.

? God created a beautiful place f
• animals to have fun with, and
Everything he needed, right? So v

? Was God able to take care of /
• do it?

? Think of one area where you ne
• need help with choosing friends
and to the teacher on time, or reso

• **Prayer:** Each devotion has a short prayer to get you started talking to God. Begin by reading the prayer with your devotion. You'll find that talking to God can be like talking to your best

Thanks, God, for giving me the promise n the Bible that if I elieve in You, You'll help me when I need help. I put my confidence in You. Amen.

friend. You'll want to add your own words to tell God other important things that are going on in your life.

• **Journal entry:** This special space is for you to think of ideas of how you can apply the main idea of the devotion to your everyday life. Each journal entry is different from the one before, so you'll have many opportunities to be creative!

DRAW A PIC
IN YOUR LIFE
LOUD WHAT y
HELP YOU WIT
JUST AS YOU

We've given you everything you need to get started. Now, it's up to you! You can read one every day, or one a week, or whenever you choose. We're sure that you'll discover that getting into God's Word can be an awesome experience! . . . Not only for today, but for every day throughout your life.

*HIS JEWISH NAME IS SAUL.

You are young, . . .
but do not let anyone treat you as if you were not important.
Be an example to show the believers how they should live.
Show them . . .
with your words,
with the way you live,
with your love,
with your faith,
and with your pure life.

I Timothy 4:12

Adam Needed Help!

IN THE BEGINNING, GOD CREATED
EVERYTHING. EACH DAY FOR SIX
DAYS HE ADDED SOMETHING
TO MAKE THE WORLD MORE
COMPLETE. HIS CREATION
PLAN WAS:

> DAY 1--HEAVEN AND EARTH
> LIGHT AND DARKNESS
> DAY AND NIGHT
> DAY 2--SKY AND CLOUDS
> DAY 3--EARTH AND SEAS
> TREES, PLANTS,
> FRUITS, AND
> FLOWERS
> DAY 4--SUN, MOON,
> AND STARS,
> THE SEASONS
> DAY 5--FISH
> AND
> BIRDS
> DAY 6--ANIMALS
> FIRST MAN
> AND FIRST
> WOMAN

ON THE SEVENTH DAY,
GOD RESTED.
GOD TOLD ADAM
THAT IT WAS HIS
JOB TO NAME ALL
THE ANIMALS AND
TEND THE GARDEN OF
EDEN. TAKING CARE OF
ALL OF THIS WAS A BIG
JOB. HE NEEDED HELP! . . .

Morell ▐▐▶

THEN the Lord God took dust from the ground and formed man from it.

The Lord breathed the breath of life into the man's nose. And the man became a living person. . . .

15The Lord God put the man in the garden of Eden to care for it and work it. . . .

18Then the Lord God said, "It is not good for the man to be alone. I will make a helper who is right for him."

19From the ground God formed every wild animal and every bird in the sky. He brought them to the man so the man could name them. Whatever the man called each living thing, that became its name. 20The man gave names to all the tame animals, to the birds in the sky and to all the wild animals. But Adam did not find a helper that was right for him. 21So the Lord God caused the man to sleep very deeply. While the man was asleep, God took one of the ribs from the man's body. Then God closed the man's skin at the place where he took the rib. 22The Lord God used the rib from the man to make a woman. Then the Lord brought the woman to the man.

23And the man said,

"Now, this is someone whose bones came from my bones.
Her body came from my body.
I will call her 'woman,'
because she was taken out of man."

From Genesis 2

? God created a beautiful place for Adam to live, lots of animals to have fun with, and plenty of good things to eat. Everything he needed, right? So why did Adam still need help?

? Was God able to take care of Adam's problem? How did He do it?

? Think of one area where you need God's help. Perhaps you need help with choosing friends, getting your homework done and to the teacher on time, or resolving a problem in your family.

> Remain in me and follow my teachings. If you do this, then you can ask for anything you want, and it will be given to you.
>
> John 15:7

Thanks, God, for giving me the promise in the Bible that if I believe in You, You'll help me when I need help. I put my confidence in You. Amen.

DRAW A PICTURE OF ONE NEED THAT YOU HAVE IN YOUR LIFE TODAY. THEN TELL GOD OUT LOUD WHAT YOUR NEED IS AND ASK HIM TO HELP YOU WITH THE SITUATION. TALK TO GOD JUST AS YOU TALK TO YOUR BEST FRIEND.

Who Me? . . . It Wasn't My Fault!

GOD TOOK ADAM AND EVE TO THE GARDEN OF EDEN AND SHOWED THEM THE BEAUTY AND FRUITFULNESS OF IT. GOD COMMANDED, "YOU MUST NOT EAT FRUIT FROM THE TREE THAT IS IN THE MIDDLE OF THE GARDEN. YOU MUST NOT EVEN TOUCH IT, OR YOU WILL DIE."

NOW the snake was the most clever of all the wild animals the Lord God had made. One day the snake spoke to the woman. He said, "Did God really say that you must not eat fruit from any tree in the garden?" ²The woman answered . . . "God told us, 'You must not eat fruit from the tree that is in the middle of the garden. . . . or you will die.'" ⁴But the snake said to the woman, "You will not die. ⁵God knows that if you eat the fruit from that tree, you will learn about good and evil. Then you will be like God!" ⁶The woman saw that the tree was beautiful. She saw that its fruit was good to eat and that it would make her wise. So she took some of its fruit and ate it. She also gave some of the fruit to her husband, and he ate it. ⁷Then, it was as if the man's and the woman's eyes were opened. . . . ⁸Then they heard the Lord God walking in the garden. . . . during the cool part of the day. And the man and his wife hid from the Lord God among the trees in the garden. ⁹But the Lord God called to the man. The Lord said, "Where are you?" ¹⁰The man answered, "I heard you walking in the garden. I was afraid. . . . So I hid." ¹¹God said to the man, " . . . Did you eat fruit from that tree? I commanded you not to eat from that tree." ¹²The man said, "You gave this woman to me. She gave me fruit from the tree. So I ate it." ¹³Then the Lord God said to the woman, "What have you done?" She answered, "The snake tricked me. So I ate the fruit."

From Genesis 3

12

❓ What lie did the snake tell Eve? Did she believe the lie?

❓ How did she get Adam involved? When God asked them about eating the fruit, what did Adam and Eve tell God?

❓ All of us do things we shouldn't. Sometimes we choose to make bad choices; sometimes we don't plan on doing wrong, it just happens. In either case, we need to be honest enough to say, "I did wrong. I'm sorry."

'M AFRAID!

QUICK—LET'S HIDE!

🔑 God, examine me and know my heart. Test me and know my thoughts. See if there is any bad thing in me. Lead me in the way you set long ago.

Psalm 139:23, 24

Prayer: Thank You, God, for loving me even when I don't always make right choices. Help me to be honest enough to say "I'm sorry" when I'm wrong. Thanks for listening.
Amen.

BECAUSE ADAM AND EVE DISOBEYED GOD, GOD TOLD EVE THAT SHE WOULD HAVE GREAT PAIN WHEN SHE DELIVERED A BABY AND THAT HER HUSBAND WOULD RULE OVER HER. HE TOLD ADAM HE WOULD HAVE TO SWEAT AND WORK HARD TO GET FOOD, AND LATER WHEN HE DIED, HIS BODY WOULD GO BACK TO DUST. ADAM AND EVE ALSO HAD TO LEAVE THE BEAUTIFUL GARDEN. GOD PUT ANGELS AND A FLAMING SWORD AT THE ENTRANCE TO KEEP THEM OUT. THE RESULTS OF SIN ARE ALWAYS BAD.

THINK OF A BAD CHOICE YOU MADE THIS WEEK. MAYBE YOU HURT SOMEONE'S FEELINGS, BORROWED SOMETHING YOU SHOULDN'T HAVE, OR SAID SOMETHING THAT WAS ONLY HALF TRUE. HOW DOES THINKING ABOUT THAT TIME MAKE YOU FEEL RIGHT NOW? WRITE A SHORT NOTE TO GOD TELLING HIM HOW YOU FEEL AND WHAT YOU PLAN TO DO TO MAKE THINGS RIGHT.

DEAR GOD,

LOVE,

14

Anger!!!

ADAM AND EVE HAD TWO BOYS, CAIN AND ABEL. AS THEY GREW UP, ABEL TOOK CARE OF THE SHEEP AND CAIN BECAME A FARMER. WHEN IT WAS TIME TO GIVE A SACRIFICE TO THE LORD . . .

CAIN brought a gift to God. He brought some food from the ground. [4]Abel brought the best parts of his best sheep. The Lord accepted Abel and his gift. [5]But God did not accept Cain and his gift. Cain became very angry and looked unhappy.

[6]The Lord asked Cain, "Why are you angry? Why do you look so unhappy? [7]If you do good, I will accept you. But if you do not do good, sin is already to attack you. Sin wants you. But you must rule over it."

[8]Cain said to his brother Abel, "Let's go out into the field." So Cain and Abel went into the field. Then Cain attacked his brother Abel and killed him.

[9]Later, the Lord said to Cain, "Where is your brother Abel?"

Cain answered, "I don't know. Is it my job to take care of my brother?"

[10]Then the Lord said, "What have you done? Your brother's blood is on the ground. That blood is like a voice that tells me what happened. [11]And now you will be cursed in your work with the ground. It is the same ground where your brother's blood fell. Your hands killed him. [12]You will work the ground. But it will not grow good crops for you anymore. You will wander around on the earth."

From Genesis 4

GAVE GOD AS MUCH AS E DID! I'LL GET EVEN!

Out of Control!!!!!

AT LAST—WE'RE ALONE! THIS IS MY CHANCE!

? What do you think God meant when He told Cain that he must "rule over" being tempted to commit sin? Did Cain have a choice whether or not to kill his brother?

? Self-discipline is the willingness to correct or control yourself in order to make yourself a better person. Was Cain self-disciplined? How could he have changed the story's sad ending?

? Most of the time we don't say to ourselves, "I'm going to murder my brother." Usually sin starts as a small seed — such as Cain's being jealous because Abel's gift was accepted. Cain's out-of-control anger grew until he committed murder. Do you have an area in your life where you feel things are getting out of control?

More!▐▐▐▶

I—I DON'T KNOW. AM I MY BROTHER'S KEEPER?

GOD KNOWS I HAVE KILLED ABEL!

> Don't be proud but accept God's teaching that is planted in your hearts.... Do what God's teaching says; do not just listen and do nothing.
>
> James 1:21b, 22

Prayer: Dear God, sometimes I'm not very disciplined and don't do what Your Word tells me to do. Remind me when I'm in confusing situations to act as You would act, and say what You would say. Amen.

WHAT IS AN AREA OF YOUR LIFE WHERE YOU THINK THINGS ARE GETTING OUT OF CONTROL? SOME EXAMPLES ARE: YOU'RE NOT GETTING ALONG WITH SOMEONE IN CLASS, HOMEWORK IS NOT TURNED IN ON TIME, YOU'RE ARGUING MORE WITH MOM OR DAD LATELY, ETC. WRITE DOWN ONE THING YOU COULD DO TO HELP THE SITUATION.

MY PROBLEM IS: _____

ONE THING I COULD DO TO HELP MAKE THE SITUATION BETTER IS: _____

YOU AND YOUR BEST FRIEND ARE ENTERING DIFFERENT PROJECTS IN YOUR SCHOOL'S SCIENCE FAIR. EVERYONE LOVES HIS PROJECT, INCLUDING THE TEACHER (WHO USED TO BE YOUR FAVORITE TEACHER!). NO ONE GIVES YOUR PROJECT EVEN A SECOND GLANCE. YOU KNOW IT WON'T WIN ANY PRIZES. WHAT IS ONE THING THAT YOU COULD DO TO STOP THIS INCIDENT FROM RUINING YOUR FRIENDSHIP?

Lord, You Want Me to Build What?

PEOPLE ON THE EARTH WERE VERY WICKED. VIOLENCE WAS EVERYWHERE. GOD BECAME SORRY THAT HE MADE HUMAN BEINGS AND DECIDED TO DESTROY EVERY LIVING THING, EXCEPT FOR NOAH. NOAH WALKED WITH GOD AND WAS A GOOD MAN. GOD TOLD HIM

"**BUILD** a boat of cypress wood for yourself. Make rooms in it and cover it inside and outside with tar. ¹⁵This is how big I want you to build the boat: 450 feet long, 75 feet wide and 45 feet high. ¹⁶Make an opening around the top of the boat. Make it 18 inches high from the edge of the roof down. Put a door in the side of the boat. Make an upper, middle and lower deck in it. ¹⁷I will bring a flood of water on the earth. I will destroy all living things that live under the sky. This includes everything that has the breath of life. Everything on the earth will die. ¹⁸But I will make an agreement with you. You, your sons, your wife and your sons' wives will all go into the boat. ¹⁹Also, you must bring into the boat two of every living thing, male and female. Keep them alive with you. ²⁰There will be two of every kind of bird, animal and crawling thing. They will come to you to be kept alive. ²¹Also gather some of every kind of food. Store it on the boat as food for you and the animals." ²²Noah did everything that God commanded him.

More

From Genesis 6

17

POOR NOAH, HE THINKS HE CAN FLOAT A BOAT ON DRY LAND.

WHAT WILL HE THINK OF NEXT?

? This must have seemed like a strange request to Noah—build a big boat for you, your family, and animals from all over the world! Yet Noah obeyed. What questions might Noah have asked God about the job he was asked to do?

? Noah probably did not fully understand what lay ahead, yet he obeyed without complaining. He could have said, "No way, God. I'm not into boat making." What could have happened if Noah had chosen not to obey God? What would have happened to his family?

? Imagine that you are the captain of a sports team at school and one of the players decides not to obey your instructions. What could happen?

Help me understand, so I can obey your teachings. I will obey them with all my heart. Ps. 119:34

Dear Lord, help me to be obedient to those who You've placed over me. Help me to understand that they are helping me to become more like You in my actions. Amen.

SOMETIMES IT'S HARD FOR US TO OBEY A PARENT OR A TEACHER. WE DON'T SEE PROBLEMS THAT COULD COME UP DOWN THE LINE AS A RESULT OF OUR CHOOSING NOT TO OBEY. THINK OF ONE AREA WHERE IT IS HARD FOR YOU TO OBEY (KEEPING YOUR ROOM CLEAN, DOING HOMEWORK, NOT FIGHTING WITH YOUR BROTHER OR SISTER, ETC.).
THEN ANSWER THE FOLLOWING:

I HAVE TROUBLE OBEYING WHEN:

_____

IF I OBEY, THIS IS WHAT HAPPENS:

_____

IF I DON'T OBEY, THIS IS WHAT HAPPENS:

_____

TALK TO GOD ABOUT YOUR CHOICES AND PLAN TO BE OBEDIENT NEXT TIME WITH HIS HELP.

19

The Only Boat in the Whole World

WHEN ALL THE ANIMALS WERE GATHERED TO THE ARK AND NOAH AND HIS FAMILY WERE INSIDE, GOD SHUT THE DOOR. RAIN FELL FOR FORTY DAYS AND FORTY NIGHTS. ALL THE EARTH WAS COVERED WITH WATER.

LOOK! THE GREAT DOOR OF NOAH'S ARK IS CLOSING!

YES...IT'S SHUT BY A INVISIB! HAND

? Noah, his family, and all the animals were in a boat—the only boat in the entire world. They had no place to land because everything was covered with water. What are some things that Noah might have been afraid of during this time?

? Noah must have felt that God was taking a long time to clear away the water. What could Noah learn while he waited in the boat?

? Sometimes waiting is scary because we don't know how things are going to work out. What is an answer from God you are waiting for?

WATER flooded the earth for 40 days.

As the water rose, it lifted the boat off the ground. [18]The water continued to rise, and the boat floated on the water above the earth. [19]The water rose so much that even the highest mountains under the sky were covered by it. [20]The water continued to rise until it was more than 20 feet above the mountains. . . . [24]And the waters continued to cover the earth for 150 days.

Chapter 8But God remembered Noah and all the wild animals and tame animals with him in the boat. God made a wind blow over the earth. And the water went down. [2]The underground springs stopped flowing. And the clouds in the sky stopped pouring down rain. [3-4]The water that covered the earth began to go down. After 150 days the water had gone down so much that the boat touched land again. It came to rest on one of the mountains of Ararat. This was on the seventeenth day of the seventh month. [5]The water continued to go down. By the first day of the tenth month the tops of the mountains could be seen.

[6]Forty days later Noah opened the window he had made in the boat. [7]He sent out a raven. It flew here and there until the water had dried up from the earth. [8]Then Noah sent out a dove. This was to find out if the water had dried up from the ground. [9]The dove could not find a place to land because water still covered the earth. So it came back to the boat. Noah reached out his hand and took the bird. And he brought it back into the boat.

[10]After seven days Noah again sent out the dove from the boat. [11]And that evening it came back to him with a fresh olive leaf in its mouth. Then Noah knew that the ground was almost dry. [12]Seven days later he sent the dove out again. But this time it did not come back.

From Genesis 7, 8

AN OLIVE BRANCH! THAT MEANS SOME LAND MUST BE DRY AGAIN.

If we see what we are waiting for, then that is not really hope. People do not hope for something they already have. But we are hoping for something that we do not have yet. We are waiting for it patiently.

Romans 8:24b, 25

Lord, thank You for knowing what is best for me. Help me to be patient and wait for things to happen when You want them to. Amen.

Morell

21

DRAW AN OUTLINE OF A BOAT. ON THE INSIDE OF YOUR BOAT WRITE ONE PROBLEM THAT YOU WOULD LIKE GOD TO ANSWER FOR YOU. THEN TALK TO HIM ABOUT IT. .

THEN **God said to Noah,** [16]**"You and your wife, your sons and their wives should go out of the boat.** [17]Bring every animal out of the boat with you—the birds, animals and everything that crawls on the earth. Let them have many young ones and let them grow in number."

[20]. . .Then Noah built an altar to the Lord. Noah took some of all the clean birds and animals. And he burned them on the altar as offerings to God. [21]The Lord was pleased with these sacrifices. He said to himself, "I will never again curse the ground because of human beings. Their thoughts are evil even when they are young. But I will never again destroy every living thing on the earth as I did this time.

Chapter 9 And God said, "I am making an agreement between me and you and every living creature that is with you. It will continue from now on. This is the sign: [13]I am putting my rainbow in the clouds. . . . [14]When I bring clouds over the earth, a rainbow appears in the clouds. [15]Then I will remember my agreement. It is between me and you and every living thing. Floodwaters will never again destroy all life on the earth.

WHEN YOU GET AN ANSWER, WRITE THE DATE HERE.

From Genesis 8, 9

The Promise of a Rainbow

AS SOON AS NOAH LEAVES THE ARK, HE BUILDS AN ALTAR. HERE HE THANKS GOD FOR HIS CARE AND ASKS GOD'S GUIDANCE IN HELPING NOAH AND HIS FAMILY TO MAKE A NEW START. THEN GOD MAKES A PROMISE TO NOAH AND TO ALL HIS CHILDREN, FOREVER...

? When Noah and his family left the ark, what things were they thankful for?

? What promise did God make to Noah? What sign did He give Noah that we might see today on a rainy day?

? Think of four things that you can thank God for. (Think of your family, your friends, your church, your home, etc., when making your list.)

More⏵

God, thank You for doing so many wonderful things for me. I love You. Amen.

WRITE A THANK-YOU NOTE TO GOD FOR SOMETHING YOU ARE THANKFUL FOR.

DEAR GOD,
    THANK YOU FOR _____

_____

_____

_____

_____

_____

_____

        LOVE,

Leave Everything and Go

AFTER THE PERIOD OF MOURNING...

WHAT ARE YOUR PLANS FOR THE TRIBE, ABRAHAM?

NAHOR, GOD HAS CALLED ME TO TAKE MY FAMILY—LOT'S, TOO, IF HE WISHES, AND LEAVE HARAN.

THEN the Lord said to Abram,* "Leave your **country,** your relatives and your father's family. Go to the land I will show you. ²I will make you a great nation, and I will bless you. I will make you famous. And you will be a blessing to others. ³I will bless those who bless you. I will place a curse on those who harm you. And all the people on earth will be blessed through you."

LEAVE? WHERE ARE YOU GOING?

I DON'T KNOW EXACTLY—BUT GOD PROMISED TO SHOW ME AND I HAVE FAITH THAT HE WILL LEAD ME.

⁴So Abram left Haran as the Lord had told him. And Lot went with him. At this time Abram was 75 years old. ⁵Abram took his wife Sarai, his nephew Lot and everything they owned. They took all the servants they had gotten in Haran. They set out from Haran, planning to go to the land of Canaan. In time they arrived there.

⁶Abram traveled through that land. He went as far as the great tree of Moreh at Shechem. The Canaanites were living in the land at that time. ⁷The Lord appeared to Abram. The Lord said, "I will give this land to your descendants." So Abram built an altar there to the Lord, who had appeared to him. *From Genesis 12*

More⫸

* *Later God changed Abram's name to Abraham.*

25

I TELL YOU ABRAHAM IS CRAZY. GOING SOMEPLACE...BUT HE DOESN'T KNOW WHERE!

? God asked Abraham to leave his home, his relatives, all that was familiar to him. How do you think Abraham felt about making a move like that?

? Did God promise Abraham any good rewards for taking such a big step? What were they?

? As we grow older we have to face new experiences. Sometimes that's scary. Think of something you have done that seemed scary at first, but once you did it, you felt good about yourself. (Some examples could be: learning to ride your bike, diving off the diving board, being up to bat for the first time, or moving to a new school.)

Trust the Lord with all your heart. Don't depend on your own understanding. Remember the Lord in everything you do. And he will give you success.

Proverbs 3:5, 6

MAKE A LIST OF THINGS YOU WOULD LIKE TO DO THAT YOU'VE NEVER DONE BEFORE. HERE ARE SOME EXAMPLES TO GET YOU STARTED: WRITE TO SOMEONE IN A FOREIGN COUNTRY, LEARN TO PLAY A MUSICAL INSTRUMENT, MAKE FRIENDS WITH SOMEONE NEW AT SCHOOL, MAKE SOMETHING OUT OF WOOD, TAKE UP A NEW SPORT. NOW MAKE YOUR OWN LIST. ASK THE LORD TO HELP YOU DO ONE OF THE THINGS ON YOUR LIST THIS NEXT YEAR. THEN BELIEVE THAT HE WILL HELP YOU DO IT. (YOU MIGHT BE SURPRISED WHEN HE ANSWERS YOUR PRAYER!)

1

2

3

4

5

6

Thank You, God, for always being there to help me through the new experiences in my life. Help me to have the faith to trust You more each day. Amen.

27

A Bride for Isaac

WHEN ABRAHAM WAS OLD, HE CALLED HIS SERVANT TO HIS SIDE. HE MADE THE SERVANT VOW THAT HE WOULD GO TO THE COUNTRY OF ABRAHAM'S RELATIVES TO FIND A WIFE FOR HIS SON ISAAC. THE SERVANT TRAVELED TO THE LAND OF ABRAHAM'S FATHER AND THERE BY A WELL HE PRAYED TO THE LORD. . . .

ABRAHAM'S SERVANT REACHES HARAN IN THE EVENING. HE RESTS BY THE TOWN'S WELL AND SEES YOUNG WOMEN OF THE CITY COMING TO GET WATER.

O GOD, GIVE ME A SIGN! LET THE ONE WHO GIVES WATER TO ME AND MY CAMELS BE ISAAC'S BRIDE!

"LORD, you are the God of my master Abraham.

Allow me to find a wife for his son today. . . . ¹³Here I am, standing by the spring of water. The girls from the city are coming out to get water. ¹⁴I will say to one of the girls, 'Please put your jar down so I can drink.' Then let her say, 'Drink, and I will also give water to your camels.' If that happens, I will know she is the right one for your servant Isaac. And I will know that you have shown kindness to my master."

¹⁵Before the servant had finished praying, Rebekah came out of the city. . . . Rebekah was carrying her water jar on her shoulder. ¹⁶She was very pretty. She was a virgin; she had never had sexual relations with a man. She went down to the spring and filled her jar. Then she came back up. ¹⁷The servant ran to her and said, "Please give me a little water from your jar."

¹⁸Rebekah said, "Drink, sir." She quickly lowered the jar from her shoulder and gave him a drink. ¹⁹After he finished drinking, Rebekah said, "I will also pour some water for your camels." ²⁰So she quickly poured all the water from her jar into the drinking trough for the camels. Then she kept running to the well until she had given all the camels enough to drink. . . .

²⁶The servant bowed and worshiped the Lord.

From Genesis 24

> **I'LL BE GLAD TO—AND I'LL DRAW WATER FOR YOUR CAMELS, TOO.**

> **SHE IS THE ONE!**

? Did Rebekah know that if she watered the servant's camels, she would someday marry Isaac? How do you know?

? Besides giving the servant a drink, how did Rebekah show him kindness?

? We show kindness when we do nice things for people without expecting a reward or pay in return. Can you think of a time this past week when you were kind to someone or someone was kind to you? What happened?

Don't ever stop being kind and truthful. Let kindness and truth show in all you do.
Proverbs 3:3

Dear God, thank You for showing me by Your example how to be kind to others. Remind me to be kind to others each day. Amen.

Morell

MAKE A LIST OF THINGS THAT YOU COULD DO THIS WEEK TO SHOW KINDNESS TO OTHERS. (DON'T FORGET TO LIST THINGS THAT YOU COULD DO FOR MOM OR DAD, YOUR TEACHER, OR AN ELDERLY PERSON WHO LIVES ON YOUR BLOCK.)

I CAN BE KIND THIS WEEK BY:

_____

_____

_____

_____

_____

GOD HAS SURPRISES IN STORE FOR YOU WHEN YOU SHOW KINDNESS TO OTHERS.

Reverence

An Expensive Pot of Soup

WHICH ONE WILL RULE OUR TRIBE AFTER ISAAC?

ESAU—IT IS HIS BIRTHRIGHT BECAUSE HE WAS BORN FIRST.

ONE day Jacob was boiling a pot of vegetable soup. Esau came in from hunting in the fields. He was weak from hunger.

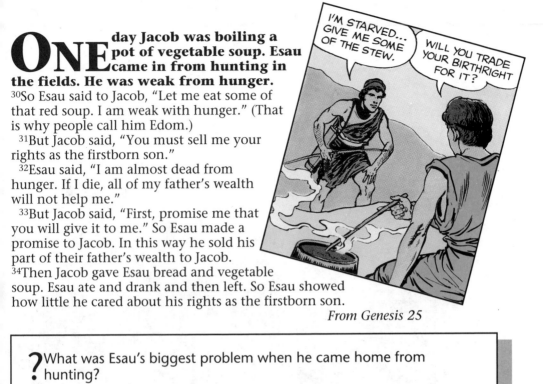

30So Esau said to Jacob, "Let me eat some of that red soup. I am weak with hunger." (That is why people call him Edom.)

31But Jacob said, "You must sell me your rights as the firstborn son."

32Esau said, "I am almost dead from hunger. If I die, all of my father's wealth will not help me."

33But Jacob said, "First, promise me that you will give it to me." So Esau made a promise to Jacob. In this way he sold his part of their father's wealth to Jacob.

34Then Jacob gave Esau bread and vegetable soup. Esau ate and drank and then left. So Esau showed how little he cared about his rights as the firstborn son.

From Genesis 25

? What was Esau's biggest problem when he came home from hunting?

? The firstborn son received twice the inheritance of any family member (Deut. 21:17), and he received special treatment from his father. Someday the son would become leader of the family. Do you think that Esau thought about what he'd be losing when he traded his inheritance for a bowl of soup?

? Esau didn't show reverence or respect for what was really important in his life. Sometimes we are like that when we don't show reverence for God and His house. We don't act as though the things of God are important to us. Name some ways that we don't show reverence to God. (Some examples are: talking while the pastor is preaching, passing notes in church, not picking up litter left in the pew, etc.)

Morell ➡

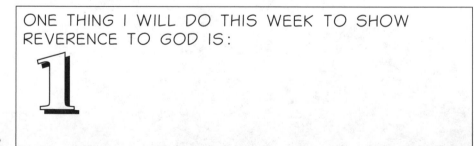

> "Remember my Sabbaths, and respect my Holy Place. I am the Lord."
> Leviticus 26:2

Dear God, thank You for loving me and giving me a church to go to. Help me always to reverence You and Your house. Amen

ONE THING I WILL DO THIS WEEK TO SHOW REVERENCE TO GOD IS:

1

The Secret Is Out

AS A BOY, JOSEPH WAS SOLD INTO SLAVERY BY HIS TEN BROTHERS. BUT GOD BLESSED JOSEPH AND HE BECAME THE GOVERNOR OF EGYPT. YEARS LATER WHEN FAMINE STRUCK THE LAND, HIS BROTHERS WENT TO EGYPT TO BUY GRAIN FROM JOSEPH. THEY DID NOT RECOGNIZE THE GOVERNOR AS BEING THEIR BROTHER JOSEPH. HE TESTS HIS BROTHERS TO SEE IF THEY HAVE CHANGED. AS A FINAL TEST, HE HAS HIS CUP PUT IN HIS YOUNGEST BROTHER'S GRAIN SACK.

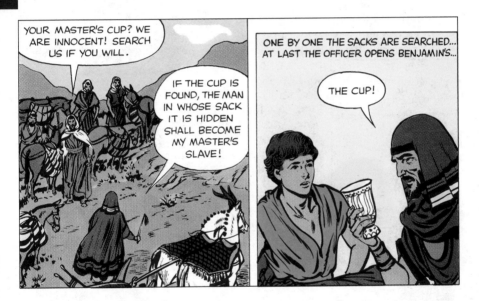

YOUR MASTER'S CUP? WE ARE INNOCENT! SEARCH US IF YOU WILL.

IF THE CUP IS FOUND, THE MAN IN WHOSE SACK IT IS HIDDEN SHALL BECOME MY MASTER'S SLAVE!

ONE BY ONE THE SACKS ARE SEARCHED... AT LAST THE OFFICER OPENS BENJAMIN'S...

THE CUP!

THE ONE IN WHOSE BAG THE CUP WAS FOUND SHALL BE MY SERVANT— THE REST OF YOU MAY RETURN TO YOUR FATHER.

IF BENJAMIN DOES NOT RETURN HOME, OUR FATHER WILL DIE OF GRIEF. LET ME BE YOUR SLAVE INSTEAD OF BENJAMIN.

THEY LISTENED IN SHOCK AS
HE SPOKE THESE WORDS.

GO! LEAVE ME ALONE WITH THESE MEN.

"**I AM** Joseph. Is my father still alive?" But the brothers could not answer him, because they were very afraid of him.

[4]So Joseph said to them, "Come close to me." So the brothers came close to him. And he said to them, "I am your brother Joseph. You sold me as a slave to go to Egypt. [5]Now don't be worried. Don't be angry with yourselves because you sold me here.

JOSEPH!

HE MUST HATE US... WHAT WILL HE DO NOW?

God sent me here ahead of you to save people's lives. [6]No food has grown on the land for two years now. And there will be five more years without planting or harvest. [7]So God sent me here ahead of you. This was to make sure you have some descendants left on earth. And it was to keep you alive in an amazing way. [8]So it was not you who sent me here, but God. God has made me the highest officer of the king of Egypt. I am in charge of his palace. I am the master of all the land of Egypt."

From Genesis 45

? If you were Joseph, what thoughts would have gone through your mind regarding your brothers during the long years between being sold and facing them as a governor? Did Joseph have the power to get revenge in the end?

? Why do you think it's so hard for us to forgive someone who has done something to hurt us?

? God's Word tells us that we are forgiven as we forgive others. How can we practice forgiving others?

I BELIEVE IT WAS GOD'S WILL THAT I CAME TO EGYPT TO SAVE YOUR LIVES— AND THE LIVES OF OTHERS— IN THIS FAMINE.

> If you forgive others for the things they do wrong, then your Father in heaven will also forgive you for the things you do wrong.
>
> Matthew 6:14

Thank You, God, for the many times You have forgiven me for things I've done wrong. Help me to be forgiving of others who hurt me with their words and actions. I want to be more like You. Amen.

THINK OF SOMETHING THAT HAPPENED THIS PAST WEEK THAT YOU NEED TO ASK FORGIVENESS FOR. PERHAPS YOU SAID OR DID SOMETHING TO HURT SOMEONE'S FEELINGS, OR YOU TOLD YOUR PARENTS SOMETHING THAT WASN'T TRUE. IN YOUR OWN WORDS, WRITE OUT HOW YOU WOULD ASK FOR FORGIVENESS FROM THAT PERSON. (BE SURE TO SAY SPECIFICALLY WHAT IT IS THAT YOU'VE DONE THAT NEEDS FORGIVE-NESS.) THEN ASK GOD TO HELP YOU GO TO THAT PERSON AND SAY THE WORDS YOU'VE WRITTEN DOWN.

Miriam and the Boat Basket

NEXT DAY THE MOTHER SETS ABO[UT] PREPARING A LITTLE BASKET.

KEEP WATCH, MIRIAM, I'M ALMOST FINISHED.

BUT **after three months, she was not able to hide the baby any longer.** So she got a basket made of reeds and covered it with tar so that it would float. She put the baby in the basket. Then she put the basket among the tall grass at the edge of the Nile River. 4The baby's sister stood a short distance away. She wanted to see what would happen to him.

LOOK—WHAT A STRANGE LITTLE BASKET! I WONDER WHAT'S INSIDE IT?

5Then the daughter of the king of Egypt came to the river. She was going to take a bath. Her servant girls were walking beside the river. She saw the basket in the tall grass. So she sent her slave girl to get it. 6The king's daughter opened the basket and saw the baby boy. He was crying, and she felt sorry for him. She said, "This is one of the Hebrew babies."

AT THIS POINT MIRIAM STEPS FORTH.

SHALL I FIND A HEBREW NURSE FOR THE BABY?

YES—BRING HER TO ME AS SOON AS YOU CAN.

7Then the baby's sister asked the king's daughter, "Would you like me to find a Hebrew woman to nurse the baby for you?"

8The king's daughter said, "Yes, please." So the girl went and got the baby's own mother.

[9]The king's daughter said to the woman, "Take this baby and nurse him for me. I will pay you." So the woman took her baby and nursed him. [10]After the child had grown older, the woman took him to the king's daughter. She adopted the baby as her own son. The king's daughter named him Moses, because she had pulled him out of the water.

From Exodus 2

? How did Miriam help both the princess and her mother?

? What might have happened to the baby if Miriam hadn't taken the initiative to speak up?

? Miriam saw an opportunity to take action and she did it quickly. Looking at the situation calmly, getting an idea for a solution, and then carrying it through was the key to Miriam saving her brother's life. Think about a problem your class is having at school (examples: the kid next to you won't stop talking, kids taking too long to come in from recess, kids getting into other kids' desks, etc.). What is one idea that you could contribute to help resolve the problem? (Share your idea with your teacher.)

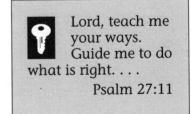

Lord, teach me your ways. Guide me to do what is right. . . .

Psalm 27:11

Lord, thank You for the abilities You have given me. Help me to think of ways to be more helpful when answers to problems are needed. Amen.

More

THINK OF ONE PROBLEM YOU ARE HAVING WITH A FAMILY MEMBER AT HOME. THINK OF ONE WAY THAT YOU COULD RESOLVE THE PROBLEM. DRAW A PICTURE OF YOUR IDEA.

SHARE YOUR IDEA WITH MOM OR DAD AND SEE IF YOU CAN ALL WORK TOGETHER TO RESOLVE THE PROBLEM.

That Bush Is on Fire!

HERE AM I!

ONE day Moses was taking care of Jethro's sheep. Jethro was the priest of Midian and also Moses' father-in-law. Moses led the sheep to the west side of the desert. He came to Sinai, the mountain of God. ²There the angel of the Lord appeared to Moses in flames of fire coming out of a bush. Moses saw that the bush was on fire, but it was not burning up. ³So Moses said, "I will go closer to this strange thing. How can a bush continue burning without burning up?"

⁴The Lord saw Moses was coming to look at the bush. So God called to him from the bush, "Moses, Moses!"

And Moses said, "Here I am."

⁵Then God said, "Do not come any closer. Take off your sandals. You are standing on holy ground. ⁶I am the God of your ancestors. I am the God of Abraham, the God of Isaac and the God of Jacob." Moses covered his face because he was afraid to look at God. ⁹I have heard the cries of the people of Israel. I have seen the way the Egyptians have made life hard for them. ¹⁰So now I am sending you to the king of Egypt. Go! Bring my people, the Israelites, out of Egypt!"

¹¹But Moses said to God, "I am not a great man! Why should I be the one to go to the king and lead the Israelites out of Egypt?"

¹²God said, "I will be with you. This will be the proof that I am sending you: You will lead the people out of Egypt. Then all of you will worship me on this mountain."

From Exodus 3

More▐▐▐▐▶

? What was unusual about the bush that Moses saw?

? Someone or something that is set apart—being consecrated or dedicated to God—is referred to as "holy" in the Bible. What did God call the place where Moses was standing?

? God called Moses to be set apart to do a special job. What was that job?

? We as Christians are set apart or chosen by God to do special things for Him. We are not usually asked to go before a king or president to bring deliverance to a nation, but there are many smaller ways that we can show Jesus' love to those around us. (Some examples are: doing something nice for a neighbor or your mom and dad!, writing a note to cheer someone up, baking cookies for a student away at school, etc.) What is one thing that you could do this week?

But you are chosen people. . . .You are a holy nation. You are a nation that belongs to God alone. God chose you to tell about the wonderful things he has done.

I Peter 2:9

Thank You, God, for making me special to You. Help me to think of ways to share Your love with others.

Amen.

PRETEND THAT YOU ARE STARTING A NEW CLUB--THE CHOSEN KIDS' CLUB (CKC). MAKE A LIST OF FRIENDS WHO COULD BELONG TO THE CLUB, AND BESIDE EACH NAME WRITE ONE THING THAT PERSON COULD DO TO SHARE JESUS' LOVE WITH SOMEONE ELSE.

1 _____

2 _____

3 _____

4 _____

5 _____

TALK TO YOUR FRIENDS AND SEE IF THEY WOULD LIKE TO START A CKC. THERE ARE LOTS OF WAYS THAT KIDS CAN BE INVOLVED IN SHARING GOD'S LOVE!

Songs of Joy

MEANWHILE...BACK IN PHARAOH'S PALACE...

IT WAS A MISTAKE TO LET THOSE HEBREW SLAVES GO—WHO WILL DO OUR WORK FOR US NOW?

IT ISN'T TOO LATE—LOOK!

THE ROUTE THEY TOOK WILL LEAD THEM INTO THIS TRAP.

EXCELLENT—WE'LL STRIKE AT ONCE. THOSE SLAVES WILL SOON BE BACK AT WORK—MAKING MORE BRICKS THAN BEFORE!

WHY DID YOU BRING US OUT HERE TO DIE?

IT'S YOUR FAULT, MOSES! WE'RE TRAPPED!

THE ISRAELITES FACED THE RED SEA. THE EGYPTIAN ARMY CHARGED THEM FROM BEHIND. WHAT COULD THE ISRAELITES DO? . . . MOSES HELD OUT HIS HAND OVER THE SEA AND THE LORD SPLIT THE SEA.

BUT **Moses answered, "Don't be afraid!** Stand still and see the Lord save you today. You will never see these Egyptians again after today.

AWED BY THE SIGHT, THE HEBREWS RUSH JOYFULLY ACROSS THE PATH IN THE SEA.

²¹Moses held his hand over the sea. All that night the Lord drove back the sea with a strong east wind. And so he made the sea become dry ground. The water was split. ²²And the Israelites went through the sea on dry land. A wall of water was on both sides. ²³Then all the king's horses, chariots and chariot drivers followed them into the sea. . . . ²⁷So Moses raised his hand over the sea. And at dawn the water became deep again. . . . ²⁸All the king's army . . . was covered. Not one of them survived. . . .

³⁰So that day the Lord saved the Israelites from the Egyptians. . . .³¹When the people of Israel saw the great power that the Lord had used against the Egyptians, they feared the Lord. And they trusted the Lord and his servant Moses.

Chapter 15Then Aaron's sister Miriam, who was a prophetess, took a tambourine in her hand. All the women followed her, playing tambourines and dancing. ²¹Miriam told them:

"Sing to the Lord
because he is worthy of great honor.
He has thrown the horse and its rider
into the sea."

From Exodus 14, 15

IN TERROR THEY TRY TO TURN BACK... BUT THE WIND DIES, AND THE WATERS RETURN. ALL OF PHARAOH'S MEN ARE CAUGHT IN THE RUSHING SEA.

? Did the Israelites have reason to rejoice? Why?

? The Israelites were glad that God kept them from being captured, but what else did they learn about God's ability to take care of them?

? It's easy to be happy when special things happen in our lives. But we can experience a deeper joy in our hearts when we realize that no matter what's happening—good or bad—God is there loving us, taking care of us. List two things that have happened in your life in the last month that maybe weren't so great. How did God help you through those times?

Thanks, God, for always being there when I need You—in good times and bad. Help me to feel Your joy and strength today. Amen.

Don't be sad. The joy of the Lord will make you strong.

Nehemiah 8:10b

WHEN I FEEL THE JOY OF THE LORD IN MY HEART, MY FACE LOOKS LIKE THIS: (DRAW A PICTURE OF YOUR FACE.)

Who's the Boss Here, Anyway?

MIRIAM **and Aaron began to talk against Moses,** who had married a Cushite. ²They said to themselves, "Is Moses the only one the Lord speaks through? Doesn't he speak through us?" And the Lord heard this.

³(Now Moses was very humble. He was the least proud person on earth.)

⁴So the Lord suddenly spoke to Moses, Aaron and Miriam. He said, "All three of you come to the Meeting Tent now." So they went. ⁵The Lord came down in a pillar of cloud. He stood at the entrance to the Tent. He called to Aaron and Miriam, and they both came near. ⁶He said, "Listen to my words:

THEN GOD SPEAKS FROM A CLOUD, AND TELLS THEM THAT HE HAS CHOSEN MOSES TO LEAD THE PEOPLE OF ISRAEL. WHEN THE CLOUD DISAPPEARS, MIRIAM AND AARON GET THE SHOCK OF THEIR LIVES.

¹⁰ Then Aaron turned toward Miriam. She was as white as snow. She had a harmful skin disease. ¹¹Aaron said to Moses, "Please, my master, forgive us for our foolish sin. . . ."

¹³So Moses cried out to the Lord, "God, please heal her!"

From Numbers 12

HEAL HER NOW, O GOD, I BEG OF THEE.

OH! NO! WHY DID I SPEAK AGAINST MOSES? HELP ME! HELP ME!

? How did God tell Miriam and Aaron who was really in charge?

? What resulted when they rebelled against Moses? What did they do to make things right with Moses?

? Sometimes it's easy to criticize the people who are in charge — our parents, teachers, youth leaders. We don't see all the different sides to every decision they have to make. Rather than rebel against that person, what is a better way to handle the situation?

Let us examine and look at what we have done. Then let us return to the Lord.
Lamentations 3:40

God, sometimes I rebel against those who You've put over me. Help me to repent and ask forgiveness when I don't act in a way that is pleasing to You. Amen.

Morell ▶

TAKE A MINUTE TO THINK ABOUT A TIME WHEN YOU REBELLED AGAINST SOMEONE WHO WAS IN CHARGE. HOW DID YOU HANDLE THE SITUATION? IF YOU FEEL THAT YOU SHOULD ASK FORGIVENESS FOR YOUR ACTIONS, WRITE DOWN TWO SENTENCES THAT YOU COULD TELL THAT PERSON.

_____
_____
_____
_____
_____
_____
_____
_____
_____
_____
_____

ASK GOD TO HELP YOU FIND AN OPPORTUNITY TO TELL HIM OR HER YOUR WORDS IN PERSON.

LOOK AT THAT CITY!

AND THE SIZE OF THOSE WALLS!

+

A FEW MILES AWAY...

LOOK— GIANTS!

THERE'S NOT A MAN IN OUR CAMP WHO COULD STAND UP AGAINST ONE OF THEM!

=

BUT THE OTHER TEN SCOUTS DISAGREE WITH JOSHUA AND CALEB.

NO! BY THE SIDE OF THOSE GIANTS WE ARE AS PUNY AS GRASSHOPPERS!

THEY'D WIPE US OUT TO A MAN—AND MAKE SLAVES OF OUR CHILDREN.

Spies in the Land

THEY **came back to Moses and Aaron** and all the Israelites at Kadesh. . . . "We went to the land where you sent us. It is a land where much food grows! Here is some of its fruit. ²⁸But the people who live there are strong. Their cities are walled and large."

³⁰Then Caleb told the people near Moses to be quiet. Caleb said, "We should go up and take the land for ourselves. We can do it."

³¹But the men who had gone with him said, "We can't attack those people. They are stronger than

we are." ³²And those men gave the Israelites a bad report about the land they explored. They said, "The land would eat us up. All the people we saw are very tall . . . We felt like grass-hoppers. And we looked like grass-hoppers to them."

Chapter 14 That night all the people in the camp began crying loudly . . . "We should have died in Egypt. Or we should have died in the desert. ³Why is the Lord bringing us to this land? We will be killed with swords. Our wives and children will be taken away. We would be better off going back to Egypt."

⁵Then Moses and Aaron bowed facedown in front of all the Israelites gathered there. . . . They tore their clothes. ⁷They said to all of the Israelites, "The land we went to explore is very good. ⁸If the Lord is pleased with us, he will lead us into that land. He will give us that land where much food grows. ⁹Don't turn against the Lord! Don't be afraid of the people in that land! We will chew them up. They have no protection, but we have the Lord. So don't be afraid of them."

From Numbers 13, 14

? What were the good things about the new land? . . . the bad things?

? Why was it easier to believe the bad report? Do you think it made a difference that more spies gave a bad report than the few who gave a good report?

? The spies told Moses that they felt like grasshoppers next to the men in Canaan. The devil tries to make us feel like the size of grasshoppers when we look at things we are afraid of (examples: being afraid of the dark, afraid to meet new people, afraid of being lonely or rejected). We feel like we will never get over our fear. But if we put our trust in God, He will help us conquer our fears. Think of one fear that you would like God to help you overcome.

If you trust the Lord, you will be safe.

Proverbs 29:25

Lord, thank You for caring about me. Help me to trust that You will take care of the "grasshoppers" in my life. Amen.

SOMETIMES IT'S EASIER TO BELIEVE A BAD REPORT AND NOT TRY SOMETHING NEW THAN TO TRUST GOD TO HELP YOU DO IT. THINK OF SOMETHING YOU WOULD LIKE TO DO BUT HAVE BEEN AFRAID TO TRY (EXAMPLES: TAKE SWIMMING LESSONS OR JOIN LITTLE LEAGUE). WRITE ONE GOOD THING AND ONE BAD THING THAT YOU WILL KNOW IF YOU DO THIS EXAMPLE:

SOMETHING NEW: TAKE SWIMMING LESSONS
SOMETHING GOOD: I WILL LEARN TO SWIM.
SOMETHING BAD: I WILL HAVE TO GO TO A LESSON EVERY MORNING FOR TWO WEEKS.

YOUR LIST:

SOMETHING NEW: _____

SOMETHING GOOD: _____

SOMETHING BAD: _____

Rahab Takes a Chance

WHEN JOSHUA'S TWO SPIES ENTER JERICHO THEY AVOID THE PUBLIC INN AND SEEK LODGING IN THE HOUSE OF A WOMAN NAMED RAHAB.

WE ARE STRANGERS IN YOUR CITY—MAY WE HAVE A ROOM HERE FOR THE NIGHT?

YES—

THE KING'S SOLDIER IS SUSPICIOUS OF THESE MEN! I'LL FIND OUT WHAT BRINGS THEM HERE.

WHEN THE KING FOUND OUT JOSHUA'S MEN WERE IN TOWN. HE SENT HIS MEN TO GO TAKE THEM PRISONER.

I HEAR FOOTSTEPS— QUICK—I'LL HIDE YOU ON THE ROOF.

More!

49

HIDE OUT IN THE MOUNTAINS FOR THREE DAYS—AFTER THAT IT WILL BE SAFE FOR YOU TO CROSS THE RIVER TO YOUR OWN CAMP.

WHEN THE ATTACK COMES, KEEP YOUR FAMILY IN THE HOUSE ...AND TIE THIS RED ROPE IN YOUR WINDOW SO OUR MEN WILL KNOW WHERE YOU LIVE!

RAHAB HID THE SCOUTS ON THE ROOF OF HER HOUSE. IN RETURN FOR PROTECTING THEM, RAHAB SAID . . .

"**So now, make me a promise before the Lord.** Promise that you will show kindness to my family just as I showed you kindness. Give me some proof that you will do this. [13]Promise me you will allow my family to live. Save my father, mother, brothers, sisters and all of their families from death."

[14]The men agreed. They said, "We will trade our lives for your lives. Don't tell anyone what we are doing. When the Lord gives us our land, we will be kind to you. You may trust us."

[15]The house Rahab lived in was built on the city wall. So she used a rope to let the men down through a window.

[18]"You are using a red rope to help us escape. When we return to this land, you must tie it in the window through which you let us down. Bring your father, mother, brothers and all your family into your house. [19]We can keep everyone safe who stays in this house. If anyone in your house is hurt, we will be responsible. If anyone goes out of your house and is killed, it is his own fault. We cannot be responsible for him."

Chapter 6 [6]Joshua saved Rahab the prostitute, her family and all who were with her. He let them live. This was because Rahab had helped the men he had sent to spy out Jericho. Rahab still lives among the Israelites today.

From Joshua 2, 6

? How did Rahab help the two men? What promise did the men give Rahab?

? Everything goes more smoothly when all cooperate to get the work done. In this case, the scouts and Rahab worked together to get necessary information back to the Israelite leader, Joshua. What would have happened if Rahab turned the scouts over to the king's men?

? Working together with a friend makes the job seem fun and takes less time. Ask a friend to help you work on a job around your house (examples: putting away the clean dishes, raking leaves, cleaning the garage, etc.). Write down the time it took for the two of you to do the job. Then go to your friend's house and help him or her with a similar job. Again, write the time down. Which job took the least amount of working-together time?

Dear God,
thank You for giving
me friends so that we can
work together to do things that
honor You. Help me always to be a
willing worker. Amen.

"I tell you that if two of you on earth agree about something, then you can pray for it. And the thing you ask for will be done for you by my Father in heaven."

Matthew 18:19

YOU CAN COOPERATE WITH A FRIEND IN DOING FUN THINGS, TOO. TOGETHER MAKE A CARD OR DRAW A PICTURE TO SEND SOMEONE IN YOUR CHURCH WHO HAS BEEN SICK. WHEN YOU'RE FINISHED WITH YOUR PROJECT, MAKE A LARGE ICE-CREAM SUNDAE OR ANOTHER TREAT THAT YOU CAN SPLIT. DRAW A PICTURE OF YOU AND YOUR FRIEND COOPERATING TOGETHER IN EATING!

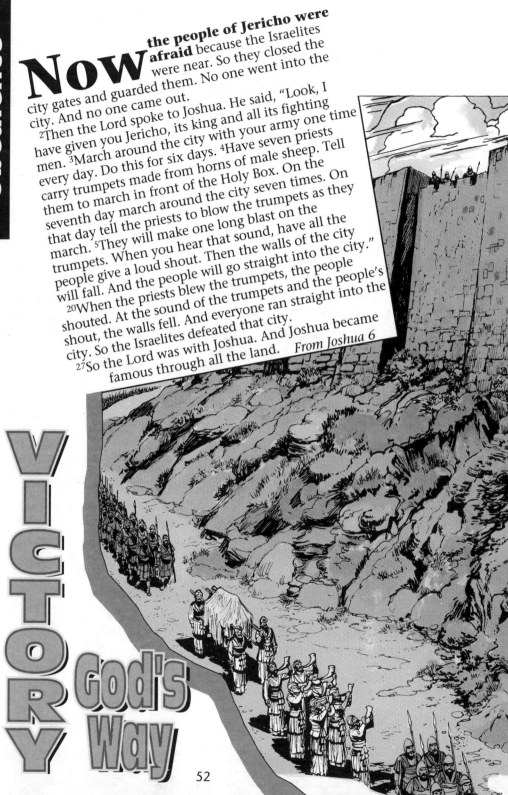

NOW the people of Jericho were **afraid** because the Israelites were near. So they closed the city gates and guarded them. No one went into the city. And no one came out. ²Then the Lord spoke to Joshua. He said, "Look, I have given you Jericho, its king and all its fighting men. ³March around the city with your army one time every day. Do this for six days. ⁴Have seven priests carry trumpets made from horns of male sheep. Tell them to march in front of the Holy Box. On the seventh day march around the city seven times. On that day tell the priests to blow the trumpets as they march. ⁵They will make one long blast on the trumpets. When you hear that sound, have all the people give a loud shout. Then the walls of the city will fall. And the people will go straight into the city." ²⁰When the priests blew the trumpets, the people shouted. At the sound of the trumpets and the people's shout, the walls fell. So the Israelites defeated that city. And everyone ran straight into the city. ²⁷So the Lord was with Joshua. And Joshua became famous through all the land. *From Joshua 6*

VICTORY God's Way

52

? After the first day of marching, what if Joshua would have said, "I'm tired! It's a long trip marching around Jericho. I think we'll only march one more day." What would have happened?

? Why were the instructions that God gave Joshua so unusual? (Remember: Joshua was the leader of the whole Israelite army.) Do soldiers normally fight this way?

? Following God's orders is very important to our Christian growth. If we want to be like Him, we have to do what He says in His Word. Sometimes the orders seem strange to us. For example, in Matthew 18:21, 22, how many times are we suppose to forgive someone who does something against us? How is this different from the way most people think?

More

> Help me obey your commands because that makes me happy.
>
> Psalm 119:35

Thank You, God, for teaching me Your ways. Help me to follow Your directions even when they seem strange to me. Amen.

LET'S INVESTIGATE OTHER THINGS GOD'S WORD TELLS US TO DO. LOOK UP THESE VERSES IN YOUR BIBLE AND THEN WRITE A SHORT SENTENCE ABOUT HOW YOU CAN FOLLOW GOD'S DIRECTIONS IN YOUR LIFE.

➪ MATTHEW 5:44--
I CAN PRAY FOR PEOPLE WHO GO AGAINST ME.

➪ MATTHEW 7:12--

➪ LUKE 6:38--

ASK GOD TO HELP YOU FOLLOW WHAT HIS WORD TELLS US TO DO.

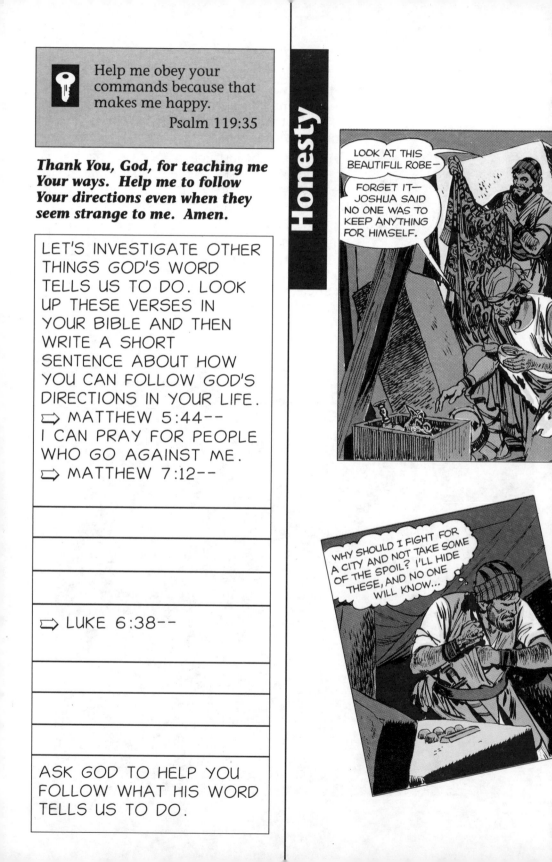

A Secret Hidden in a Tent

"DON'T take any of **the things that are to be destroyed** as an offering to the Lord. If you take them and bring them into our camp, then you yourselves will be destroyed. You will also bring trouble to all of Israel. ¹⁹All the silver and gold and things made from bronze and iron belong to the Lord. They must be saved for him."

Chapter 7But the people of Israel did not obey the Lord. There was a man from the tribe of Judah named Achan. . . . Achan kept some of the things that were to be given to the Lord. So the Lord became very angry at the Israelites.

From Joshua 6, 7

THAT NIGHT WHILE THE REST OF THE CAMP SLEEPS HE BURIES HIS STOLEN TREASURE.

THIS WILL HELP ME GET STARTED IN THIS NEW LAND.

HO, LOOK AT THEM RUN. THEY'RE AFRAID TO FIGHT.

SO THESE ARE THE BRAVE ISRAELITES WHO TOOK JERICHO!

LATER, WHEN THE ARMY ATTACKED THE SMALL CITY OF AI, THE SOLDIERS WERE ROUTED, AND JOSHUA WAS SHOCKED. HE ASKED THE LORD WHY, AND GOD SAID THAT IT WAS BECAUSE SOMEONE HAD DISOBEYED.

More!💪➡

IT IS TRUE—I SINNED AGAINST GOD AND MY PEOPLE.

NOW WE STAND RIGHT WITH GOD.

EARLY the next morning Joshua led all of Israel before the Lord. All of the tribes stood before him. And the Lord chose the tribe of Judah. [17]So all the family groups of Judah stood before the Lord. The Lord then chose the family group of Zerah. And all the families of Zerah stood before the Lord. Then the family of Zimri was chosen. [18]And Joshua told all the men in that family to come before the Lord. The Lord chose Achan son of Carmi. . . .

[19]Then Joshua said to Achan, "My son, you should tell the truth. Confess to the Lord, the God of Israel. Tell me what you did. Don't try to hide anything from me."

But if we confess our sins, he will forgive our sins. We can trust God. He does what is right. He will make us clean from all the wrongs we have done.

I John 1:9

God, help me always to be honest with You, and ask forgiveness when I'm wrong. Amen.

? What was the command that Joshua gave the Israelites? Who was supposed to get the captured goods?

? What did Achan do with the robe, gold and silver? Did his dishonesty go unnoticed?

? God sees everything we do. When we do things that are wrong, we need to confess and tell the truth. Achan not only did not confess when he took the items, but he didn't come forward when Joshua was questioning the people. Think of something that you have not been completely honest about. What can you do to make things right with God?

WRITE A NOTE TO GOD EXPLAINING A TIME WHEN YOU WERE NOT HONEST. THEN READ THE NOTE ALOUD TO GOD, AND CLOSE BY ASKING HIM TO FORGIVE YOU.

DEAR GOD,

Ruth Finds a New Home

ONE DAY Ruth, the woman from Moab, said to Naomi, **"Let me go to the fields.** Maybe someone will be kind and let me gather the grain he leaves in his field."

Naomi said, "Go, my daughter."

[3]So Ruth went to the fields. She followed the workers who were cutting the grain. And she gathered the grain that they had left. It just so happened that the field belonged to Boaz. . . .

[8]Then Boaz said to Ruth, "Listen, my daughter. Stay here in my field to gather grain for yourself. Do not go to any other person's field. Continue following behind my women workers. [9]Watch to see which fields they go to and follow them. I have warned the young men not to bother you. When you are thirsty, you may go and drink. Take water from the water jugs that the servants have filled."

[10]Then Ruth bowed low with her face to the ground. She said to Boaz, "I am a stranger. Why have you been so kind to notice me?"

[11]Boaz answered her, "I know about all the help you have given to Naomi, your mother-in-law. You helped her even after your husband died. You left your father and mother and your own country. You came to this nation where you did not know anyone. [12]The Lord will reward you for all you have done. You will be paid in full by the Lord, the God of Israel. You have come to him as a little bird finds shelter under the wings of its mother."

From Ruth 2

HER NAME IS RUTH—SHE IS THE MOABITE WOMAN WHO TAKES CARE OF HER MOTHER-IN-LAW, NAOMI.

HOW BEAUTIFUL SHE IS!

? What did Ruth do to help Naomi?

? What special thing did Boaz do for Ruth when she gathered grain in his field?

? Ruth showed loyalty by leaving her homeland to travel with and care for Naomi. No matter what happened, Ruth would not leave Naomi. A true friend shows loyalty by sticking close by you no matter what happens. Think about three qualities you would like to have in a friend (example: a friend should listen when you feel like talking about your problems, or a friend is someone you can share any secret with).

DROP SOME GRAIN ON PURPOSE FOR HER TO PICK UP. AND SEE THAT NO HARM COMES TO HER!

HAVE NO FEAR, BOAZ. SHE WILL BE SAFE—AND SHE WILL FIND ALL THE GRAIN SHE NEEDS.

A person who tries to live right and be loyal finds life, success and honor.

Proverbs 21:21

God, thank You for giving me family and friends who care about me. Help me to show loyalty to them by saying kind things to encourage them. Amen.

WE SHOW LOYALTY TO OUR FAMILY BY DEFENDING IT WHEN OTHERS SAY HURTFUL WORDS AGAINST IT. YOU CAN BUILD STRONG LOYALTY BY SAYING POSITIVE THINGS ABOUT ONE ANOTHER TO MAKE EACH MEMBER FEEL IMPORTANT TO THE FAMILY. WRITE ONE POSITIVE THING ABOUT EACH MEMBER OF YOUR FAMILY.

ON SEPARATE PIECES OF PAPER, WRITE THE POSITIVE COMMENTS. THEN HIDE EACH NOTE UNDER THE PILLOW OF THE PERSON FOR WHOM THE COMMENT WAS INTENDED.

59

A Promise for Hannah

After they had eaten their meal in Shiloh, Hannah got up. Now Eli the priest was sitting on a chair near the entrance to the Lord's Holy Tent. [10]Hannah was very sad. She cried much and prayed to the Lord. [11]She made a promise. She said,

"Lord of heaven's armies, see how bad I feel. Remember me! Don't forget me. If you will give me a son, I will give him back to you all his life. And no one will ever use a razor to cut his hair."

[12]While Hannah kept praying, Eli watched her mouth. [13]She was praying in her heart. Her lips moved, but her voice was not heard. So Eli thought she was drunk. [14]He said to her, "Stop getting drunk! Throw away your wine!"

ANGRILY HE ACCUSES HER...

NO! NO! I AM NOT DRUNK, I AM UNHAPPY; AND IN MY SORROW I HAVE POURED OUT MY HEART TO GOD, ASKING HIM TO HELP ME.

[15]Hannah answered, "No, master, I have not drunk any wine or beer. I am a woman who is deeply troubled. I was telling the Lord about all my problems. [16]Don't think of me as an evil woman. I have been praying because of my many troubles and much sadness."

[17]Eli answered, "Go in peace. May the God of Israel give you what you asked of him."

[18]Hannah said, "I want to be pleasing to you always." Then she left and ate something. She was not sad anymore.

From I Samuel 1

60

? How did Hannah let God know what she wanted?

? What promise did Eli give Hannah?

? Sometimes there are situations in our lives that seem impossible. But God is able to help us with any problem. All we have to do is to pray and ask God for His help. What is one thing you would like God to work out in your life?

Remain in me and follow my teachings. If you do this, then you can ask for anything you want, and it will be given to you.

John 15:7

Lord, help me to pray to You for the things I need. Thank You for always being there to answer. Amen.

More!➡

WHEN PEOPLE SPEAK THEIR NEEDS, WE CALL THEM PRAYER REQUESTS. A REQUEST IS SOMETHING WE ARE ASKING GOD TO TAKE CARE OF. WRITE SEVERAL PRAYER REQUESTS ON THE LINES BELOW.

MY REQUESTS ARE:

_____

_____

_____

_____

_____

_____

_____

_____

_____

_____

_____

THANK YOU, GOD, FOR ANSWERING PRAYERS.

MY NAME:

Wisdom

The King Makes a Terrible Mistake

SAUL **waited seven days,** because Samuel had said he would meet him then. But Samuel did not come to Gilgal. And the soldiers began to leave.

⁹So Saul said, "Bring me the whole burnt offering and the fellowship offerings." Then Saul offered the whole burnt offering. ¹⁰Just as he finished, Samuel arrived. Saul went to meet him.

¹¹Samuel asked, "What have you done?"

Saul answered, "I saw the soldiers leaving me, and you were not here. The Philistines were gathering at Micmash. ¹²Then I thought, 'The Philistines will come against me at Gilgal. And I haven't asked for the Lord's approval.' So I forced myself to offer the whole burnt offering."

¹³Samuel said, "You acted foolishly! You haven't obeyed God's command. If you had obeyed him, God would make your kingdom continue in Israel forever. ¹⁴But now your kingdom will not continue. The Lord has looked for the kind of man he wants. The Lord has appointed him to become ruler of his people. He is doing this because you haven't obeyed his command."

From I Samuel 13

TAKE THIRTY THOUSAND CHARIOTS, SIX THOUSAND HORSEMEN AND ALL OUR INFANTRY—SET UP A CAMP AT MICHMASH. FROM THERE WE CAN SEND OUT RAIDING PARTIES THAT WILL DRAW SAUL FROM HIS STRONGHOLD AT GILGAL.

THE PHILISTINES OUTNUMBER US BY THOUSANDS. I'M HIDING OUT UNTIL THIS IS OVER.

THERE'S A PIT DOWN THE VALLEY— I'LL HIDE THERE.

THE MEN ARE LOSING THEIR NERVE. WE CAN'T WAIT MUCH LONGER FOR SAMUEL TO COME AND OFFER THE SACRIFICE TO GOD.

YOU'RE RIGHT. WE'LL WAIT NO LONGER. I'LL MAKE THE OFFERING!

? Saul took things into his own hands and didn't wait for Samuel. What did Saul do that angered Samuel?

? What did Samuel tell Saul?

? When God doesn't answer as fast as we'd like Him to, sometimes we make bad choices to work things out ourselves. Think of a time when you made a bad choice to accomplish a goal (examples: copied someone else's homework, covered up for a friend's wrongdoing, joined others in making fun of someone even though you really didn't want to do it). How did you feel about making the bad choice?

More!▮▮▮▶

> *Dear God, thank You for Your Word that teaches us how to live. Help me to make wise choices as I'm learning to be like You. Amen.*

> "Now, my children, listen to me. Those who follow my ways are happy. Listen to my teaching, and you will be wise. Do not ignore it."
>
> Proverbs 8:32, 33

LET'S DO A QUICK CHECK. THE NEXT TIME YOU ARE FACED WITH A DIFFICULT DECISION, ASK YOURSELF THESE QUESTIONS.

WILL MY ACTIONS BE:
- ☐ GOOD FOR ME?
- ☐ GOOD FOR THE OTHER PERSON INVOLVED?
- ☐ PLEASING TO GOD?

ASKING THESE QUESTIONS WILL HELP YOU TO ACT WISELY.

WRITE A PROMISE TELLING GOD YOU WILL THINK BEFORE YOU ACT THE NEXT TIME A DIFFICULT DECISION COMES UP.

_____

_____

_____

_____

_____

A Giant? No Problem!

SEND OUT A MAN WHO DARES TO FIGHT ME. IF HE KILLS ME, THE PHILISTINES WILL BE YOUR SERVANTS, BUT IF I KILL HIM, YOU WILL BE OUR SERVANTS.

EVERY DAY THAT GIANT DEFIES US. I HAVE OFFERED A HANDSOME REWARD —EVEN MY DAUGHTER IN MARRIAGE— BUT NOT ONE SOLDIER IN MY WHOLE ARMY WILL ACCEPT THE CHALLENGE.

I CAN'T WEAR THIS— I'M NOT USED TO FIGHTING IN ARMOR. BESIDES, MY PLAN IS NOT TO DEFEND MYSELF, BUT TO ATTACK!

A SHEPHERD BOY! YOU CAN'T FIGHT A GIANT!

More!⫸

65

HE **took his stick in his hand.** And he chose five smooth stones from a stream. He put them in his pouch and held his sling in his hand. Then he went to meet Goliath.

[41]At the same time, the Philistine was coming closer to David. The man who held his shield walked in front of him. [42]Goliath looked at David. He saw that David was only a boy, tanned and handsome. He looked down at David with disgust. [43]He said, "Do you think I am a dog, that you come at me with a stick?" He used his gods' names to curse David. [44]He said to David, "Come here. I'll feed your body to the birds of the air and the wild animals!"

[45]But David said to him, "You come to me using a sword, a large spear and a small spear. But I come to you in the name of the Lord of heaven's armies.... You have spoken out against him. [46]Today the Lord will give you to me. I'll kill you, and I'll cut off your head.... Then all the world will know there is a God in Israel! [47]Everyone gathered here

AM I A DOG, THAT YOU COME AT ME WITH STICKS AND STONES?

From I Samuel 17

will know the Lord does not need swords or spears to save people. The battle belongs to him! And he will help us defeat all of you."

[48]As Goliath came near to attack him, David ran quickly to meet him. [49]He took a stone from his pouch. He put it into his sling and slung it. The stone hit the Philistine on his forehead and sank into it. Goliath fell facedown on the ground.

[50]So David defeated the Philistine with only a sling and a stone! He hit him and killed him. He did not even have a sword in his hand. [51]David ran and stood beside the Philistine. He took Goliath's sword out of its holder and killed him. Then he cut off Goliath's head.

When the Philistines saw that their champion was dead, they turned and ran.

? Why wasn't Goliath afraid of David? Why wasn't David afraid of Goliath?

? What were the differences between David and Goliath?

? David's purpose was clear—anyone who spoke against the Lord God of Israel must be brought down. David never wavered; he never doubted God's ability to help him complete the task. What he knew of God strengthened him for the job.

? Take a watch with a second hand. For one minute, say as many things that you know about God as you can (examples: God answers prayer, He loves people, He died on the cross so that we can be saved, etc.).

Lord, teach me what you want me to do. And I will live by your truth.

Psalm 86:11

Lord, help me purpose in my heart to serve You with my thoughts, my words, my actions. Daily give me strength to do what is right according to Your Word. Amen.

GOLIATH'S DEAD!

DRAW FIVE STONES. ON EACH STONE, WRITE ONE WAY THAT GOD HELPS YOU TO BECOME STRONG IN HIM. SOME EXAMPLES ARE: GOD ANSWERS MY PRAYERS, GOD GIVES ME STRENGTH, GOD GIVES ME HIS WORD, ETC.

WHEN YOU FEEL DISCOURAGED, TURN TO THIS PAGE AND READ ALOUD THESE FIVE THINGS. BY DOING THIS, GOD WILL STRENGTHEN AND HELP YOU.

Jonathan Saves a Friend's Life

W HEN **David finished talking with Saul, Jonathan felt very close to David.** He loved David as much as he loved himself. ²Saul kept David with him from that day on. He did not let David go home to his father's house. ³Jonathan made an agreement with David. He did this because he loved David as much as himself. ⁴He took off his coat and gave it to David. He also gave David his uniform, including his sword, bow and belt. ⁹So Saul watched David closely from then on. He was jealous of him.

THANK YOU, JONATHAN. GOD IS MY WITNESS THAT I WILL BE YOUR FRIEND UNTIL DEATH.

Chapter 19Saul told his son Jonathan and all his servants to kill David. But Jonathan cared very much for David. ²So he warned David, "My father Saul is looking for a chance to kill you. Watch out in the morning. Hide in a secret place. ³I will go out and stand with my father in the field where you are hiding. I'll talk to him about you. Then I'll let you know what I find out."

⁴Jonathan talked to Saul his father. He said good things about David. Jonathan said, "You are the king. Don't do wrong to your servant David. He did nothing wrong to you. What he did has helped you greatly. ⁵David risked his life when he killed Goliath the Philistine. The Lord won a great victory for all Israel. You saw it, and you were happy. Why would you do wrong against David? He's innocent. There's no reason to kill him!"

⁶Saul listened to Jonathan. Then he made this promise: "As surely as the Lord lives, David won't be put to death."

From I Samuel 18, 19

? What did Jonathan do to protect David?

? Jonathan didn't have to stick up for David. He could have smuggled him out of the country instead. Why do you think Jonathan took the problem right to the king?

? Being a friend means helping someone become the person God has intended him or her to be. Sometimes this means that you may have to step back and let your friend get the glory or as in the case of Jonathan, step in to protect your friend. What is one thing you've done to help a friend?

A friend loves you all the time.
Proverbs 17:17

Which prayer fits you best? Choose one:

Dear God, thank You for the friends You've given me. Help me to encourage them to serve You. Amen.

Dear God, I need a good friend. Help me to be a good friend to those around me so that I can develop a friendship with someone special. Thanks, God. Amen

More!

THINK ABOUT YOUR
BEST FRIEND.

WHAT DO YOU LIKE
ABOUT HIM OR HER?

WHAT TALENTS OR
ABILITIES DO YOU
THINK GOD HAS GIVEN
YOUR FRIEND?

HOW CAN YOU HELP
YOUR FRIEND PRACTICE
USING HIS OR HER
ABILITIES FOR GOD?

NOW **Saul had chased the Philistines away.** Then he was told, "David is in the Desert of En Gedi." ²So he chose 3,000 men from all Israel. He took these men and began looking for David and his men. They looked near the Rocks of the Wild Goats.

³Saul came to the sheep pens beside the road. A cave was there, and he went in to relieve himself. Now David and his men were hiding far back in the cave. ⁴The men said to David, "Today is the day the Lord talked about! The Lord told you, 'I will give your enemy to you. You can do anything you want with him.'"

Then David crawled near Saul. He cut off a corner of Saul's robe. But Saul did not notice him. ⁵Later David felt guilty because he had cut off a corner of Saul's robe. ⁶He said to his men, "May the Lord keep me from doing such a thing to my master! Saul is the Lord's appointed king. I should not do anything against him, because he is the Lord's appointed king!" ⁷David used these words to stop his men. He did not let them attack Saul. Then Saul left the cave and went his way.

⁸When David came out of the cave, he shouted to Saul, "My master and king!" Saul looked back, and David bowed facedown on the ground. ⁹He said to Saul, "Why do you listen when people say, "David plans to harm you'? ¹⁰You have seen something with your own eyes today. You have seen how the Lord put you in my power in the cave. But I refused to kill you. I was merciful to you. I said, "I won't harm my master, because he is the Lord's appointed king.' ¹¹My father, look at this piece of your robe in my hand! I cut off the corner of your robe, but I didn't kill you. Now understand and know I am not planning any evil against you.". . .

¹⁶David finished saying these words. Then Saul asked, "Is that your voice, David my son?" And he cried loudly. ¹⁷He said, "You are right, and I am wrong. . . . May the Lord reward you because you were good to me today. ²⁰I know you will surely be king. You will rule the kingdom of Israel.

HE'S YOUR WIFE'S FATHER— SO IF YOU DON'T WANT TO KILL HIM, I'LL DO IT FOR YOU.

NO— HE WAS CHOSEN BY GOD TO BE OUR KING. IT IS NOT FOR US TO DECIDE WHEN HE WILL DIE.

More!▮▮▮➡

From I Samuel 24

? What did David's men want him to do?

? What reason did David give for not killing Saul?

? God has placed people over us to teach us and protect us — people like our parents, our pastor, our teachers. God has made them responsible for our souls. To resist the authorities over us goes against God's plan. Think of a time when you went against someone who was in charge. What happened?

Respect those people . . . who lead you in the Lord and teach you. Respect them with a very special love because of the work they do with you.
I Thessalonians 5:12, 13

Lord, sometimes it's hard to always obey those who are put in charge. Give me a willing heart so that I show those over me respect. Amen.

ON THE LEFT SIDE OF THE SPACE BELOW, DRAW A PICTURE OF YOUR FACE WHEN YOU DON'T WANT TO DO WHAT YOUR TEACHER WANTS YOU TO DO. ON THE RIGHT SIDE, DRAW HOW YOU THINK GOD WOULD WANT YOU TO LOOK IN THE SAME SITUATION.

AFTER they had crossed over,

Elijah said to Elisha, "What can I do for you before I am taken from you?"

Elisha said, "Leave me a double share of your spirit."

[10]Elijah said, "You have asked a hard thing. But if you see me when I am taken from you, it will be yours. If you don't, it won't happen."

[11]Elijah and Elisha were still walking and talking. Then a chariot and horses of fire appeared. The chariot and horses of fire separated Elijah from Elisha. Then Elijah went up to heaven in a whirlwind. [12]Elisha saw it and shouted, "My father! My father! The chariots of Israel and their horsemen!" Elisha did not see him anymore. Elisha grabbed his own clothes and tore them to show how sad he was.

[13]He picked up Elijah's coat that had fallen from him. Then Elisha returned and stood on the bank of the Jordan. [14]Elisha hit the water with Elijah's coat. He said, "Where is the Lord, the God of Elijah?" When he hit the water, it divided to the right and to the left. Then Elisha crossed over.

From II Kings 2

ELIJAH! ELIJAH! I SEE NOW—THE POWER THAT PROTECTED AND GUIDED YOU IS GREATER THAN ALL THE ARMIES OF EARTH!

Whoever helps
others will himself
be helped.
Proverbs 11:25

Lord, help me to show
Your love by being
concerned about others.
Remind me that if I help
others, I will be helped
when I am discouraged.
Amen.

? Why did Elisha not want to leave Elijah, even for a minute?

? What happened to Elijah?

? Elisha showed concern for Elijah by always being there by his side. Elisha probably knew that he would not receive money as an inheritance from Elijah, yet he wanted the power to do God's work as Elijah had done. Is there someone in your family that you are worried or concerned about? If so, what could you do to help that person?

THINK OF SOMEONE IN YOUR CHURCH WHO NEEDS ENCOURAGEMENT. WRITE OUT THREE SENTENCES THAT COULD CHEER THAT PERSON UP. THEN CALL THAT PERSON ON THE TELEPHONE AND SAY THE WORDS YOU'VE WRITTEN.

75

Miracle of Oil

YOUR HUSBAND OWED ME MONEY WHEN HE WAS ALIVE. PAY ME WHAT HE OWED, OR I'LL TAKE YOUR SONS AS SLAVES!

THE wife of a man from a group of the prophets came to Elisha. She said,

"Your servant, my husband, is dead! You know he honored the Lord. But now the man he owes money to is coming to take my two boys. He will make them his slaves!"

THERE, THAT'S THE LAST JAR WE HAVE -- AND MINE IS STILL FULL. IT'S A MIRACLE.

²Elisha answered, "How can I help you? Tell me, what do you have in your house?"

The woman said, "I don't have anything there except a pot of oil."

³Then Elisha said, "Go and get empty jars from all your neighbors. Don't ask for just a few. ⁴Then you must go into your house and close the door. Only you and your sons will be there. Then pour oil into all the jars. Set the full ones to one side."

⁵She left Elisha and shut the door. Only she and her sons were in the house. As they brought the jars to her, she poured the oil. ⁶When the jars were all full, she said to her son, "Bring me another jar."

But he said, "There are no more jars." Then the oil stopped flowing.

⁷She went and told Elisha. Elisha said to her, "Go. Sell the oil and pay what you owe. You and your sons can live on what is left."

76

From II Kings 4

? What miracle did Elisha do for the woman?

? Why do you think Elisha didn't just give the woman money instead of having her and her children work for it?

? Elisha heard the woman's problem and had compassion for her. Not only did he feel pity, but he went on to help her out of her poverty. When we see people with special needs or problems, we need to do more than feel sorry for them. We need to take action to help. Think of a way that you could encourage someone living in a nursing home or a person who is homeless.

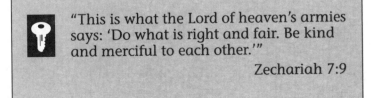

"This is what the Lord of heaven's armies says: 'Do what is right and fair. Be kind and merciful to each other.'"

Zechariah 7:9

God, help me to think of ways to show compassion to those around me. Help me to remember that because You show compassion for me, I need to show compassion to others. Amen.

More⊪➡

REMEMBER THE CHOSEN KIDS' CLUB (SEE PAGE 40)? ASK YOUR FRIENDS FOR IDEAS ON HOW YOUR GROUP COULD SHOW COMPASSION TO SOMEONE IN YOUR NEIGHBORHOOD (EXAMPLES: RAKING LEAVES OR SHOVELING SNOW FOR A DISABLED PERSON, BABY-SITTING KIDS IN THE BACKYARD FOR A PARENT WHO NEEDS A BREAK, ETC.). ASK YOUR PARENTS FOR ADVICE AND HELP.

Courage

ESTHER WAS CHOSEN TO BE THE QUEEN OF PERSIA. SHE WAS JEWISH AND HAD NOT TOLD ANYONE HER BACKGROUND. HAMAN, A PERSON OF HIGH RANK IN THE KINGDOM, ORGANIZED AN EVIL PLOT TO DESTROY ALL THE JEWS. ESTHER'S COUSIN MORDECAI WARNED HER BY SENDING A MESSENGER WITH THE NEWS. . . .

THEN Esther told Mordecai . . . [11]"No man or woman may go to the king in the inner courtyard without being called. There is only one law about this. Anyone who enters must be put to death. But if the king holds out his gold scepter, that person may live. And I have not been called to go to the king for 30 days."

[12]And Esther's message was given to Mordecai. [13]Then Mordecai gave orders to say to Esther: "Just because you live in the king's palace, don't think that out of all the Jews you alone will escape. [14]You might keep quiet at this time. Then someone else will help and save the Jews. But you and your father's family will all die. And who knows, you may have been chosen queen for just such a time as this."

[15]Then Esther sent this answer to Mordecai: [16]"Go and get all the Jews in Susa together. For my sake, give up eating. Do not eat or drink for three days, night and day. I and my servant girls will also give up eating. Then I will go to the king, even though it is against the law. And if I die, I die."

A Queen Risks Her Life

SURPRISED AS HE IS BY HER SUDDEN APPEARANCE, THE KING IS PLEASED AT THE SIGHT OF HIS BEAUTIFUL QUEEN. HE HOLDS OUT HIS SCEPTOR TO SHOW THAT SHE IS FORGIVEN, AND ASKS WHAT SHE WANTS.

I ASK THAT YOU AND HAMAN COME TO A DINNER THAT I SHALL PREPARE FOR YOU.

So the king and Haman went in to eat with Queen Esther. ²They were drinking wine. And the king said to Esther on this second day also, "What are you asking for? I will give it to you. What is it you want? I will give you as much as half of my kingdom."

³Then Queen Esther answered, "My king, I hope you are pleased with me. If it pleases you, let me live. This is what I ask. And let my people live, too. This is what I want. ⁴I ask this because my people and I have been sold to be destroyed. We are to be killed and completely wiped out. . . ."

⁵Then King Xerxes asked Queen Esther, "Who is he? Where is he? Who has done such a thing?"

⁶Esther said, "A man who is against us! Our enemy is this wicked Haman!"

Then Haman was filled with terror before the king and queen. . . . ⁹Harbona was one of the eunuchs there serving the king. He said, "Look, a platform for hanging people stands near Haman's house. It is 75 feet high. This is the one Haman had prepared for Mordecai, who gave the warning that saved the king."

The king said, "Hang Haman on it!" ¹⁰So they hanged Haman on the platform he had prepared for Mordecai.

From Esther 4, 7

79

? What might have happened to Esther if the king wouldn't have extended his scepter to her?

? Mordecai reminded Esther that she, too, was a Jew and would die. But what wonderful opportunity did he present to Esther?

? What a choice!—Die because of the order or die because the king wouldn't accept her presence in the throne room. It took a lot of courage for Esther to go before the king. Think of someone you know or have read about who showed a lot of courage in the face of danger. What was the choice he or she had to face? How did the situation turn out?

MORDECAI IS YOUR COUSIN? I'LL PUT HIM IN HAMAN'S PLACE --SECOND IN POWER IN ALL OF MY KINGDOM. WITH HAMAN OUT OF THE WAY, NO ONE WILL DARE TO HARM EITHER OF YOU.

Have courage. May the Lord be with those who do what is right.

II Chronicles 19:11

Lord, help me to have the courage to stand up for what's right. Give me the strength I need to go against friends when I know they want to do wrong. Amen.

ESTHER TOOK THE RISK EVEN THOUGH SHE KNEW THINGS MIGHT NOT WORK OUT AS SHE PLANNED. THINK OF A SITUATION WHERE YOU MIGHT NEED TO GO AGAINST SOMEONE TO TAKE A STAND FOR RIGHT. SOME EXAMPLES ARE: WHEN BIGGER KIDS ARE HASSLING A SMALLER KID AND YOU NEED TO STEP IN, WHEN SOMEONE WANTS TO SHOPLIFT A CANDY BAR AND YOU DON'T WANT TO BE A PART OF THE ACTION, OR WHEN A FRIEND WANTS TO CHEAT ON A TEST AND YOU DON'T THINK IT'S RIGHT. DRAW A PICTURE OF HOW YOU WOULD HANDLE THE SITUATION.

I'd Rather Eat Vegetables

DANIEL **decided not to eat the king's food and wine** because that would make him unclean. So he asked Ashpenaz for permission not to make himself unclean in this way.

⁹God made Ashpenaz want to be kind and merciful to Daniel. ¹⁰But Ashpenaz said to Daniel, "I am afraid of my master, the king. He ordered me to give you this food and drink. If you don't eat this food, you will begin to look worse than other young men your age. The king will see this. And he will cut off my head because of you."

¹¹Ashpenaz had ordered a guard to watch Daniel, Hananiah, Mishael and Azariah. ¹²Daniel said to the guard, "Please give us this test for ten days: Don't give us anything but vegetables to eat and water to drink. ¹³Then after ten days compare us with the other young men who eat the king's food. See for yourself who looks healthier. Then you judge for yourself how you want to treat us, your servants."

¹⁴So the guard agreed to test them for ten days. ¹⁵After ten days they looked very healthy. They looked better than all of the young men who ate the king's food. ¹⁶So the guard took away the king's special food and wine. He gave Daniel, Hananiah, Mishael and Azariah vegetables instead.

¹⁷God gave these four men wisdom and the ability to learn. They learned many kinds of things people had written and studied. Daniel could also understand all kinds of visions and dreams.

¹⁸The end of the three years came. And Ashpenaz brought all of the young men to King Nebuchadnezzar. ¹⁹The king talked to them. He found that none of the young men were as good as Daniel, Hananiah, Mishael and Azariah. So those four young men became the king's servants. ²⁰Every time the king asked them about something important, they showed much wisdom and understanding.

From Daniel 1

More ▶

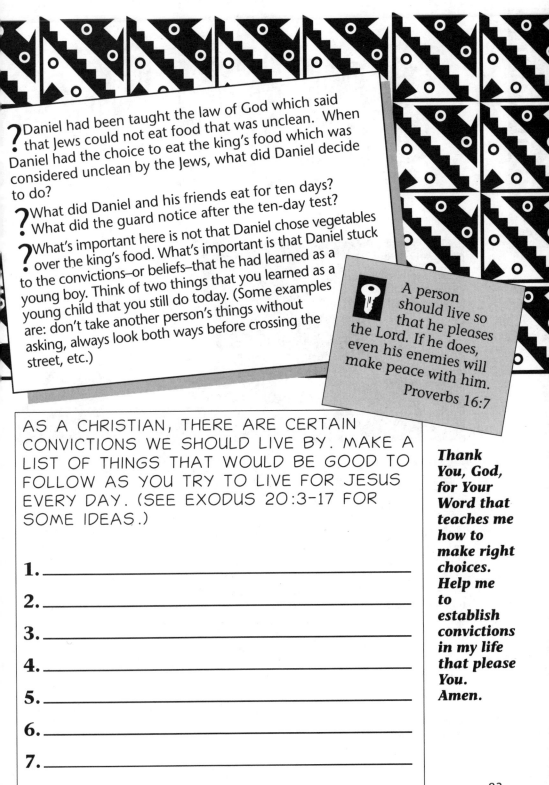

? Daniel had been taught the law of God which said that Jews could not eat food that was unclean. When Daniel had the choice to eat the king's food which was considered unclean by the Jews, what did Daniel decide to do?

? What did Daniel and his friends eat for ten days? What did the guard notice after the ten-day test?

? What's important here is not that Daniel chose vegetables over the king's food. What's important is that Daniel stuck to the convictions—or beliefs—that he had learned as a young boy. Think of two things that you learned as a young child that you still do today. (Some examples are: don't take another person's things without asking, always look both ways before crossing the street, etc.)

A person should live so that he pleases the Lord. If he does, even his enemies will make peace with him.
Proverbs 16:7

AS A CHRISTIAN, THERE ARE CERTAIN CONVICTIONS WE SHOULD LIVE BY. MAKE A LIST OF THINGS THAT WOULD BE GOOD TO FOLLOW AS YOU TRY TO LIVE FOR JESUS EVERY DAY. (SEE EXODUS 20:3-17 FOR SOME IDEAS.)

1. _____

2. _____

3. _____

4. _____

5. _____

6. _____

7. _____

Thank You, God, for Your Word that teaches me how to make right choices. Help me to establish convictions in my life that please You. Amen.

A Very Hot Spot!

MUSIC FILLS THE AIR -- SOLEMNLY THE OFFICIALS OF BABYLON BOW DOWN AND WORSHIP THE GOLDEN STATUE -- ALL BUT SHADRACH, MESHACH, AND ABEDNEGO.

SEE? THEY REFUSE TO BOW DOWN!

THE KING

became very angry. . . . [16]Shadrach, Meshach and Abednego answered the king. They said, "Nebuchadnezzar, we do not need to defend ourselves to you. [17]You can throw us into the blazing furnace. The God we serve is able to save us from the furnace and your power. If he does this, it is good. [18]But even if God does not save us, we want you, our king, to know this: We will not serve your gods. We will not worship the gold statue you have set up."

[19]Then Nebuchadnezzar was furious with Shadrach, Meshach and Abednego. He ordered the furnace to be heated seven times hotter than usual. [20]Then he commanded some of the strongest soldiers in his army to tie up Shadrach, Meshach and Abednego. The king told the soldiers to throw them into the blazing furnace.

[21]So Shadrach, Meshach and Abednego were tied up and thrown into the blazing furnace. They were still wearing their robes, trousers, turbans and other clothes. [22]The king was very angry when he gave the command. And the furnace was made very hot. The fire was so hot that the flames killed the strong soldiers who took Shadrach, Meshach and Abednego there. [23]Firmly tied, Shadrach, Meshach and Abednego fell into the blazing furnace.   *From Daniel 3*

? Do you think it was hard for the three Hebrews to keep standing when everyone else was bowing down to the statue? Why or why not?

? Were they sure that God would keep them from burning up? How do you know?

? Sometimes being committed to God means having to stand alone when you're with friends at school. Can you think of a time when your friends wanted to do something you knew would get you in trouble? How did you feel? Did you stand up to them or did you do what they wanted to do?

BUT WHEN THE KING LOOKS INTO THE FURNACE...

THEY'RE ALIVE! NOT EVEN TOUCHED BY THE FLAMES! AND, DIDN'T WE CAST **THREE** INTO THE FIRE?

WE DID, O KING.

Teach me to do what you want, because you are my God. Let your good Spirit lead me on level ground.

Psalm 143:10

God, thank You for being there when I need You. Help me to commit myself to You and stand firm on the teachings of Your Word. Amen.

More!➤

WE WORSHIP GOD BY DOING DIFFERENT THINGS. WE BUILD OUR RELATIONSHIP WITH GOD ONE STEP AT A TIME. LOOK AT THE LIST BELOW. CHECK ONE THING THAT YOU WILL PROMISE TO DO FOR GOD THIS WEEK.

LORD, THIS WEEK I WILL: (CHECK ONE)

❏ READ FIVE VERSES IN MY BIBLE EVERY DAY.
❏ TALK TO YOU IN PRAYER FIVE MINUTES EVERY DAY.
❏ EARN MONEY BY DOING AN EXTRA JOB AND THEN GIVE IT IN THE OFFERING NEXT SUNDAY.
❏ OBEY MY PARENTS WITHOUT ARGUING OR TALKING BACK THIS WEEK.
❏ OTHER IDEAS I HAVE:

_____

_____

_____

YOUR SPECIAL KID,

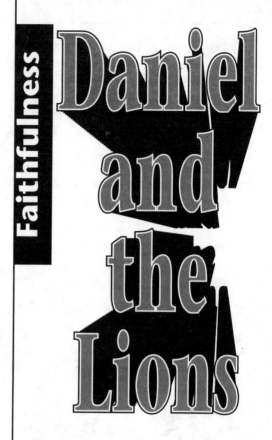

Faithfulness

Daniel and the Lions

DANIEL WAS FAITHFUL TO GOD. THREE TIMES EACH DAY HE WOULD PRAY. THE MEN HE WORKED WITH WERE JEALOUS OF HIS GOOD RECORD AND WANTED TO GET HIM IN TROUBLE WITH THE BOSS, KING DARIUS. BUT DANIEL WAS TRUSTWORTHY AND A GOOD WORKER. SO THE MEN PLOTTED AGAINST HIM AND HAD THE KING SIGN AN ORDER THAT NO ONE COULD PRAY TO ANY GOD BUT THE KING'S GOD. BUT THAT DIDN'T STOP DANIEL FROM PRAYING TO HIS GOD. . . .

A FEW MINUTES LATER DANIEL, WHO BROKE THE KING'S LAW BY PRAYING TO GOD, IS CAST INTO THE LIONS' DEN.

MAY THE GOD WHOM YOU SERVE PROTECT YOU.

KING Darius . . . did not eat that night. He did not have any

entertainment brought to entertain him. And he could not sleep.

¹⁹The next morning King Darius got up at dawn. He hurried to the lions' den. ²⁰As he came near the den, he was worried. He called out to Daniel. He said, "Daniel, servant of the living God! Has your God that you always worship been able to save you from the lions?"

²¹Daniel answered, "My king, live forever! ²²My God sent his angel·to close the lions' mouths. They have not hurt me, because my God knows I am innocent. I never did anything wrong to you, my king."

²³King Darius was very happy. He told his servants to lift Daniel out of the lions' den. So they lifted him out and did not find any injury on him. This was because Daniel had trusted in his God.

²⁵Then King Darius wrote a letter. It was to all people and all nations, to those who spoke every language in the world:

I wish you great wealth.

²⁶I am making a new law. This law is for people in every part of my kingdom. All of you must fear and respect the God of Daniel.

Daniel's God is the living God.
He lives forever.
His kingdom will never be destroyed.
His rule will never end.
²⁷God rescues and saves people.
God does mighty miracles
in heaven and on earth.
God saved Daniel
from the power of the lions.

MY GOD HAS SHUT THE LIONS' MOUTHS!

From Daniel 6

? What did Daniel do to show faithfulness to God?

? God showed faithfulness to Daniel by helping him. What did God do?

? Showing faithfulness means that a person can be counted on to do a certain thing. For instance, God could count on Daniel to pray three times each day. Can your parents count on you to do a certain job every day (or almost every day!)? What is that job?

 If you are faithful, I will give you the crown of life.
Revelation 2:10b

Dear God, thank You for always being there when I need to talk to someone. Help me to show my love for You by being faithful in the things I do for You and others. Amen.

WHAT ARE WAYS THAT WE CAN BE FAITHFUL TO GOD? SOME EXAMPLES WOULD BE GOING TO CHURCH EVERY SUNDAY, PRAYING AND READING GOD'S WORD, BEING NICE TO OTHERS. . . . THE LIST COULD GO ON AND ON. DRAW A PICTURE OF ONE WAY THAT YOU CAN SHOW YOUR LOVE FOR GOD EVERY DAY.

A Gift from a Stable

MARY, THIS IS NO PLACE FOR YOU.

IT'S ALL RIGHT, JOSEPH. I'M THANKFUL FOR WHATEVER SHELTER WE CAN FIND.

MARY gave birth to her first son. There were no rooms left in the inn. So she wrapped the baby with cloths and laid him in a box where animals are fed.

⁸That night, some shepherds were in the fields nearby watching their sheep. ⁹An angel of the Lord stood before them. The glory of the Lord was shining around them, and suddenly they became very frightened. ¹⁰The angel said to them, "Don't be afraid, because I am bringing you some good news. It will be a joy to all the people. ¹¹Today your Savior was born in David's town. He is Christ, the Lord. ¹²This is how you will know him: You will find a baby wrapped in cloths and lying in a feeding box." ¹³Then a very large group of angels from heaven joined the first angel. All the angels were praising God.

From Luke 2

DON'T BE AFRAID, BECAUSE I AM BRINGING YOU SOME GOOD NEWS. IT WILL BE A JOY TO ALL THE PEOPLE. TODAY YOUR SAVIOR WAS BORN IN DAVID'S TOWN. HE IS CHRIST, THE LORD. THIS IS HOW YOU WILL KNOW HIM: YOU WILL FIND A BABY WRAPPED IN CLOTHS AND LYING IN A FEEDING BOX.

More!⫸

THEN THE SKY IS FILLED WITH A GREAT CHOIR OF ANGELS -- SINGING THEIR PRAISE TO GOD.

Glory to God in the highest, and on earth peace, good will toward men.

? What do people do immediately before a baby is born? What might friends and relatives do for the new baby?

? Do you think that Mary might have wondered if something was wrong with the plan when she had to have her baby in a stable?

? The Bible tells us in Romans 6:23, "But God gives us a free gift—life forever in Christ Jesus our Lord." Jesus was the greatest gift that God gave the world. When Jesus was older He took all our sins and paid for them by shedding His blood on the cross. Now we have the chance to live with Him forever in heaven.

AN ANGEL TOLD US THAT THE SAVIOR HAS BEEN BORN. MAY WE SEE HIM?

A Gift from a Stable

A Gift from a Stable

A Gift from a Stable

Thanks, God, for loving me so much that You made a way for me to live with You forever. Help me to love You more each day, and serve You with my words and actions. Amen.

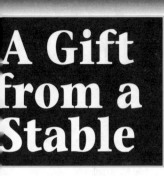
"She will give birth to a son. You will name the son Jesus. Give him that name because he will save his people from their sins."

Matthew 1:21

IN YOUR OWN WORDS, WRITE A THANK-YOU NOTE TO GOD FOR GIVING US THE GREATEST GIFT OF ALL--HIS SON.

Worship

Worshiping with Gifts

IT IS A SIGN FROM GOD THAT THE GREAT KING OF THE JEWS HAS BEEN BORN.

LET US GO TO JERUSALEM AND FIND THE KING.

JESUS **was born in the town of Bethlehem** in Judea during the time when Herod was king. After Jesus was born, some wise men from the east came to Jerusalem. 2They asked, "Where is the baby who was born to be the king of the Jews? We saw his star in the east. We came to worship him."

3When King Herod heard about this new king of the Jews, he was troubled. And all the people in Jerusalem were worried too. 4Herod called a meeting of all the leading priests and teachers of the law. He asked them where the Christ would be born. 5They answered, "In the town of Bethlehem in Judea. The prophet wrote about this in the Scriptures:

6'But you, Bethlehem, in the land of Judah,
    you are important among the rulers of
        Judah.
A ruler will come from you.
    He will be like a shepherd for my people,
        the Israelites.'"

. . . 9The wise men heard the king and then left. They saw the same star they had seen in the east. It went before them until it stopped above the place where the child was. 10When the wise men saw the star, they were filled with joy. 11They went to the house where the child was and saw him with his mother, Mary. They bowed down and worshiped the child. They opened the gifts they brought for him. They gave him treasures of gold, frankincense, and myrrh.

From Matthew 2

IS THERE ANYTHING IN THE SACRED BOOKS TELLING ABOUT A BABY WHO WILL BECOME KING OF THE JEWS?

YES, THE SCRIPTURES SAY HE WILL BE BORN IN BETHLEHEM.

? The wise men worshiped Jesus by kneeling before Him and giving Him expensive gifts. God doesn't expect us to do the same. Why?

? Have you ever really wanted to talk to God but felt awkward because of the place you were in or the people you were with? What are some ways to worship God other than speaking words in a prayer? (Examples: helping others, singing praise songs, telling others about Jesus, etc.)

? One way the wise men worshiped was by each giving the baby a different gift. Each of us has different gifts and talents that we can give to God as worship. Name two things that you could give as worship to God.

Thank You, God, for always being there when I want to talk to You. Help me to think of ways that I can show You how much I love You. Amen.

Praise the Lord for the glory of his name. Worship the Lord because he is holy.

Psalm 29:2

More!

WE CAN WORSHIP GOD
IN MANY WAYS. WE CAN
PRAISE HIM WITH OUR
WORDS AND WITH OUR
ACTIONS. DRAW ONE
WAY THAT YOU CAN
WORSHIP GOD.

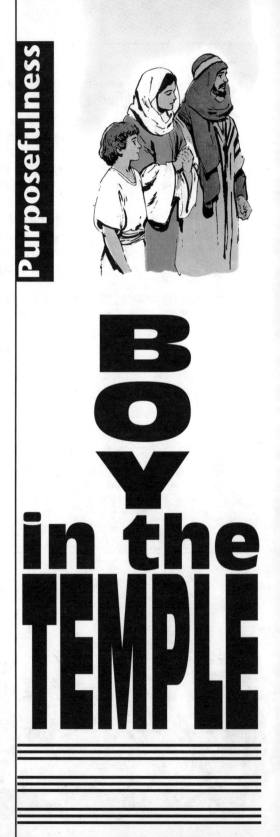

BOY in the TEMPLE

JOSEPH, WHERE IS JESUS?

HE'S WITH HIS FRIENDS. I'LL FIND HIM.

EVERY year Jesus' parents went to Jerusalem for the

Passover Feast. 42When Jesus was 12 years old, they went to the feast as they always did. 43When the feast days were over, they went home. The boy Jesus stayed behind in Jerusalem, but his parents did not know it. 44Joseph and Mary traveled for a whole day. They thought that Jesus was with them in the group. Then they began to look for him among their family and friends, 45but they did not find him. So they went back to Jerusalem to look for him there. 46After three days they found him. Jesus was sitting in the Temple with the religious teachers, listening to them and asking them questions. 47All who heard him were amazed at his understanding and wise answers. 48When Jesus' parents saw him, they were amazed. His mother said to him, "Son, why did you do this to us? Your father and I were very worried about you. We have been looking for you."

49Jesus asked, "Why did you have to look for me? You should have known that I must be where my Father's work is!" 50But they did not understand the meaning of what he said.

51Jesus went with them to Nazareth and obeyed them. His mother was still thinking about all that had happened. 52Jesus continued to learn more and more and to grow physically. People liked him, and he pleased God.

From Luke 2

WE ARE SURPRISED AT YOUR SON'S KNOWLEDGE OF THE SCRIPTURES. HIS QUESTIONS SHOW THAT HE HAS THOUGHT A GREAT DEAL ABOUT GOD AND HIS LAWS FOR MAN.

JESUS IS NOT LIKE ANYONE ELSE. EVEN I, HIS MOTHER, DO NOT UNDERSTAND EVERYTHING ABOUT HIM.

More!

95

? Do you think that Jesus intended to hide from His parents? Why or why not?

? Why did Jesus stay at the temple so long?

? Jesus had a purpose in talking to the teachers — He wanted to learn more about God's work. If you could be anything you wanted to be in God's work — a teacher, minister, musician, missionary, choir director, etc. — what would you like to be? Why?

In all the work you are doing, work the best you can. Work as if you were working for the Lord, not for men.
Colossians 3:23

Dear Lord, help me to set a goal to serve You with my whole heart. And then give me strength each day to keep working toward that goal. Amen.

A TRACK RUNNER DOESN'T DECIDE TO SIT DOWN AND EAT A SANDWICH IN THE MIDDLE OF A RACE. HE SETS HIS EYES ON THE FINISH LINE AND DOESN'T QUIT UNTIL HE REACHES IT. WE WOULD SAY THAT RUNNER IS PURPOSEFUL. THINK OF A GOAL YOU WOULD LIKE TO REACH THIS WEEK (GETTING AN ASSIGNMENT DONE, DOING A JOB FOR SOMEONE ELSE, EARNING EXTRA MONEY, ETC.) WHAT WILL IT TAKE FOR YOU TO REACH THAT GOAL?

No More Wine!

Twodays later there was **a wedding in the town of Cana** in Galilee. Jesus' mother was there. [2]Jesus and his followers were also invited to the wedding. [3]When all the wine was gone, Jesus' mother said to him, "They have no more wine."

[4]Jesus answered, "Dear woman, why come to me? My time has not yet come."

[5]His mother said to the servants, "Do whatever he tells you to do."

[6]In that place there were six stone water jars. The Jews used jars like these in their washing ceremony. Each jar held about 20 or 30 gallons.

[7]Jesus said to the servants, "Fill the jars with water." So they filled the jars to the top.

[8]Then he said to them, "Now take some out and give it to the master of the feast."

So the servants took the water to the master. [9]When he tasted it, the water had become wine. He did not know where the wine came from. But the servants who brought the water knew. The master of the wedding called the bridegroom [10]and said to him, "People always serve the best wine first. Later, after the guests have been drinking a lot, they serve the cheaper wine. But you have saved the best wine till now."

From John 2

DURING THE FEAST MARY DISCOVERS SOMETHING THAT WILL EMBARRASS THE GROOM -- THERE IS NO MORE WINE. SHE TELLS JESUS, THEN SHE GOES TO THE SERVANTS.

DO WHATEVER HE TELLS YOU.

?What did Jesus do to help the master of the feast?

?Besides providing something more to drink, what was special about the wine in the six jars?

?Helping others is something that pleases God and can be done by people of all ages–young and old. Think of a time when you helped someone. How did your helping make his or her job easier?

He will not forget the work you did and the love you showed for him by helping his people. And he will remember that you are still helping them.

Hebrews 6:10

Dear God, help me to see the needs of people who need Your help. Then show me ways to help them. Amen.

WHAT IS ONE THING YOU COULD DO TO HELP SOMEONE THIS WEEK? DRAW A PICTURE OF YOU AS YOU GIVE THAT HELP.

A Late-Night Talk

Nicodemus, a judge of the Jewish Supreme Court, has a problem he can't solve. People in Jerusalem are asking, "Is Jesus the savior who will overthrow the Romans and set up God's kingdom in Palestine?"

Nicodemus isn't sure, and he wonders: "What must a man do to enter God's kingdom?" He has to find out. So secretly-- by night-- he goes to the place where Jesus is staying, and Jesus answers his question even before he asks it...

A MAN MUST BE BORN OVER AGAIN TO ENTER GOD'S KINGDOM.

BORN AGAIN? HOW CAN I BE BORN AGAIN WHEN I AM OLD?

THERE
was a man named Nicodemus who was one of the Pharisees. He was an important Jewish leader. ²One night Nicodemus came to Jesus. He said, "Teacher, we know that you are a teacher sent from God. No one can do the miracles you do, unless God is with him."

³Jesus answered, "I tell you the truth. Unless one is born again, he cannot be in God's kingdom."

⁴Nicodemus said, "But if a man is already old, how can he be born again? He cannot enter his mother's body again. So how can he be born a second time?"

⁵But Jesus answered, "I tell you the truth. Unless one is born from water and the Spirit, he cannot enter God's kingdom. ⁶A person's body is born from his human parents. But a person's spiritual life is born from the Spirit. ⁷Don't be surprised when I tell you, 'You must all be born again.' ⁸The wind blows where it wants to go. You hear the wind blow. But you don't know where the wind comes from or where it is going. It is the same with every person who is born from the Spirit."

⁹Nicodemus asked, "How can all this be possible?"

¹⁰Jesus said, "You are an important teacher in Israel. But you still don't understand these things? ¹¹I tell you the truth. We talk about what we know. We tell about what we have seen. But you don't accept what we tell you. ¹²I have told you about things here on earth, but you do not believe me. So surely you will not believe me if I tell you about the things of heaven! ¹³The only one who has ever gone up to heaven is the One who came down from heaven—the Son of Man. . . .

¹⁶"For God loved the world so much that he gave his only Son. God gave his Son so that whoever believes in him may not be lost, but have eternal life.

From John 3

? What did Nicodemus want to know from Jesus?

? Did Nicodemus really understand what Jesus was trying to tell him? How do you know?

? Sometimes it's hard for us to believe something unless we actually see it. Nicodemus couldn't see someone being born again so he couldn't believe it could happen. What is something you know about God that you cannot see?

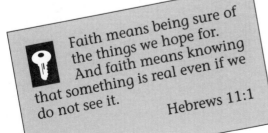

Faith means being sure of the things we hope for. And faith means knowing that something is real even if we do not see it.

Hebrews 11:1

Lord, help me to believe You are there and that You can help me in difficult times. Amen.

More▐▐▐▶

WHEN IT'S HARD TO
BELIEVE THAT GOD IS
THERE TO HELP YOU,
READ BIBLE VERSES OUT
LOUD. AS YOUR EARS
HEAR GOD'S WORDS,
YOUR FAITH IN HIM WILL
GROW AND YOU WILL BE
ENCOURAGED. LOOK UP
THESE VERSES AND
READ THEM OUT LOUD.
THEN WRITE WHAT THE
VERSE MEANS TO YOU.

⇨ DEUTERONOMY 31:6
GOD WILL NEVER LEAVE ME
OR FORGET ABOUT ME.
⇨ PSALM 46:1

⇨ ISAIAH 41:13

⇨ JOHN 14:13

⇨ I PETER 5:7

Enthusiasm

A JEW! DOE[S]
HE KNOW J[EWS]
AREN'T WELC[OME]
IN SAMARI[A]

Talk of the Town

IN **Samaria Jesus came to the town called Sychar.** This town is near the field that Jacob gave to his son Joseph. [6]Jacob's well was there. Jesus was tired from his long trip. So he sat down beside the well. It was about noon. [7]A Samaritan woman came to the well to get some water. Jesus said to her, "Please give me a drink." [8](This happened while Jesus' followers were in town buying some food.)

[9]The woman said, "I am surprised that you ask me for a drink. You are a Jew and I am a Samaritan." (Jews are not friends with Samaritans.)

[10]Jesus said, "You don't know what God gives. And you don't know who asked you for a drink. If you knew, you would have asked me, and I would have given you living water."

[11]The woman said, "Sir, where will you get that living water? The well is very deep, and you have nothing to get water with. [12]Are you greater than Jacob, our father? Jacob is the one who gave us this well. He drank from it himself. Also, his sons and flocks drank from this well."

[13]Jesus answered, "Every person who drinks this water will be thirsty again. [14]But whoever drinks the water I give will never be thirsty again. The water I give will become a spring of water flowing inside him. It will give him eternal life."

[15]The woman said to him, "Sir, give me this water. Then I will never be thirsty again. And I will not have to come back here to get more water."

. . .[25]The woman said, "I know that the Messiah is coming." (Messiah is the One called Christ.) "When the Messiah comes, he will explain everything to us."

[26]Then Jesus said, "He is talking to you now. I am he."

. . .[28]Then the woman left her water jar and went back to town. She said to the people, [29]"A man told me everything I have ever done. Come see him. Maybe he is the Christ!" [30]So the people left the town and went to see Jesus.

From John 4

? Did the woman understand what the "living water" was that Jesus spoke of? What makes you think so?

? What happened when the woman realized that Jesus was the Messiah she had been looking for?

? When the woman heard all that Jesus said, she got excited. She ran into town and told everybody. Her enthusiasm was contagious because all the people came out to see the man she spoke of. How do you react when you are really excited about something?

COME! SEE A MAN WHO HAS TOLD ME THINGS ABOUT MY LIFE THAT NO STRANGER COULD KNOW. HE IS THE PROMISED MESSIAH! THE SAVIOR!

🔑 I can do all things through Christ because he gives me strength.
Philippians 4:13

Dear God, thank You for giving me strength each day to do the things required of me. Help me to work cheerfully and with enthusiasm because I know that everything I do is for You. Amen.

DRAW TWO CIRCLES. IN THE CIRCLE ON THE LEFT, DRAW A PICTURE OF YOUR FACE AS YOU USUALLY LOOK WHEN MOM OR DAD HAS A JOB FOR YOU TO DO. ON THE RIGHT, DRAW A PICTURE OF YOUR FACE WHEN YOU ARE REALLY ENTHUSED AND EXCITED ABOUT SOMETHING. DO THE TWO FACES MATCH? HOW CAN YOU SHOW MORE ENTHUSIASM FOR THE JOBS PEOPLE ASK YOU TO DO?

the Roof THROUGH

So **many people gathered to hear him preach that the house was full.** There was no place to stand, not even outside the door. Jesus was teaching them. ³Some people came, bringing a paralyzed man to Jesus. Four of them were carrying the paralyzed man. ⁴But they could not get to Jesus because of the crowd. So they went to the roof above Jesus and made a hole in the roof. Then they lowered the mat with the paralyzed man on it. ⁵Jesus saw that these men had great faith. So he said to the paralyzed man, "Young man, your sins are forgiven."

⁶Some of the teachers of the law were sitting there. They saw what Jesus did, and they said to themselves, ⁷"Why does this man say things like that? He is saying things that are against God. Only God can forgive sins."

⁸At once Jesus knew what these teachers of the law were thinking. So he said to them, "Why are you thinking these things? ⁹Which is easier: to tell this paralyzed man, 'Your sins are forgiven,' or to tell him, 'Stand up. Take your mat and walk'? ¹⁰But I will prove to you that the Son of Man has authority on earth to forgive sins." So Jesus said to the paralyzed man, ¹¹"I tell you, stand up. Take your mat and go home." ¹² Immediately the paralyzed man stood up. He took his mat and walked out while everyone was watching him.

The people were amazed and praised God. They said, "We have never seen anything like this!"

From Mark 2

What might the four men have thought when they saw such a large crowd outside the house where Jesus was teaching?

In this story, who had great faith—the paralyzed man or his friends?

Being a responsible person means that you are willing to do what you say you'll do. The four men didn't give up when they saw the large crowd, but took the responsibility to get their friend to Jesus. Think of an instance when you took responsibility for a friend — perhaps you promised to have your parents pick him up, help with homework, etc. How did it make you feel to help?

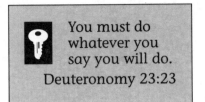

You must do whatever you say you will do.
Deuteronomy 23:23

Lord, help me to be responsible about the words I say and the things I do. Remind me to keep the promises I make. Amen.

WHAT YOU SAY IS SO IMPORTANT. PEOPLE EXPECT YOU TO KEEP YOUR WORD. IF YOU DON'T, THEY THINK THAT YOU ARE NOT A RESPONSIBLE PERSON. SOMETIMES WE BREAK OUR PROMISE AND NEED TO ASK FORGIVENESS, BUT GOD WANTS US TO KEEP TRYING TO IMPROVE. HERE IS A WAY TO START. FILL OUT THIS RESPONSIBILITY CARD.

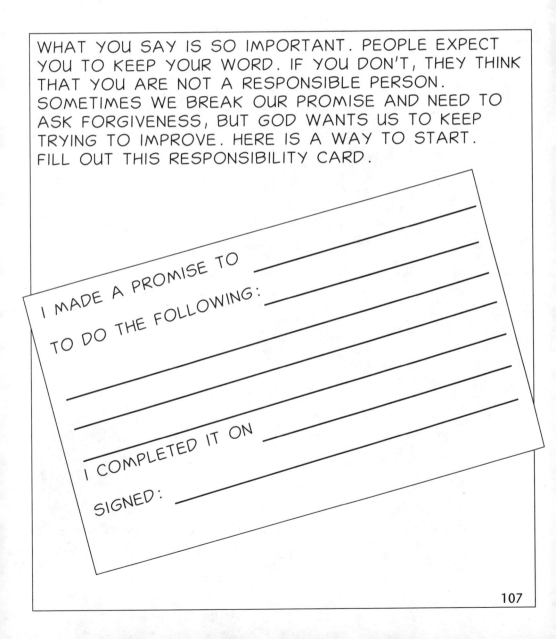

I MADE A PROMISE TO _____

TO DO THE FOLLOWING: _____

_____

_____

I COMPLETED IT ON _____

SIGNED: _____

A Job Well Done for No $$$

JESUS **left there and went into their synagogue.** ¹⁰In the synagogue, there was a man with a crippled hand. Some Jews there were looking for a reason to accuse Jesus of doing wrong. So they asked him, "Is it right to heal on the Sabbath day?"

¹¹Jesus answered, "If any of you has a sheep, and it falls into a ditch on the Sabbath day, then you will take the sheep and help it out of the ditch. ¹²Surely a man is more important than a sheep. So the law of Moses allows people to do good things on the Sabbath day."

¹³Then Jesus said to the man with the crippled hand, "Let me see your hand." The man put his hand out, and the hand became well again, the same as the other hand. ¹⁴But the Pharisees left and made plans to kill Jesus.

From Matthew 12

? What was Jesus trying to prove to the Pharisees?

? Did Jesus heal the man because He knew that the man would pay Him BIG BUCKS to have his hand made well?

? Jesus did a lot of good things for people. He didn't expect payment. Think of two things that you've done in the last month where you did it just because you wanted to be nice to someone.

So love your enemies. Do good to them, and lend to them without hoping to get anything back.

Luke 6:35

Dear God, help me get ideas for doing good things for others that will please You. Thanks. Amen.

IN TODAY'S WORLD EVERYONE EXPECTS TO GET PAID FOR EVERYTHING THEY DO. BUT JESUS TOLD US TO DO GOOD THINGS EVEN TO OUR ENEMIES. THAT'S A TALL ORDER! PAYMENT DOESN'T ALWAYS COME IN THE FORM OF DOLLARS AND CENTS. THINGS LIKE FRIENDSHIP, HAVING OTHERS RESPECT YOU, AND HAVING GOD SEE THAT WE'RE PRACTICING HIS INSTRUCTIONS CAN BE ADDED BENEFITS.
COMPLETE THE FOLLOWING STATEMENT.
ON THE DATE OF

_____

I, _____
DID SOMETHING GOOD
FOR _____

THE THING I DID WAS:

_____

I RECEIVED NO PAY, BUT I THINK THE BENEFITS TO ME FOR DOING THIS JOB WERE:

WHEN I DID THIS, I WAS PRACTICING GOD'S GOODNESS.

SIGNED, _____

IT'S THE KIND OF A NIGHT WHEN A SUDDEN STORM COULD HIT.

Caught in a Storm

THAT evening, Jesus said to his followers, **"Come with me across the lake."** 36He and the followers left the people there. They went in the boat that Jesus was already sitting in. There were also other boats with them. 37A very strong wind came up on the lake. The waves began coming over the sides and into the boat. It was almost full of water. 38Jesus was at the back of the boat, sleeping with his head on a pillow. The followers went to him and woke him. They said, "Teacher, do you care about us? We will drown!"

39Jesus stood up and commanded the wind and the waves to stop. He said, "Quiet! Be still!" Then the wind stopped, and the lake became calm.

40Jesus said to his followers, "Why are you afraid? Do you still have no faith?"

41The followers were very afraid and asked each other, "What kind of man is this? Even the wind and the waves obey him!"

From Mark 4

LOWER THE SAIL!

HELP! E BEING AMPED!

MASTER! DON'T YOU CARE IF WE DROWN?

Morel▶

? Why were the disciples afraid?

? What was Jesus doing at the back of the boat? When the disciples talked to Him, what did Jesus do about the storm?

? Peacefulness is the sense of feeling at rest even though you may be going through some difficult things. Every day we face things that seem to take our peace away. What are some things that keep you from being at peace? Some examples could be: fighting with your brother, being bullied by someone at school, etc.

PEACE, BE STILL!

I pray that the God who gives hope will fill you with much joy and peace while you trust in him.
Romans 15:13

Dear God, thank You for being there when I feel I have no peace in my life. Remind me that even when things go wrong, You are always there for me. Amen.

DRAW AN OUTLINE OF A BOAT WITH JESUS AND YOU INSIDE. AROUND THE BOAT DRAW BIG WAVES AND WRITE THINGS IN THE WATER THAT TAKE AWAY YOUR PEACE--ANGER, JEALOUSY, PROBLEMS, FIGHTING, ETC. WHEN YOU FEEL THAT YOU HAVE NO PEACE, TURN TO THIS PAGE AND REMIND YOURSELF THAT JESUS IS ALWAYS THERE WITH YOU.

A small Answer to a Big Problem

Resourcefulness

AFTER **this, Jesus went across Lake Galilee** (or, Lake Tiberias). ²Many people followed him because they saw the miracles he did to heal the sick. ³Jesus went up on a hill and there sat down with his followers. ⁴It was almost the time for the Jewish Passover Feast.

⁵Jesus looked up and saw a large crowd coming toward him. He said to Philip,

"Where can we buy bread for all these people to eat?" ⁶(Jesus asked Philip this question to test him. Jesus already knew what he planned to do.)

⁷Philip answered, "We would all have to work a month to buy enough bread for each person here to have only a little piece."

⁸Another follower there was Andrew. He was Simon Peter's brother. Andrew said, ⁹"Here is a boy with five loaves of barley bread and two little fish. But that is not enough for so many people."

¹⁰Jesus said, "Tell the people to sit down." This was a very grassy place. There were about 5,000 men who sat down there. ¹¹Then Jesus took the loaves of bread. He thanked God for the bread and gave it to the people who were sitting there. He did the same with the fish. He gave them as much as they wanted.

¹²They all had enough to eat. When they had finished, Jesus said to his followers, "Gather the pieces of fish and bread that were not eaten. Don't waste anything." ¹³So they gathered up the pieces that were left. They filled 12 large baskets with the pieces that were left of the five barley loaves.

From John 6

More!▶

? When the young boy offered his lunch to Jesus, do you think he expected it to feed 5,000 men (not to mention the women and children)? Why?

? What did Jesus do with the small lunch?

? Sometimes a situation seems impossible. But when we ask for God's help, He will give us ideas for ways to solve the problem. Think about a situation where you want to have more free time but you still have to do homework and chores around the house. Name two ways that will help you to organize your work so that you'll get it done faster.

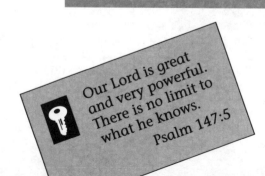

Our Lord is great and very powerful. There is no limit to what he knows.
Psalm 147:5

Thanks, God, for giving me the abilities and talents to think up ways to get things done. Help me to remember that You are always there to give me new ideas when I face a problem.   Amen.

LOOK! EVERYONE HERE IS GETTING ALL THE FOOD HE WANTS.

IT'S A MIRACLE!

GATHER UP THE FOOD THAT REMAINS.

A RESOURCEFUL PERSON DEVISES WAYS AND MEANS TO GET A JOB ACCOMPLISHED. THINK ABOUT YOUR BEDROOM (WHOA! LET'S NOT!). WRITE DOWN A THREE-STEP PLAN TO EVACUATE THE MESS AND MAKE YOUR MOM HAPPY. CONSIDER WHAT WOULD BE THE MOST TIME-EFFICIENT WAY SO THAT YOU CAN QUICKLY GET TO MORE IMPORTANT ISSUES--PLAYING BASEBALL, RIDING YOUR BIKE, ETC.

PROJECT: MESS EVACUATION
MY PLAN IS TO:

1.

2.

3.

TIME TAKEN TO ACCOMPLISH THE JOB:

SIGNED,

_____ ,

A VERY RESOURCEFUL PERSON

WALKING ON WATER

THEN **Jesus made his followers get into the boat.** He told them to go ahead of him to the other side of the lake. Jesus stayed there to tell the people they could go home. 23After he said good-bye to them, he went alone up into the hills to pray. It was late, and Jesus was there alone. 24By this time, the boat was already far away on the lake. The boat was having trouble because of the waves, and the wind was blowing against it.

25Between three and six o'clock in the morning, Jesus' followers were still in the boat. Jesus came to them. He was walking on the water. 26When the followers saw him walking on the water, they were afraid. They said, "It's a ghost!" and cried out in fear.

27But Jesus quickly spoke to them. He said, "Have courage! It is I! Don't be afraid."

28Peter said, "Lord, if that is really you, then tell me to come to you on the water."

29Jesus said, "Come."

And Peter left the boat and walked on the water to Jesus. 30But when Peter saw the wind and the waves, he became afraid and began to sink. He shouted, "Lord, save me!"

31Then Jesus reached out his hand and caught Peter. Jesus said, "Your faith is small. Why did you doubt?"

32After Peter and Jesus were in the boat, the wind became calm. 33Then those who were in the boat worshiped Jesus and said, "Truly you are the Son of God!"

From Matthew 14

SUDDENLY THEY LOOK UP TO SEE A FIGURE WALKING ON THE WATER. "A SPIRIT!" THEY CRY IN TERROR. ACROSS THE WAVES A CALM VOICE CALLS OUT: "IT IS I; DON'T BE AFRAID."

LORD! IF IT IS YOU, TELL ME TO COME TO YOU.

COME!

INSTANTLY PETER JUMPS FROM THE BOAT AND STARTS WALKING TOWARD JESUS. BUT WHEN HE SEES THE POWER OF THE WIND, HE LOSES FAITH— AND BEGINS TO SINK...

? What did Peter say to Jesus when he knew the image on the water was not a ghost?

? What did Peter do when Jesus told him to come?

? It took a lot of courage for Peter to get out of the boat. He had to trust that Jesus would take care of him. Think of an example in your life—maybe someone was in an accident or really sick or maybe your dad lost his job—where you had to have courage and just keep believing that God would take care of the situation. How did you feel? Were you a little scared?

Lord, thank You for being there when I need You. Help me to keep my eyes on You and not on my problems. Give me courage and make me strong. Amen.

Lord, you are my shield. You are my wonderful God who gives me courage. I will pray to the Lord. And he will answer me from his holy mountain.

Psalm 3:3, 4

More!

AS LONG AS PETER LOOKED AT JESUS, HE HAD COURAGE. WHEN HE STARTED LOOKING AT THE WIND AND THE WAVES, HE STARTED TO SINK. DRAW A PICTURE OF YOURSELF FULL OF COURAGE. THE NEXT TIME YOU FEEL DOWN AND NEED ENCOURAGEMENT, TURN TO THIS PAGE AND REMIND YOURSELF THAT GOD IS IN CONTROL.

THEN a teacher of the law stood up.

He was trying to test Jesus. He said, "Teacher, what must I do to get life forever?"

26Jesus said to him, "What is written in the law? What do you read there?"

27The man answered, "Love the Lord your God. Love him with all your heart, all your soul, all your strength, and all your mind." Also, "You must love your neighbor as you love yourself."

28Jesus said to him, "Your answer is right. Do this and you will have life forever."

29But the man wanted to show that the way he was living was right. So he said to Jesus, "And who is my neighbor?"

30To answer this question, Jesus said, "A man was going down the road from Jerusalem to Jericho. Some robbers attacked him. They tore off his clothes and beat him. Then they left him lying there, almost dead.

A Samaritan Comes to the Rescue

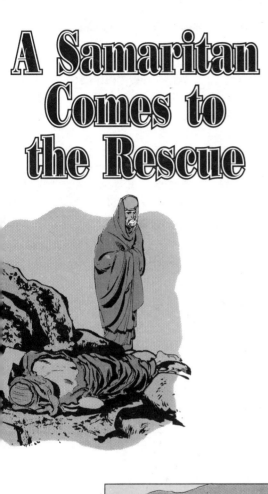

³¹It happened that a Jewish priest was going down that road. When the priest saw the man, he walked by on the other side of the road. ³²Next, a Levite came there. He went over and looked at the man. Then he walked by on the other side of the road. ³³Then a Samaritan traveling down the road came to where the hurt man was lying. He saw the man and felt very sorry for him. ³⁴The Samaritan went to him and poured olive oil and wine on his wounds and bandaged them. He put the hurt man on his own donkey and took him to an inn. At the inn, the Samaritan took care of him. ³⁵The next day, the Samaritan brought out two silver coins and gave them to the innkeeper. The Samaritan said, "Take care of this man. If you spend more money on him, I will pay it back to you when I come again.' "

³⁶Then Jesus said, "Which one of these three men do you think was a neighbor to the man who was attacked by the robbers?"

³⁷The teacher of the law answered, "The one who helped him."

Jesus said to him, "Then go and do the same thing he did!"

From Luke 10

More!

NOW I SEE-- MY NEIGHBOR IS ANYONE WHO NEEDS ME.

? Neither the priest nor the Levite (temple worker) stopped to help the injured man. Why do you think they didn't stop?

? The Samaritan bandaged the hurt man's wounds. What else did he do to help the man?

? The Samaritan saw the man's need and immediately took action to help him. If you saw an injured person lying in the street today, what might you do to help him?

 Remember the Lord in everything you do. And he will give you success.

Proverbs 3:6

Lord, show me ways that I can help others. Then help me take action to do what You want me to do. Thanks, Lord. Amen.

A PERSON WITH INITIATIVE SEES A PROBLEM AND THEN TAKES ACTION TO RESOLVE THAT PROBLEM. THINK OF SOMEONE IN YOUR CLASS AT SCHOOL OR CHURCH WHO NEEDS A FRIEND. WRITE DOWN AN ACTION PLAN OF HOW YOU CAN HELP THAT PERSON FEEL SPECIAL.

ACTION PLAN

PERSON WHO NEEDS A FRIEND: _____

THINGS I CAN DO TO HELP THAT PERSON:

1. _____

2. _____

3. _____

DATE I WILL PUT THIS PLAN INTO ACTION: _____

SIGNED _____, CIO

(CHIEF INITIATING OFFICER)

The Son who Left Home

THEN Jesus said, "A man had two sons. 12The younger son said to his father, 'Give me my share of the property.' So the father divided the property between his two sons. 13Then the younger son gathered up all that was his and left. He traveled far away to another country. There he wasted his money in foolish living. 14He spent everything that he had. Soon after that, the land became very dry, and there was no rain. There was not enough food to eat anywhere in the country. The son was hungry and needed money. 15So he got a job with one of the citizens there. The man sent the son into the fields to feed pigs. 16The son was so hungry that he was willing to eat the food the pigs were eating. But no one gave him anything. 17The son realized that he had been very foolish. He thought, 'All of my father's servants have plenty of food. But I am here, almost dying with hunger. 18I will leave and return to my father. I'll say to him: Father, I have sinned against God and have done wrong to you. 19I am not good enough to be called your son. But let me be like one of your servants.' 20So the son left and went to his father.

"While the son was still a long way off, his father saw him coming. He felt sorry for his son. So the father ran to him, and hugged and kissed him. 21The son said, 'Father, I have sinned against God and have done wrong to you. I am not good enough to be called your son.' 22But the father said to his servants, 'Hurry! Bring the best clothes and put them on him. Also, put a ring on his finger and sandals on his feet. 23And get our fat calf and kill it. Then we can have a feast and celebrate! 24My son was dead, but now he is alive again! He was lost, but now he is found!' So they began to celebrate.

From Luke 15

FATHER, I WANT TO RUN MY OWN LIFE. PLEASE GIVE ME THE SHARE OF YOUR MONEY THAT WILL SOMEDAY BE MINE.

I HAD HOPED YOU WOULD STAY HOME AND HELP WITH THE WORK HERE-- BUT IF YOU WANT THE MONEY, YOU MAY HAVE IT.

More‼➡

? The younger son made some bad choices. What were they?

? When he made the wise choice to return to his father's house, how did his father react toward him?

? All of us make good and bad choices. Think of an example of a good choice that you made this past week. What might have happened if you had chosen differently?

Lord, help me to make wise choices. Help me not to act first and think later. Lead me to make the best choice the first time. Amen.

The Lord says, "I will make you wise. I will show you where to go. I will guide you and watch over you."

Psalm 32:8

WE SHOULD GET WISER AS WE GROW OLDER BECAUSE WE CAN LEARN FROM OUR EXPERIENCES. IF YOU ASKED THE SON IF HE'D HAVE DONE THE SAME THING OVER A SECOND TIME, HE MIGHT HAVE SAID, "NO WAY! I'LL ONLY MAKE THAT MISTAKE ONCE!" THINK OF TWO QUESTIONS YOU HAVE ABOUT A PROBLEM IN YOUR LIFE, PERHAPS WITH A FRIEND OR A FAMILY MEMBER. THEN TALK TO SOMEONE OLDER--A PARENT, TEACHER, OR PASTOR--AND ASK FOR ADVICE. ASK THIS PERSON TO PRAY WITH YOU AND THEN WRITE THE WORDS OF ADVICE HERE.

The Sad Rich Man

A Jewish leader asked Jesus, **"Good Teacher,** what must I do to get the life that continues forever?"

19Jesus said to him, "Why do you call me good? Only God is good. 20You know the commands: 'You must not be guilty of adultery. You must not murder anyone. You must not steal. You must not tell lies about your neighbor in court. Honor your father and mother.'"

21But the leader said, "I have obeyed all these commands since I was a boy!"

22When Jesus heard this, he said to him, "But there is still one more thing you need to do. Sell everything you have and give the money to the poor. You will have a reward in heaven. Then come and follow me!" 23But when the man heard this, he became very sad because he was very rich.

24When Jesus saw that the man was sad, he said, "It will be very hard for rich people to enter the kingdom of God! 25It would be easier for a camel to go through the eye of a needle than for a rich person to enter the kingdom of God!"

From Luke 18

124

BUT I HAVE KEPT THE LAWS --SINCE I WAS A BOY.

YOU NEED TO DO ONE THING MORE -- SELL ALL THAT YOU HAVE, GIVE THE MONEY TO THE POOR, AND FOLLOW ME.

? Did the man consider himself to be a good man? Why?

? What was the one thing that the man didn't want to do?

? Some people want to give only a part of their life to God. They don't want to make a total commitment. They say, "I'll give you this much, God, but not my WHOLE life." How do you think God feels about this kind of commitment?

... The Lord is our God. He is the only Lord. Love the Lord your God with all your heart, soul and strength.

Deuteronomy 6:4, 5

Thanks, God, for loving me. Help me to commit my whole life to You and be willing to do whatever You ask me to do. Amen.

More!

THINK ABOUT YOUR COMMITMENT TO GOD. DO YOU WANT TO LEARN ABOUT HIM? . . . DO THINGS FOR HIM? . . . LIVE BY HIS RULES AND PROMISES? WRITE A NOTE TO GOD ABOUT HOW YOU FEEL.

DEAR GOD:

_____

_____

_____

_____

_____

_____

_____

_____

_____

_____

_____

_____

_____

_____

_____

_____

_____

Stewardship

JESUS was going through the city of Jericho.

2In Jericho there was a man named Zacchaeus. He was a wealthy, very important tax collector. 3He wanted to see who Jesus was, but he was too short to see above the crowd. 4He ran ahead to a place where he knew Jesus would come. He climbed a sycamore tree so he could see Jesus. 5When Jesus came to that place, he looked up and saw Zacchaeus in the tree. He said to him, "Zacchaeus, hurry and come down! I must stay at your house today."

6Zacchaeus came down quickly. He was pleased to have Jesus in his house. 7All the people saw this and began to complain, "Look at the kind of man Jesus stays with. Zacchaeus is a sinner!"

8But Zacchaeus said to the Lord, "I will give half of my money to the poor. If I have cheated anyone, I will pay that person back four times more!"

9Jesus said, "Salvation has come to this house today. This man truly belongs to the family of Abraham. 10The Son of Man came to find lost people and save them."

From Luke 19

A Rich Tree Climber

I HAVE TO SEE JESUS -- AND I WILL!

? What was Zacchaeus's job?

? What did Zacchaeus say that would let you know that he didn't want to cheat people anymore?

? Being a good steward (or manager) of your money is important to God. He wants you to use money wisely and be honest in your dealings with other people. Think of some wise ways that money can be used to get God's work done. Some examples might be to help missionaries, to support the minister, to buy needed items for the church, etc.

"Give, and you will receive. . . . The way you give to others is the way God will give to you."

Luke 6:38

Lord, help me to be a good manager of my time, talents, and money. Remind me that You come first in my life and that I should always give You the best of what I have to give. Amen.

GOD WANTS US TO BE GOOD STEWARDS OR MANAGERS OF ALL OUR RESOURCES: OUR TIME, OUR TALENTS AND ABILITIES, AND OUR MONEY. WRITE ONE THING YOU COULD GIVE TO GOD IN EACH OF THESE AREAS.

FOR EXAMPLE,
TIME: SATURDAY MORNING . . . 2 HOURS
TALENT: MOWING MRS. JONES'S LAWN
MONEY: EARN TEN DOLLARS FROM JOB TO GIVE IN MISSIONS' OFFERING ON SUNDAY.

YOUR EXAMPLE:
TIME:
TALENT:
MONEY:

Wash My Stinky Feet? No Way!

JESUS **and his followers were at the evening meal.** [4]During the meal Jesus stood up and took off his outer clothing. Taking a towel, he wrapped it around his waist. [5]Then he poured water into a bowl and began to wash the followers' feet. He dried them with the towel that was wrapped around him.

[6]Jesus came to Simon Peter. But Peter said to Jesus, "Lord, are you going to wash my feet?"

[7]Jesus answered, "You don't understand what I am doing now. But you will understand later."

[8]Peter said, "No! You will never wash my feet."

Jesus answered, "If I don't wash your feet, then you are not one of my people."

[9]Simon Peter answered, "Lord, after you wash my feet, wash my hands and my head, too!"

[10]Jesus said, "After a person has had a bath, his whole body is clean. He needs only to wash his feet. And you men are clean, but not all of you." [11]Jesus knew who would turn against him. That is why Jesus said, "Not all of you are clean."

PETER AND JOHN PREPARE FOR THE FEAST, AND THAT EVENING JESUS JOINS THE TWELVE IN THE UPPER ROOM. AFTER THEY ARE SEATED JESUS KNEELS, LIKE A SERVANT, TO WASH THE FEET OF HIS DISCIPLES.

NO, LORD. I'M NOT GOOD ENOUGH TO HAVE **YOU** WAIT ON ME!

[12]When he had finished washing their feet, he put on his clothes and sat down again. Jesus asked, "Do you understand what I have just done for you? [13]You call me 'Teacher' and 'Lord.' And this is right, because that is what I am. [14]I, your Lord and Teacher, have washed your feet. So you also should wash each other's feet. [15]I did this as an example for you. So you should do as I have done for you. [16]I tell you the truth. A servant is not greater than his master. A messenger is not greater than the one who sent him. [17]If you know these things, you will be happy if you do them.

From John 13 Morell 129

?Why did Jesus wash His follower's feet?

?What did Jesus say that would give us a clue as to how we should treat each other?

?Washing stinky feet is not a job that Jesus had to do. Yet He did this to show us what humility is. Think of a dirty job that you've had to do. How did you feel while you were doing it? Did you feel like a king or company president when you were through?

Dear God, help me to remember that all people are equal in Your eyes. Help me to keep my attitude right so that the things I do will build others up. Amen.

HUMILITY IS A HARD THING FOR US TO LEARN. IT MEANS LOWERING YOURSELF SO THAT THE OTHER GUY IS BUILT UP. THINK OF A TEETER-TOTTER. YOU ARE ON ONE END; YOUR FRIEND IS ON THE OTHER END. AS YOU GO DOWN, YOUR FRIEND IS LIFTED UP. WHAT ARE SOME THINGS YOU COULD DO TO LIFT SOMEONE UP THIS WEEK?

▲

▲

▲

▲

Asleep on the Job

QUIETLY, THEY LEAVE THE UPPER ROOM. THEY WALK THROUGH THE MOONLIT STREETS OF THE CITY, OUT AN EAST GATE, AND ACROSS A VALLEY TO THE GARDEN OF GETHSEMANE ON THE MOUNT OF OLIVES.

THEN **Jesus went with his followers to a place called Gethsemane.** He said to them, "Sit here while I go over there and pray." [37]He told Peter and the two sons of Zebedee to come with him. Then Jesus began to be very sad and troubled. [38]He said to Peter and the two sons of Zebedee, "My heart is full of sorrow and breaking with sadness. Stay here with me and watch."

[39]Then Jesus walked a little farther away from them. He fell to the ground and prayed, "My Father, if it is possible, do not give me this cup of suffering. But do what you want, not what I want." [40]Then Jesus went back to his followers and found them asleep. Jesus said to Peter, "You men could not stay awake with me for one hour? [41]Stay awake and pray for strength against temptation. Your spirit wants to do what is right. But your body is weak."

[42]Then Jesus went away a second time. He prayed, "My Father, if it is not possible for this painful thing to be taken from me, and if I must do it, then I pray that what you want will be done."

[43]Then Jesus went back to the followers. Again he found them asleep, because their eyes were heavy. [44]So Jesus left them and went away one more time and prayed. This third time he prayed, he said the same thing.

[45]Then Jesus went back to the followers and said, "You are still sleeping and resting? The time has come for the Son of Man to be given to sinful people. [46]Get up. We must go.

From Matthew 26

AT THE ENTRANCE JESUS ASKS EIGHT OF THE DISCIPLES WHILE HE TAKES HIS CLOSEST DISCIPLES, PETER, JAMES, JOHN FARTHER INTO THE GARDEN.

THIS IS A SAD NIGHT FOR ME -- STAY HERE AND WATCH WHILE I GO ALONE TO PRAY.

Good people will be guided by honesty. But dishonesty will destroy those who are not trustworthy.
Proverbs 11:3

Lord, help me to be a trustworthy person. Remind me to keep the promises I make to others. Amen.

? What did Jesus tell Peter and the sons of Zebedee the first time He went to pray?

? What did Jesus find every time He came back from prayer? Could He trust them to stay awake and pray? Why?

? Being trustworthy means that you are dependable and others can count on you. When you say you'll do something, it will get done. Can people count on you to do what you promise to do? Give an example of when you kept a promise to do something for someone.

More⏩

PEOPLE LEARN TO TRUST YOU WHEN YOU CARRY OUT YOUR PROMISES. BY FOLLOWING THROUGH, YOU PROVE TO OTHERS THAT YOU ARE TRUSTWORTHY. WRITE A COUPON TO YOUR MOM OR DAD PROMISING TO DO ONE JOB BY A CERTAIN DATE. THEN COPY YOUR COUPON ON ANOTHER PIECE OF PAPER. PLACE THE COPIED COUPON BY HIS OR HER PLATE AT THE NEXT MEAL. (YOU MIGHT WANT TO ROLL IT UP AND PUT A SMALL RIBBON AROUND IT.)

JOB COUPON

TO:

JOB TO BE DONE:

COMPLETED BY

SIGNED:

Gentleness

Before His Enemies

THEN Jesus said to the crowd, "You came to get me with swords and clubs as if I were a criminal.

Every day I sat in the Temple teaching. You did not arrest me there. 56But all these things have happened so that it will be as the prophets wrote." Then all of Jesus' followers left him and ran away.

57Those men who arrested Jesus led him to the house of Caiaphas, the high priest. The teachers of the law and the older Jewish leaders were gathered there. 58Peter followed Jesus but did not go near him. He followed Jesus to the courtyard of the high priest's house. He sat down with the guards to see what would happen to Jesus.

59The leading priests and the Jewish council tried to find something false against Jesus so that they could kill him. 60Many people came and told lies about him. But the council could find no real reason to kill Jesus. Then two people came and said, 61"This man said, 'I can destroy the Temple of God and build it again in three days.' "

62Then the high priest stood up and said to Jesus, "Aren't you going to answer? Don't you have something to say about their charges against you?" 63But Jesus said nothing.

Again the high priest said to Jesus, "You must swear to this. I command you by the power of the living God to tell us the truth. Tell us, are you the Christ, the Son of God?"

64Jesus answered, "Yes, I am. But I tell you, in the future you will see the Son of Man sitting at the right hand of God, the Powerful One. And you will see him coming in clouds in the sky."

65When the high priest heard this, he was very angry. He tore his clothes and said, "This man has said things that are against God! We don't need any more witnesses. You all heard him say these things against God. 66What do you think?"

The people answered, "He is guilty, and he must die."

67Then the people there spit in Jesus' face and beat him with their fists. Others slapped Jesus. 68They said, "Prove to us that you are a prophet, you Christ! Tell us who hit you!"

From Matthew 26

More⏵

FOLLOWING HIS ARREST, JESUS IS BROUGHT TO THE PALACE OF THE HIGH PRIEST. FALSE WITNESSES BOLDLY ACCUSE HIM OF MANY THINGS --BUT THEY CAN PROVE NOTHING. FINALLY THE HIGH PRIEST QUESTIONS THE PRISONER.

ARE YOU THE CHRIST, THE SON OF GOD?

I AM.

Lord, help me to be more gentle to others. Remind me that when I fail, You are always gentle to me. Amen.

Always be humble and gentle. Be patient and accept each other with love.

Ephesians 4:2

? How did the people act toward Jesus?

? Did Jesus have the power to kill the leaders and the people if He had wanted to? How do you know?

? Being gentle means that you have the power to take control, to show force or anger, but you choose not to. What can happen when we lose our temper and get angry?

USUALLY WE ARE NOT GENTLE. WE YELL AND DEMAND OUR OWN WAY. WE THINK IF WE ACT TOUGH, WE'LL ACCOMPLISH WHAT WE WANT. THINK OF A SITUATION WHERE YOU COULD GIVE A GENTLE ANSWER INSTEAD OF DEMANDING YOUR OWN WAY. FOR EXAMPLE, INSTEAD OF YELLING AT A BROTHER OR SISTER, YOU RESPOND WITH GENTLENESS. WHAT DO YOU THINK WILL HAPPEN?

(TRY THIS NEXT TIME YOU GET INTO A FIGHT. WRITE DOWN WHAT ACTUALLY HAPPENED WHEN YOU TRIED THE GENTLE METHOD.)

"I Never Saw Him Before"

> PETER, BEFORE THE COCK CROWS YOU WILL DENY ME THREE TIMES.

> DENY MY LORD? NEVER! MY SWORD IS READY THIS MINUTE FOR THE FIRST PERSON WHO TRIES TO HARM HIM.

AT **that time, Peter was sitting in the courtyard.** A servant girl came to him and said, "You were with Jesus, that man from Galilee."

70But Peter said that he was never with Jesus. He said this to all the people there. Peter said, "I don't know what you are talking about."

71Then he left the courtyard. At the gate, another girl saw him. She said to the people there, "This man was with Jesus of Nazareth."

72Again, Peter said that he was never with Jesus. Peter said, "I swear that I don't know this man Jesus!"

73A short time later, some people standing there went to Peter. They said, "We know you are one of those men who followed Jesus. We know this because of the way you talk."

74Then Peter began to curse. He said, "May a curse fall on me if I'm not telling the truth. I don't know the man." After Peter said this, a rooster crowed. 75Then he remembered what Jesus had told him: "Before the rooster crows, you will say three times that you don't know me." Then Peter went outside and cried painfully.

From Matthew 26

Morell⯈

137

138

? What did Jesus tell Peter he would do before the rooster crowed?

? How did Peter feel after he heard the rooster?

? A faithful friend is one who is always there — in good times or bad. Peter was not a faithful friend. When the going got rough, he got scared and denied he even knew Jesus. Have you ever had someone who you thought was a friend go against you? How did it make you feel?

Dear God, thank You for being a faithful friend to me. Show me ways that I can be a good friend to others. Amen.

Some friends may ruin you. But a real friend will be more loyal than a brother.
Proverbs 18:24

DO YOU HAVE A FAITHFUL FRIEND--SOMEONE WHO IS THERE IN GOOD TIMES OR BAD? WRITE DOWN THREE THINGS THAT YOU LIKE ABOUT THAT PERSON. THEN THINK OF THREE THINGS YOU COULD DO TO SHOW THAT YOU ARE A FAITHFUL FRIEND TO YOUR FRIEND (LISTEN WHEN HE OR SHE NEEDS TO TALK, EAT LUNCH TOGETHER, ETC.).

MY FRIEND'S NAME IS: _____
I LIKE MY FRIEND BECAUSE:

1. _____
2. _____
3. _____

SOME WAYS THAT I CAN SHOW THAT I AM A FAITHFUL FRIEND ARE:

1. _____
2. _____
3. _____

Between 2 Criminals

THERE **were also two criminals led out with Jesus to be killed.** 33Jesus and the two criminals were taken to a place called the Skull. There the soldiers nailed Jesus to his cross. They also nailed the criminals to their crosses, one beside Jesus on the right and the other beside Jesus on the left. . . . 39One of the criminals began to shout insults at Jesus: "Aren't you the Christ? Then save yourself! And save us too!"

40But the other criminal stopped him. He said, "You should fear God! You are getting the same punishment as he is. 41We are punished justly; we should die. But this man has done nothing wrong!" 42Then this criminal said to Jesus, "Jesus, remember me when you come into your kingdom!"

43Then Jesus said to him, "Listen! What I say is true: Today you will be with me in paradise!"

From Luke 23

140

A good person speaks with wisdom. He says what is fair.
Psalm 37:30

God, help me treat others fairly. Remind me to say kind words and keep a good attitude when things I face seem unfair. Amen.

? What happened to Jesus and the two criminals when they were taken to the place called the Skull?

? What did one of the criminals say to let you know that he realized something wasn't fair about Jesus' punishment?

? Some things around us don't seem fair—why do good people lose their jobs or get cancer or get hit by a car? We can look at our everyday life and wonder why some people always get the special parts in plays, get to be team captain, or have so many friends. If we try, we can find unfair things all around us. Name other things that you think are unfair.

SOME THINGS IN LIFE ARE UNFAIR. WHAT MATTERS TO GOD IS HOW YOU HANDLE UNFAIR SITUATIONS. BY CHECKING WITH GOD'S WORD YOU CAN DISCOVER SOME HELPFUL KEYS TO HELP KEEP YOUR ATTITUDE ON TRACK. LOOK UP THESE SCRIPTURES. THEN WRITE A SHORT DESCRIPTION OF WHAT THE VERSE SAYS TO YOU ABOUT FAIRNESS.

☆ ACTS 10:34--TO GOD EVERYONE IS THE SAME

☆ ROMANS 12:10--

☆ PROVERBS 21:3--

☆ HEBREWS 13:16--

☆ PROVERBS 21:15--

Loving

TRULY THIS MAN WAS GOD'S SON!

GOD SO LOVED THE WORLD FOR GOD SO LOVED THE WORLD

FATHER, INTO THY HANDS I COMMIT MY SPIRIT.

IT was about noon, and the whole land became dark until three o'clock in the afternoon. 45There was no sun! The curtain in the Temple was torn into two pieces.

46Jesus cried out in a loud voice, "Father, I give you my life." After Jesus said this, he died.

47The army officer there saw what happened. He praised God, saying, "I know this was a good man!"

48Many people had gathered there to watch this thing. When they saw what happened, they returned home. They beat their chests because they were so sad.

From Luke 23

?What was unusual about what happened when Jesus died?

?How did the army officer, Jesus' followers, and the other people who were watching act when Jesus died?

?It's hard for us to understand how Jesus could take all the sins of every person who has ever lived and then die to pay for those sins with His blood. Sin could only be blotted out by sacrificing a lamb. Jesus became a lamb and gave His blood for us. What might have happened if Jesus would have decided He didn't want to die on the cross?

Morell

> You are God's children whom he loves. So try to be like God. Live a life of love. Love other people just as Christ loved us. Christ gave himself for us—he was a sweet-smelling offering and sacrifice to God.
>
> Ephesians 5:1, 2

Jesus, thank You for going to the cross to pay for my sin. Thank You for loving me. Help me to think of different ways to show You how much I love You. Amen.

GOD LOVED US SO MUCH THAT HE GAVE HIS ONLY SON SO THAT WE CAN HAVE ETERNAL LIFE WITH HIM IN HEAVEN. DRAW A PICTURE THAT SHOWS YOUR LOVE FOR GOD. YOU MIGHT LIKE TO MAKE A VALENTINE TO GOD.

A Job for Peter

Peter Peter Peter Peter Peter

PETER IS SO EAGER TO REACH JESUS THAT HE JUMPS INTO THE WATER AND SWIMS TO LAND. THE OTHERS BRING THE BOAT IN AND ANCHOR IT OFFSHORE. AFTER THE NET IS PULLED IN, JESUS CALLS TO HIS HUNGRY DISCIPLES.

COME AND EAT.

LATER, Jesus showed himself to his **followers** by Lake Galilee. This is how it happened: . . .
³Simon Peter said, "I am going out to fish."

The other followers said, "We will go with you." So they went out and got into the boat. They fished that night but caught nothing.

⁴Early the next morning Jesus stood on the shore. But the followers did not know that it was Jesus. ⁵Then he said to them, "Friends, have you caught any fish?"

They answered, "No."

⁶He said, "Throw your net into the water on the right side of the boat, and you will find some." So they did this. They caught so many fish that they could not pull the net back into the boat.

⁷The follower whom Jesus loved said to Peter, "It is the Lord!" When Peter heard him say this, he wrapped his coat around himself. (Peter had taken his clothes off.) Then he jumped into the water. ⁸The other followers went to shore in the boat, dragging the net full of fish.

From John 21

More!➡

145

They were not very far from shore, only about 100 yards. 9When the followers stepped out of the boat and onto the shore, they saw a fire of hot coals. There were fish on the fire, and there was bread.

10Then Jesus said, "Bring some of the fish that you caught."

11Simon Peter went into the boat and pulled the net to the shore. It was full of big fish. There were 153. Even though there were so many, the net did not tear. 12Jesus said to them, "Come and eat." None of the followers dared ask him, "Who are you?" They knew it was the Lord. 13Jesus came and took the bread and gave it to them. He also gave them the fish . . . .

15When they finished eating, Jesus said to Simon Peter, "Simon son of John do you love me more than these?"

He answered, "Yes, Lord, you know that I love you."

Jesus said, "Take care of my lambs."

16Again Jesus said, "Simon son of John do you love me?"

He answered, "Yes, Lord, you know that I love you."

Jesus said, "Take care of my sheep."

17A third time he said, "Simon son of John do you love me?"

Peter was hurt because Jesus asked him the third time, "Do you love me?" Peter said, "Lord, you know everything. You know that I love you!"

He said to him, "Take care of my sheep."

? How many fish did they catch after following Jesus' suggestion? Why do you think Jesus told them to cast their net on the other side of the boat?

? How many times did Jesus ask Peter the question, "Do you love Me?"

? Jesus may have been testing Peter's loyalty by asking him the same question so many times. Sometimes it's easy to give a quick answer and not think about what we are saying. If a friend asked you, "Are you really my friend?", what would that question mean to you? Does it mean more than just saying "Hi!" at school?

 He guards those who are fair to others. He protects those who are loyal to him.

Proverbs 2:8

Dear God, thank You for showing Your love to me every day. Help me to show loyalty to You by trying to do things that please You. Give me more ideas through Your Word on how I can do this. Thanks. Amen.

JESUS WANTED PETER TO GO BEYOND SAYING THAT HE LOVED JESUS. HE WANTED PETER TO PROVE HIS LOYALTY WITH ACTION--TAKE CARE OF HIS SHEEP (OR HIS FOLLOWERS). JESUS WANTS MORE THAN AN "I LOVE YOU" FROM YOU. HE WANTS YOU TO TAKE ACTION TO SHOW YOUR LOYALTY TO HIM. NAME SOME WAYS THAT YOU CAN SHOW YOUR LOVE AND LOYALTY TO THE LORD.

1 _____

2 _____

3 _____

4 _____

5 _____

6 _____

It's Hard to Wait

AFTER his **death, [Jesus] showed himself** to them and . . . spoke to them about the Kingdom of God. . . . [4]He said, "The Father has made you a promise . . . . Wait here to receive this promise. . . . The Holy Spirit will come to you. Then you will receive power. You will be my witnesses—in Jerusalem, in all of Judea, in Samaria, and in every part of the world."

Chapter 2When the day of Pentecost came, they were all together in one place. [2]Suddenly a noise came from heaven. It sounded like a strong wind blowing. This noise filled the whole house where they were sitting. . . . [4]They were all filled with the Holy Spirit, and they began to speak different languages. The Holy Spirit was giving them the power to speak these languages.

[5]There were some religious Jews staying in Jerusalem who were from every country in the world.

[38]Peter said to them, "Change your hearts and lives and be baptized, each one of you, in the name of Jesus Christ for the forgiveness of your sins. And you will receive the gift of the Holy Spirit. [39]This promise is for you. It is also for your children and for all who are far away. It is for everyone the Lord our God calls to himself."

From Acts 1, 2

THE ANGELS DISAPPEAR, AND PETER TURNS TO THE OTHERS.

LET'S DO WHAT JESUS TOLD US TO DO-- GO BACK TO JERUSALEM AND WAIT FOR THE POWER HE PROMISED TO SEND US BEFORE WE BEGIN HIS WORK.

So THE DISCIPLES WHO HAD ONCE FLED FOR FEAR OF BEING ARRESTED AS FRIENDS OF JESUS, RETURN TO THE CITY-- KNOWING THAT JESUS IS DEPENDING ON THEM TO CARRY ON THE WORK FOR WHICH HE WAS CRUCIFIED.

? What were Jesus' followers waiting for?

? What would this promise enable them to do?

? Whether we know what's in the future or not, waiting is the hardest part. Think of a time that you had to wait for a long time to receive something special.

 My brothers, you will have many kinds of troubles. But when these things happen, you should be very happy. . . . This will give you patience.

James 1:2, 3

Lord, help me to learn patience so that I can speak and act in a way that will always please You. Thanks. Amen.

More!!!⟶

SOMETIMES GOD USES WAITING TO HELP US LEARN PATIENCE. PATIENCE IS THE ABILITY TO GO THROUGH PROBLEMS WITH A CALM ATTITUDE, WITHOUT COMPLAINING. IT ALLOWS US THE TIME TO HEAR THE OTHER SIDE OF THE STORY BEFORE SAYING ANGRY WORDS WE WILL REGRET. WRITE GOD A NOTE AND TELL HIM ABOUT ONE PROBLEM YOU'RE HAVING TROUBLE WORKING OUT. ASK HIM FOR PATIENCE TO SOLVE THE PROBLEM HIS WAY.

DEAR GOD:

3000 in a Day

ON THE FIRST DAY OF THE NEW TESTAMENT CHURCH, 3,000 PEOPLE WERE ADDED TO THE NUMBER OF BELIEVERS IN JESUS CHRIST. NEW BELIEVERS WERE EVERYWHERE, ALL HAVING A GREAT TIME. . . .

THEY spent their time learning the apostles' teaching. And they continued to share, to break bread, and to pray together.

⁴³The apostles were doing many miracles and signs. And everyone felt great respect for God. ⁴⁴All the believers stayed together. They shared everything. ⁴⁵They sold their land and the things they owned. Then they divided the money and gave it to those people who needed it. ⁴⁶The believers met together in the Temple every day. They all had the same purpose. They broke bread in their homes, happy to share their food with joyful hearts. ⁴⁷They praised God, and all the people liked them. More and more people were being saved every day; the Lord was adding those people to the group of believers.

More▐▌▌➡

From Acts 2

? What were some of the things the new believers did?

? How did they feel about sharing their money and food?

? Fellowship means the getting together of two or more people who share similar beliefs or feelings. Christians experience this in a special way because they believe in Jesus. Think of all the ways that Christians have fellowship together. How many can you list? (Examples: Sunday school class, church dinners, having someone over to your house, etc.)

Lord, help me to share myself with other Christians. Show me ways to encourage others and give me ideas to help them get closer to You. Amen.

... You should meet together and encourage each other. Do this even more as you see the Day coming.
Hebrews 10:25b

CALL A SPECIAL MEETING OF THE CKC (SEE PAGE 40) FOR THE PURPOSE OF HAVING FELLOWSHIP. ASSIGN SOMEONE TO READ A BIBLE VERSE, SOMEONE TO TELL THE GROUP ABOUT SOMETHING SPECIAL GOD DID, AND SOMEONE TO SAY A PRAYER. TELL EVERYONE TO BRING SOMETHING GOOD TO EAT. THEN PLAN TO HAVE A GREAT TIME! ORGANIZE YOUR PLANS HERE.

Miracle at the Gate

ONE AFTERNOON WHEN PETER AND JOHN GO TO THE TEMPLE FOR PRAYER THEY FIND A LAME MAN BEGGING AT THE BEAUTIFUL GATE.

HAVE MERCY-- A COIN FOR THE POOR.

ONE day Peter and John **went to the Temple.** It was three o'clock in the afternoon. This was the time for the daily prayer service. 2There, at the Temple gate called Beautiful Gate, was a man who had been crippled all his life. Every day he was carried to this gate to beg. He would ask for money from the people going into the Temple. 3The man saw Peter and John going into the Temple and asked them for money. 4Peter and John looked straight at him and said, "Look at us!" 5The man looked at them; he thought they were going to give him some money. 6But Peter said, "I don't have any silver or gold, but I do have something else I can give you: By the power of Jesus Christ from Nazareth—stand up and walk!" 7Then Peter took the man's right hand and lifted him up. Immediately the man's feet and ankles became strong. 8He jumped up, stood on his feet, and began to walk. He went into the Temple with them, walking and jumping, and praising God. 9-10All the people recognized him. They knew he was the crippled man who always sat by the Beautiful Gate begging for money. Now they saw this same man walking and praising God. The people were amazed. They could not understand how this could happen.

I HAVE NO MONEY, BUT I'LL GIVE YOU WHAT I HAVE. IN THE NAME OF JESUS CHRIST, RISE UP AND WALK!

From Acts 3

More➠

? What did the crippled man expect to get from Peter and John? What did they give him instead?

? What did the man do when he was able to walk?

? When we praise God we are expressing words of thanks and love to Him. Think of five things that you can thank God for.

Lord, thank You for always being there to watch over me and provide for my needs. Help me to praise You in all that I do. Amen.

 Let everything that breathes praise the Lord. Praise the Lord!

Psalm 150:6

WE CAN PRAISE GOD BY TELLING HIM WHAT A GREAT GOD HE IS. PRETEND THAT THIS SPACE IS A POSTER. WRITE WORDS OR PHRASES THAT DESCRIBE HOW YOU FEEL ABOUT GOD. SOME EXAMPLES ARE: YOU'RE A GREAT GOD! SUPER! PRAISE THE LORD!

To Preach or Not To Preach

WHILE Peter and John **were speaking to the people,** a group of men came up to them. There were Jewish priests, the captain of the soldiers that guarded the Temple, and some Sadducees. [2]They were upset because the two apostles were teaching the people. Peter and John were preaching that people will rise from death through the power of Jesus. [3]The Jewish leaders grabbed Peter and John and put them in jail. It was already night, so they kept them in jail until the next day. [4]But many of those who heard Peter and John preach believed the things they said. There were now about 5,000 men in the group of believers.

YOU ARE UNDER ARREST!

[5]The next day the Jewish leaders, the older Jewish leaders, and the teachers of the law met in Jerusalem. [6]Annas the high priest, Caiaphas, John, and Alexander were there. Everyone from the high priest's family was there. [7]They made Peter and John stand before them. The Jewish leaders asked them: "By what power or authority did you do this?"

[8]Then Peter was filled with the Holy Spirit. He said to them, "Rulers of the people and you older leaders, [9]are you questioning us about a good thing that was done to a crippled man? Are you asking us who made him well? [10]We want all of you and all the Jewish people to know that this man was made well by the power of Jesus Christ from Nazareth!

. . .[12]Jesus is the only One who can save people. His name is the only power in the world that has been given to save people. And we must be saved through him!"

[13]The Jewish leaders saw that Peter and John were not afraid to speak. They understood that these men had no special training or education. So they were amazed. Then they realized that Peter and John had been with Jesus. [14]They saw the crippled man standing there beside the two apostles. They saw that the man was healed. So they could say nothing against them . . . .

[18]They told them not to speak or to teach at all in the name of Jesus. [19]But Peter and John answered them, "What do you think is right? What would God want? Should we obey you or God? [20]We cannot keep quiet. We must speak about what we have seen and heard."

From Acts 4

THE NEXT MORNING THEY ARE BROUGHT BEFORE THE SANHEDRIN, THE SAME JEWISH COURT THAT CONDEMNED JESUS TO DEATH. BESIDE THEM--PERFECTLY WELL-- STANDS THE MAN WHO HAD BEEN LAME FROM BIRTH.

BY WHAT POWER AND IN WHOSE NAME HAVE YOU HEALED THIS MAN?

? Why did the group of men put Peter and John in jail?

? God wanted Peter and John to preach to people who needed to know Jesus, yet they had to go through some bad things. What did they experience?

WHETHER IT IS RIGHT IN THE EYES OF GOD FOR US TO OBEY HIM OR YOU, YOU MUST DECIDE. BUT WE HAVE TO KEEP ON PREACHING WHAT WE HAVE SEEN AND HEARD.

? It takes courage to stand up for what is right, and sometimes in doing that we may have to go through some tough stuff ourselves. Think of a time when you told the truth about something and because of doing so received bad treatment from others. An example: because of your honesty some kids at school wouldn't speak to you, or maybe you had to face a punishment.

Lord, give me the courage to stand up for what's right, regardless of the consequences. Help me to remember that no matter how bad things look, You are in control of my life and You are always there by my side. Amen.

So do not lose the courage that you had in the past. It has a great reward. You must hold on, so you can do what God wants and receive what he has promised.

Hebrews 10:35, 36

157

SOMETIMES IT'S HARD TO HAVE COURAGE BECAUSE YOU FEEL ALL ALONE. DRAW A PICTURE OF YOU. THEN DRAW A PICTURE OF JESUS STANDING RIGHT BESIDE YOU. REMEMBER THAT GOD IS ALWAYS THERE TO GIVE YOU THE COURAGE YOU NEED FOR ANY SITUATION.

A man named Ananias and his wife Sapphira sold some land. 2But he gave only part of the money to the apostles. He secretly kept some of it for himself. His wife knew about this, and she agreed to it.

3Peter said, "Ananias, why did you let Satan rule your heart? You lied to the Holy Spirit. Why did you keep part of the money you received for the land for yourself? 4Before you sold the land, it belonged to you. And even after you sold it, you could have used the money any way you wanted. Why did you think of doing this? You lied to God, not to men!" 5-6When Ananias heard this, he fell down and died. Some young men came in, wrapped up his body, carried it out, and buried it. And everyone who heard about this was filled with fear.

7About three hours later his wife came in. She did not know what had happened. 8Peter said to her, "Tell me how much money you got for your field. Was it this much?"

Sapphira answered, "Yes, that was the price."

9Peter said to her, "Why did you and your husband agree to test the Spirit of the Lord? Look! The men who buried your husband are at the door! They will carry you out." 10At that moment Sapphira fell down by his feet and died. The young men came in and saw that she was dead. They carried her out and buried her beside her husband. 11The whole church and all the others who heard about these things were filled with fear.

From Acts 5

? What did Ananias and Sapphira agree to do?

? Did they have to give all the money to the church? (See verse 4.)

? Sometimes we are more interested in how things look to others than we are in being honest. Sure, they sold their land and gave money to the church, but they wanted Peter to think that they gave ALL the money. Jeff wants his mom to think that he's spent hours on his homework, when really he spent most of the time in his room reading the comics. Is this honest? Why or why not?

Dear God,
show me ways to be
more honest with the people
around me. Help me to check myself
every day to make sure that my life follows
the example You gave me.   Amen.

The honest person will live safely. But the one who is dishonest will be caught.

Proverbs 10:9

THINK FOR A MOMENT ABOUT HOW HONEST YOU HAVE BEEN LATELY WITH YOUR FRIENDS, YOUR TEACHERS, AND YOUR FAMILY. WHAT IS ONE WAY THAT YOU COULD IMPROVE IN THIS AREA? WRITE DOWN YOUR PLAN IN A PRAYER TO GOD.

DEAR GOD:

DEDICATED TO THE RIGHT CAUSE

IN **Jerusalem Saul was still trying to frighten the followers of the Lord by saying he would kill them.** So he went to the high priest ²and asked him to write letters to the synagogues in the city of Damascus. Saul wanted the high priest to give him the authority to find people in Damascus who were followers of Christ's Way. If he found any there, men or women, he would arrest them and bring them back to Jerusalem.

³So Saul went to Damascus. As he came near the city, a bright light from heaven suddenly flashed around him. ⁴Saul fell to the ground. He heard a voice saying to him, "Saul, Saul! Why are you doing things against me?"

⁵Saul said, "Who are you, Lord?"

The voice answered, "I am Jesus. I am the One you are trying to hurt. ⁶Get up now and go into the city. Someone there will tell you what you must do."

⁷The men traveling with Saul stood there, but they said nothing. They heard the voice, but they saw no one. ⁸Saul got up from the ground. He opened his eyes, but he could not see. So the men with Saul took his hand and led him into Damascus.

PAUL, WHAT'S THE MATTER?

MY EYES—I CAN'T SEE! HELP ME INTO THE CITY.

IN TIME PAUL BECOMES THE MOST BRILLIANT PUPIL OF THE FAMOUS TEACHER, GAMALIEL. TOGETHER THEY DISCUSS THE SCRIPTURES-- ESPECIALLY THE PARTS THAT TELL ABOUT THE COMING OF THE SAVIOR.

LIKE KING DAVID, HE WILL MAKE OUR COUNTRY STRONG AND POWERFUL. IF ONLY HE WOULD COME NOW-- I'D SPEND MY LIFE SERVING HIM.

161

More!!!⏵

⁹For three days Saul could not see, and he did not eat or drink.

¹⁰There was a follower of Jesus in Damascus named Ananias. The Lord spoke to Ananias in a vision, "Ananias!" Ananias answered, "Here I am, Lord."

¹¹The Lord said to him, "Get up and go to the street called Straight Street. Find the house of Judas. Ask for a man named Saul from the city of Tarsus. He is there now, praying. ¹²Saul has seen a vision. In it a man named Ananias comes to him and lays his hands on him. Then he sees again."

¹³But Ananias answered, "Lord, many people have told me about this man and the terrible things he did to your people in Jerusalem. ¹⁴Now he has come here to Damascus. The leading priests have given him the power to arrest everyone who worships you."

¹⁵But the Lord said to Ananias, "Go! I have chosen Saul for an important work. He must tell about me to non-Jews, to kings, and to the people of Israel. ¹⁶I will show him how much he must suffer for my name." *From Acts 9*

GO, FOR I HAVE CHOSEN HIM TO TAKE MY NAME BEFORE THE GENTILES, AND KINGS, AND THE CHILDREN OF ISRAEL.

ANANIAS, GET UP. GO TO THE HOUSE OF JUDAS ON THE STREET CALLED STRAIGHT. ASK FOR A MAN NAMED PAUL. HE IS PRAYING, AND HE HAS SEEN YOU COMING TO RESTORE HIS SIGHT.

LORD, I HAVE HEARD OF THIS MAN AND THE EVIL HE HAS DONE TO YOUR FOLLOWERS IN JERUSALEM.

? Why did Saul want to find Jesus' followers in Damascus?

? After Saul became a Christian, how did he act toward Christians?

? A dedicated person is one who goes after something with his or her whole heart. Saul was dedicated to killing Christians because he felt strongly that that was the right thing to do. Name some areas where a person can be dedicated. Some examples are: sports, music, being a minister or a teacher, etc.

Dear God, help me to stay dedicated to the right cause—serving You. Thank You for Your Word that can help me to keep on track and not get into areas that wouldn't please You. Amen.

So brothers, since God has shown us great mercy, I beg you to offer your lives as a living sacrifice to him. Your offering must be only for God and pleasing to him.

Romans 12:1

PAUL WAS DEDICATED TO THE WRONG CAUSE WHEN HE KILLED THE CHRISTIANS. BUT WHEN JESUS SPOKE TO HIM ON THE ROAD TO DAMASCUS, HE BECAME DEDICATED TO THE RIGHT CAUSE--HELPING PEOPLE BECOME CHRISTIANS. HOW CAN YOU BECOME MORE DEDICATED TO JESUS? THINK OF TWO THINGS YOU COULD DO WITH YOUR WHOLE HEART TO SHOW GOD THAT YOU MEAN BUSINESS!

1.

2.

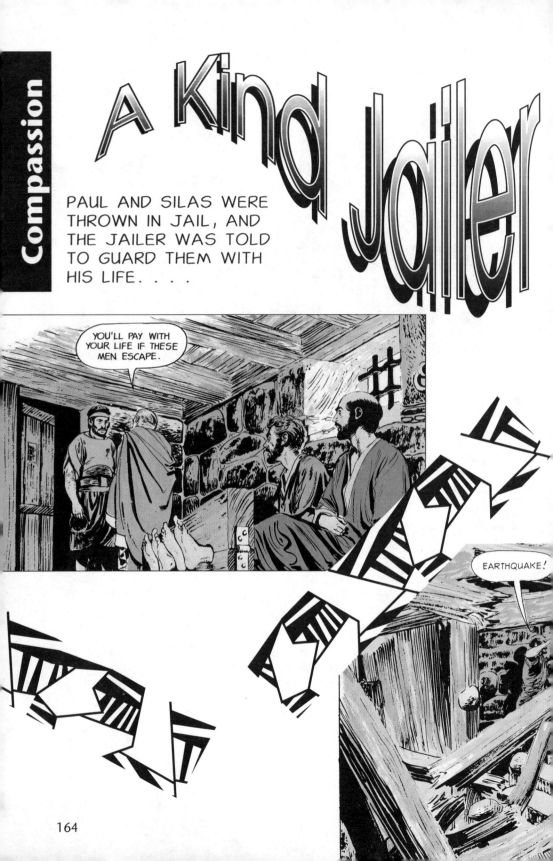

THEY'RE GONE! I MIGHT AS WELL KILL MYSELF.

NO! NO! WE'RE ALL HERE!

THE QUAKE IS OVER. THE JAILER RUSHES INTO THE DUNGEON, AFRAID THAT HIS PRISONERS HAVE ESCAPED.

ABOUT midnight Paul and Silas

were praying and singing songs to God. The other prisoners were listening to them. 26Suddenly, there was a big earthquake. It was so strong that it shook the foundation of the jail. Then all the doors of the jail broke open. All the prisoners were freed from their chains. 27The jailer woke up and saw that the jail doors were open. He thought that the prisoners had already escaped. So he got his sword and was about to kill himself. 28But Paul shouted, "Don't hurt yourself! We are all here!"

29The jailer told someone to bring a light. Then he ran inside. Shaking with fear, he fell down before Paul and Silas. 30Then he brought them outside and said, "Men, what must I do to be saved?"

31They said to him, "Believe in the Lord Jesus and you will be saved—you and all the people in your house." 32So Paul and Silas told the message of the Lord to the jailer and all the people in his house. 33At that hour of the night the jailer took Paul and Silas and washed their wounds. Then he and all his people were baptized immediately. 34After this the jailer took Paul and Silas home and gave them food. He and his family were very happy because they now believed in God.

From Acts 16

WHAT MUST I DO TO BE SAVED?

BELIEVE ON THE LORD JESUS CHRIST.

? What happened at midnight that made the jailer afraid?

? What was the jailer's reaction to what Paul and Silas told him?

? When the jailer heard about Jesus, it changed his life. He changed from a hardened jailer to a man full of compassion. He washed Paul and Silas's wounds and took them home and gave them food. The more we know about Jesus, the more we want to help others. Think of a time when you helped someone who was in need.

Lord, thank You for always caring about the needs of people. Use me to show compassion to those who need help so that they see Your love through the way I act toward them. Amen.

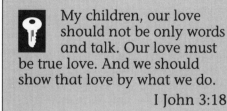
My children, our love should not be only words and talk. Our love must be true love. And we should show that love by what we do.

I John 3:18

WHEN GOD'S LOVE FILLS OUR HEART, WE WANT TO DO NICE THINGS FOR PEOPLE. WE FEEL COMPASSION FOR PEOPLE IN TROUBLE AND WANT TO HELP THEM. THINK OF SOMEONE IN YOUR CHURCH OR NEIGHBORHOOD WHO COULD REALLY USE SOME HELP (MAYBE THEY NEED CHEERING UP OR THEIR YARD RAKED OR THEIR PLANTS WATERED). ASK GOD TO SHOW YOU WAYS TO HELP THAT PERSON AND THEN OFFER YOUR HELP. WRITE YOUR IDEAS HERE.

1.

2.

3.

4.

5.

Perseverence

"**I** have been in prison. . . I have been hurt . . . in beatings. I have been near death many times 24Five times the Jews have given me their punishment of 39 lashes with a whip. 25Three different times I was beaten with rods. One time they tried to kill me with stones. Three times I was in ships that were wrecked, and one of these times I spent the night and the next day in the sea. 26I have gone on many travels. And I have been in danger from rivers, from thieves, from my own people, the Jews, and from those who are not Jews. I have been in danger in cities, in places where no one lives, and on the sea. . . . 27I have done hard and tiring work, and many times I did not sleep. I have been hungry and thirsty. Many times I have been without food. I have been cold and without clothes."

From II Corinthians 11

"**My** life is being given as an offering to God. The time has come for me to leave this life. 7I have fought the good fight. I have finished the race. I have kept the faith. 8Now, a crown is waiting for me. I will get that crown for being right with God. The Lord is the judge who judges rightly, and he will give me the crown on that Day. He will give that crown not only to me but to all those who have waited with love for him to come again."

From II Timothy 4

Finishing the Race

More!⟩⟩⟩

? Did Paul live an easy life because he was a Christian? How do you know?

? What was Paul's attitude about the life he had lived? (See II Timothy 4:6.) Did he complain to God?

? Paul used the illustration of finishing a race to talk about the end of his life. When you think of running a race, what are some things that happen that make you want to stop running?

 God is working in you to help you want to do what pleases him. Then he gives you the power to do it.

Philippians 2:13

Lord, help me to keep following You and obeying Your Word no matter what happens in my life. Thanks, God, for giving me the strength to keep trying. Amen.

PAUL'S GOAL WAS TO RECEIVE A CROWN THAT THE LORD WOULD GIVE HIM IN HEAVEN. IT IS IMPORTANT FOR US TO KEEP OUR GOAL IN MIND. THEN WHEN PROBLEMS COME, WE CAN REMEMBER THAT GOD HAS PREPARED A GREAT REWARD FOR US IN HEAVEN. DRAW A PICTURE OF YOURSELF RUNNING TOWARD A FINISH LINE WHERE A BEAUTIFUL CROWN WAITS FOR YOU.

W9-AHJ-637

There's No Justice
Just Court Costs©

By
Lawrence B. Fox

TABLE OF CONTENTS

DISCLAIMER

Any similarity between the characters depicted in this book and actual individuals is purely coincidental. The characters reflected in this book are fictional and are not meant to describe actual persons, either living or deceased.

DEDICATION

This book is dedicated to the memory of Clinton Budd Palmer,

President Judge of the Court of Common Pleas of

Northampton County, Pennsylvania.

ACKNOWLEDGEMENT

Two friends assisted with the preparation of this book. Their enthusiastic and unwavering support made publication a reality.

Cathy Rudolph typed the original manuscript and its countless revisions.

Dianne Pelaggi's insightful editorial comments kept my energies focused in the proper direction.

I am truly blessed to have worked with these two professionals.

Cover photographs by Bethlehem Photo Graphics

WWW.BETHPHOTO.COM

INTRODUCTION

"Quiet Please — Court in Session" signs stood as lonely sentinels at each end of the second floor hallway of the Northampton County Courthouse. They didn't seem to be necessary, since I was the only person in the hallway, and I was just passing through on my way to the recorder of deeds office.

Suddenly the exterior doors leading to courtroom No. 1 burst open, and a torrent of people poured forth, with the speed and animation usually reserved for school kids at dismissal time. A spectrum of emotions was reflected upon the faces of the courtroom spectators who now filled the hallway, spectators engaged in animated discourse, oblivious to the *Quiet Please* signs. A few in the crowd appeared ecstatic, while others seemed close to tears. One group looked confused. Another radiated a sense of vindication.

An exasperated woman wearing a large green hat with a feather in the brim waved her arms about as she stood in the midst of a circle of friends. "I can't believe it! Is there no Justice?" she screamed. She pointed an indignant finger in the air, as if preparing to pose as the model for a bronze statue.

While I had not been in the courtroom to witness firsthand the verdict, I quickly concluded that she had not fared very well as a litigant.

"That judge is an ass!" she concluded. "I've lost all faith in the system!"

It was about this point in time that I overheard a different evaluation of the same court proceedings. A man wearing a threadbare sport coat three sizes too large for his slender frame was conducting his own post-trial review with a group of his close associates.

"At last — Justice!" the victor proclaimed, a smile beaming from his triumphant face. "This restores my faith in the system. That judge is a scholar!" A few of his supporters began to applaud.

I had just learned an important lesson about the most elusive of legal concepts — Justice. For the first time, I could now accurately define it: *Justice* occurs when your opponent loses; *Injustice* occurs when your opponent wins. From this axiom follow other interrelated corollaries:

1. Justice and Injustice can and do usually occur in equal amounts simultaneously in the same courtroom during the same proceeding.

2. There is only so much Justice to go around. If someone finds some, somebody else loses an equivalent amount. This is known as "equal justice under the law."

3. Perfect Justice occurs when the bum you sued pays the judgment, and doesn't take an appeal. For him there is no Justice, just court costs.

"I demand Justice," one of my clients once screamed at a judge, after deciding I had failed to make the point during my summation.

"We'll have none of that in here!" His Honor shouted back, and he was right - my client didn't find any at all.

As a result, some people look for Justice elsewhere — in the workplace, in church, in the military, or on the farm. This book also reviews such quests in detail.

Everything you are about to read is mostly true, except where I've lied a little. In some instances the names may have been changed, but that's not in an endeavor to protect anyone in particular. Rather, my memory just isn't what it use to be.

Most of the people whose foibles are reported in this collection have lived and worked in the neighboring jurisdictions of Northampton and Lehigh Counties, in the Commonwealth of Pennsylvania. That doesn't necessarily bode well for these two counties. If you ever choose to visit either of these places, however, you will find what I am about to describe is considered by most folks around here to be quite normal.

Many of the characters you are about to meet have been my clients. Nonetheless, I don't think the attorney-client privilege applies since I rarely got paid. That's because I lost most of my cases, and people who are dragged off to jail generally are not inclined to pay for services rendered, no matter how skillfully performed. In those rare instances when I gained an acquittal, I still didn't get paid.

"Why should I pay you?" was the usual response. "I was innocent — they shouldn't have arrested me in the first place." This is how one practices law in eastern Pennsylvania. It's also why Perry Mason and other high profile attorneys who have never had difficulty paying their office overhead chose to set up office far, far away in California.

The judge has just ascended the bench. Why not sit here next to me, and we'll see if there's any more *Justice* left for His Honor to dish out.

At Bethlehem, Pennsylvania, 1999

xv

CHAPTER ONE: MY FIRST TRIAL

Incompetence is a trait with which one is usually born. Some attorneys, however, with time and practice, fully develop this natural skill as the hallmark of their entire careers. And so it was with me. After being hatched from law school like a baby turtle heading from the beach for the first time into the unknown ocean, upon passing the bar examination, I instinctively directed my steps toward the county courthouse, serenely unaware of the dangerous shoals lurking therein.

Back when I was attending law school, the argument that every criminal defendant, even those who were indigent, had a constitutional right to the assistance of legal counsel, was still being hotly debated in the appellate courts. Even at the time of my admission to the local bar, our county still had no taxpayer-subsidized Office of the Public Defender staffed with free lawyers standing at the ready to serve the impoverished. Rather, the Court determined on a case-by-case basis whether an accused defendant required legal assistance. If such aid were found to be necessary, the judge before whom the trial was pending would try to convince some luckless attorney to take the case on a gratis basis.

During the summer before I was to graduate, I learned how to "search titles" — the science of reviewing the accuracy and ownership of real estate as recorded at the local courthouse. I knew lawyers with established practices would hire me to perform this time-consuming task when their clients sought to purchase real estate. Title searching would help me pay the rent until I stumbled upon a client or two of my own.

Less than 48 hours after learning that I had passed the state bar examination, I was inducted as the newest member of our local bar, and within hours after the official court admission ceremony, I found myself standing in the recorder of deeds office, dressed in my one and only suit, struggling to complete a title search on time. I was finally a lawyer, broke, and facing seven years of student loans. With the exception of the admission ceremony, I had never stood before a judge in my life.

That was about to change. I had to go to the bathroom, so I left the recorder of deeds office for the journey down the long second floor marble corridor. Courtroom No. 1, the large ornate chamber over which the President Judge presided, was located on my left, about 100 feet before my goal, the men's room. The two huge oak doors were drawn wide open. Back then air conditioning had not yet been installed, so all the windows and doors were propped open to let air drawn by large ceiling fans find its way through the building. I decided to peek into the courtroom, hopeful that I might catch a glimpse of some real lawyers at work.

There in all his splendor sat the President Judge, adorned in his austere black robe. The bench upon which he was seated towered at least four feet above the mere mortals subserviently scurrying below him. He was the only one in a position to see me as I leaned in from behind the open doors. Everyone else was obediently facing him, similar to a faithful church congregation, attentively fixed upon the minister at the pulpit.

That's when I caught His Honor's attention, for he raised his head ever so slightly to see above his bifocals. For a split second our eyes met, after which a slight grin overtook his previously solemn judicial face. And then he did it. He motioned with the index finger of his left hand, just as my second grade teacher used to do whenever I had transgressed. I looked behind me to see if His

2

Honor was motioning for someone else, but I was alone. I inched into full view and pointed at my chest. Was the judge actually motioning to me? He nodded his head ever so slightly, the way only President Judges do, so I accepted his kind invitation and advanced into the hall of justice.

I walked cautiously down the center aisle of the courtroom, past the 20 or 30 pews filled with several hundred potential jurors. As I approached the bench, I noted that the fidgeting and whispering which had only seconds before filled the room had now abruptly ceased. I could feel the penetration of a thousand eyeballs. Who was this interloper, this pretender, seeking audience with the court?

My journey ended at the judge's elevated bench. There I stood before tipstaffs, stenographers, court clerks, sheriff's deputies, bailiffs, and real lawyers, unaware why I had been summoned. His Honor decided to speak. Judges can do that whenever they want.

"Forgive me, young man, but didn't I admit you into the Bar yesterday as this county's newest attorney?"

"Yes," I whispered, grateful that my pants were a dark color.

"How very fortunate for both of us," Judge Porter mused.

"Do you see that gentleman seated over there?"

The judge pointed in the direction of a tired-looking, unshaven bum slumped at what I would soon learn was the defense table. His Honor had motioned with the very same finger he used to ensnare me just moments ago. The judge, I would also quickly learn, had more power emanating from that one finger than most sorcerers possess in their entire bodies.

"He's your newest client. Be ready for trial in 15 minutes."

With those words, Judge Porter abruptly stood up and withdrew into his chambers. Judges do that a lot, too, I would learn.

"Court is in recess for 15 minutes," the court crier announced as the assembled multitude once again began its animated conversation.

I decided I better introduce myself to my newest client who served the dual role of being my only client. I may have lacked trial experience, but this deficit was offset by the fact that I was able to give this case my undivided attention.

Joe Hummel did not project an image designed to capture the sympathy of a jury. His stained bowling shirt barely covered a sizeable potbelly that protruded from his 65-year-old frame. His pants had grease stains. The whole grizzly ensemble was held together by a belt I couldn't see. And his 6 o'clock shadow wasn't helping matters much.

The court clerk presented me with a file — my client's criminal file. Was I representing a mass murderer? A bank robber? A gangster?

"I didn't do it," Hummel insisted as we sat side by side at the defense table.

"Do what?" I asked the accused, as I tried unsuccessfully to glean from the file the nature of the felonious act he had allegedly committed.

"Drunk drivin'," Hummel confirmed. "I'm innocent. I want you to make sure I get Justice."

No one had ever requested this of me. I began to realize that I had inadvertently, while searching for a toilet, stumbled upon something much bigger and perhaps more important — Truth, Justice, and the American Way.

I sensed Hummel's indignation at having been wrongfully accused. I took him at his word, for he certainly had no reason to lie to me. After all, I was his lawyer.

As I continued leafing through his file, some of the data reflected upon sworn affidavits, the indictment, and the official laboratory report, caught my attention. I decided to confront my client with the allegations.

"The police report relates that your car left the roadway at a high rate of speed and struck a tree located over 100 yards from the shoulder of the highway. . . "

"I can explain that. . ."

". . . And that when the police arrived, you appeared to be highly intoxicated. . ."

"I can explain that, too. . ."

4

". . .And that your blood-alcohol level was twice the legal limit. . ."

"That may have been, counselor, but I ain't guilty. I would never drink and drive. People could get hurt. Don't you want to hear my side of the story?"

Hummel's sincerity touched me as I looked into his blue eyes, the left iris of which appeared to be just a shade or two darker than the right.

"Of course I do," I noted apologetically.

Delighted to have discovered a captive audience upon which to test his defense, Hummel launched into a dramatic narrative of his vehicular accident, and his resulting arrest.

"It's like this, see, it was Saturday night, and I had just finished buying a case of beer at the mall. I was driving home, minding my own business, when all of a sudden this deer scampers out on the road, not 500 feet in front of my car, and starts staring into my high beams. I got exactly one second to decide if I'm going to slaughter Bambi, or veer hard to the right. I'm an animal lover just as much as the next guy. So I swerve, lose control of the car, go down an embankment into the woods, and hit a tree. I totaled my wife's new car."

"Were you injured?"

"Not 'til I got home. She was real mad. I knew she would be, and so as I sat there in the dark woods watchin' steam rise from the busted radiator, I thinks to myself — it sure would be nice to have somethin' to take the edge off 'til the cops arrive. And that's when the idea come to me. . ."

"The beer?"

"Right, counselor. The beer! I figured, why not have a snort or two just to brace me. So I reached behind to the back seat and glory be, discovered not a single bottle was broken. I pops one open, and boy it tasted good. So did the second."

"How many beers did it take to help you relax?"

"Maybe 12. Maybe 15. Anyway, after a while, I stopped counting. So there I am sitting behind the wheel, minding my own business, when this cop shows up, shines a light in my face, says I'm drunk, and arrests me. Imagine my surprise!"

5

Hummel took a long emotional breath before continuing his saga. "You believe me, don't you? I want a trial, and Justice. Now here's the proof that I'm an innocent man. . ."

"Mr. Hummel," I interrupted, "all that talk about beer has reminded me how I ended up here in the first place. In two short minutes, the judge is returning, and I have to go to the bathroom."

Hummel appeared disappointed, but sympathetic.

"I'll tell you when you get back. OK?"

"OK," I said over my shoulder. I figured I'd be safe from judges, defendants, and tipstaffs, if only for a moment, were I to find the solitude of the men's room. Unfortunately, such was not the case. Attorney Vanderbilt, the lawyer who gave me the title search assignment, spotted me as I approached the bathroom door.

"Is the title search done? Settlement is tomorrow, son. I'm relying on you."

"The title search? Oh, yes, the title search. Well, you see, I'm in trial, and as a result. . ."

"That's not possible, son," Vanderbilt corrected me. "The only judge in town this week is Porter, and he and I have a tee-off time at the country club every Thursday at 2:00 p.m. Today is Thursday, and he hasn't missed a game in seven years."

What good would it do to debate the judge's golf schedule with learned counsel? I visited the facilities, and returned to Courtroom No. 1, at the side of Mr. Hummel, still seated at the defense table. Most of the 200 potential jurors had also found their way back into the courtroom, and were now studying my every move, their eyes following me as if I were a tennis ball at the U.S. Open.

"Like I was sayin'," Hummel began, "the real proof that I'm innocent is this. . ."

"All rise," the tipstaff announced.

I instinctively stood up, as did the masses, for Judge Porter had again entered the courtroom. He nestled into his overstuffed, green-leather-swivel-high-backed judge's chair.

"Please be seated," the tipstaff directed.

This, by the way, is all I recall ever seeing tipstaffs do: tell

6

people to stand or to sit, perhaps twice a day. And for that expenditure of energy they receive accrued credit toward a county pension, full health benefits, and a staff to tip. Go figure.

"Gentlemen," Judge Porter began, "have you been able to dispose of this matter?"

Some fellow dressed in a three piece suit similar to mine, a studious looking man about two years older than I, possibly an attorney, stood up at what I would soon learn was the prosecutor's table.

"May we have the Court's indulgence for a moment?"

"Certainly, Mr. Ritter," His Honor assured the man, who was now heading my way.

"I'm Assistant District Attorney Michael Ritter," the prosecutor whispered in my direction, as he hunched over the defense table and stuck out a bony hand. "Now listen: Hummel here is going to plead guilty, in return for which I agree to his probation, a $100.00 fine on the drunk driving, a $50.00 fine on the reckless driving, and a six-month suspension of his driving privileges. Then we'll be out of here in 15 minutes, and the jury panel can go home, since this is the last case on the docket. Agreed?"

Hummel tapped me on the shoulder. He, too, whispered as he joined the informal huddle. I could hear the judge's fingers impatiently drumming on his elevated oak bench.

"Nutin' doin'," the defendant proclaimed.

"OK, I'll drop the reckless driving charge and the $50.00 fine," Ritter countered, "but that's the best I can do. Now let's go before you annoy the judge!"

Ritter returned to his seat, confident that an agreement had been reached. I, on the other hand, was not as optimistic. I hardly knew Mr. Hummel, but if ever an individual yearned for a trial, Hummel fit the bill.

"I ain't pleadin' to something I didn't do," Hummel whispered in my ear.

"Gentlemen, please approach the bench," Judge Porter commanded. I followed Ritter's footsteps. "Do we have a plea?" His Honor inquired of me.

"I don't believe so, Your Honor," I advised the Court.

Ritter stared at me in disbelief, his shock exceeded only by that of the judge.

"Mr. Fox," Judge Porter instructed me, "when I asked you to be 'ready for trial,' that was just my little way of bringing some humor into an otherwise dull day. I didn't expect you to take me seriously. If you plead your client, we all go home, including Mr. Hummel. If you are misguided enough to test the limits of the system, and you fail, Hummel will get six months in the slammer, and I'll find some way to arrange that you are his cell mate. Get the picture, Counselor?"

"Well, you see, Judge, my client is innocent, and he wants Justice," I began to explain.

"If it's Justice he wants, then tell him to live long enough to see his children have kids. There isn't much Justice left around here. I distributed most of it last week."

"May I have a moment with my client, Your Honor?" I asked.

"Take all the time you need," the judge assured me.

I advised Hummel that he might want to reconsider his demand for a jury trial.

"I'd rather go to jail than plead to somethin' I didn't do," he asserted. "Don't you believe me?"

I did. I returned to the bench, to the waiting judge and to the assistant district attorney.

"Mr. Hummel wants a jury trial, Your Honor."

The judge, who had been picturing the green on the par-3 seventh hole, now focused upon my words.

"I have a foursome with a 2:00 p.m. tee-off time. It's now 11:15 a.m. How long will this trial take?"

"I don't really know, Judge," I admitted. "This is my very first trial."

The judge leaned back in his squeaky chair. "Let's pick a jury, gentlemen," he ordered, as he sat dejected and solemn. "Mr. Ritter,

8

please return to your seat. Mr. Fox, please remain here at side-bar for a moment. I have a minor matter to discuss with you."

I could have sworn that Ritter gave me a microscopic wink as he turned toward the prosecutor's table. I was left standing alone to incur the wrath of the Court. But Judge Porter was now serene and reconciliatory in his demeanor.

"Mr. Fox, I'm about to miss a golf game for the first time in seven years," His Honor mumbled.

"I am truly sorry," I assured the Court. "Is there anything I can do?"

"Actually, there is," Porter confirmed. "There is a potential juror in the third row. She's got the biggest set of hooters this side of the Mississippi. Ritter knows enough to put her on the jury. Now you know enough not to raise an objection. Right?"

I turned to survey the third row of potential jurors. The presence of a well-endowed platinum blonde gave a special glow to the entire room. "I think I understand, Sir," I advised the Court, as I returned to the defense table.

Picking a jury proved to be easy. Ritter and I positioned Ms. Hooters front and center, whereupon the judge's prior agitation appeared to quickly subside as he quietly stared in her direction.

"He won't give you much trouble now," Ritter noted from his seat at the prosecutor's table. In fact, Judge Porter would prove to be helpful on occasion to the defense.

Ritter called Pennsylvania State Trooper Martin Johnson as his first witness. The trooper had a jutting Clark Kent square jaw. A John Wayne swagger. He was resplendent in his tailored gray uniform, complete with gun, badge, nameplate, and spit-shined shoes. No doubt about it, he was the poster boy for Truth, Justice, and the American Way.

All state troopers attend state trooper school. That's where they learn to square their jaws and to swagger. They also learn a new language for use during court appearances. As an example, they are taught that defendants who are arrested for drunk driving "walk with a staggered gait, have slurred speech, wear disheveled clothes, and appear to have bloodshot eyes." Nobody really knows what any of that phraseology means, but it's quite effective on the witness stand.

After soliciting the usual formalities of name, rank, and serial number, Ritter began in earnest the direct examination of his star witness. Trooper Johnson advised the jury that on the evening in question, he was called to the scene of a one-car accident. Upon his arrival, he noted a single white male sitting behind the wheel of a late model Oldsmobile that appeared to have been totaled. What was left of the front end of the car had imbedded itself into a large tree. The headlights beamed into the woods. Steam was rising from the radiator.

The driver did not appear to be injured. To the contrary, he seemed to be rather jovial and offered the trooper a beer. The trooper asked the driver, who identified himself as Joseph Hummel, to exit the vehicle in preparation for a field sobriety test. But Hummel was unable to perform the simple maneuvers. Assistant district attorney Ritter continued with his direct examination.

"Did anything noteworthy occur as the defendant emerged from his car?"

"Yes. Had I not caught him, he would have fallen on his face. It was then that I noticed that his shirt was moist with beer. His breath smelled as if he had been drinking. I found 15 empty beer bottles in the car."

Hummel tugged at my sleeve. "I never litter," he whispered to me. "It ain't legal."

"I asked the defendant to touch his nose with his right third finger. He was unable to do so. His speech was slurred, and he had a staggered gait. His clothes were disheveled. I directed my flashlight into the defendant's eyes. They were bloodshot from drinking," the witness confirmed.

Judge Porter snapped his gaze away from Ms. Hooters for a second, and turned to me.

"Mr. Fox?"

I stood at attention. "Yes, Your Honor?"

"Don't you want to object? It really is a perfect time for you to object."

"It is?"

"Trust me on this one, counselor. I won't lead you astray."

The big picture was starting to come into focus, and so I summoned up all my courage, and did it:

"I object!" I said, although I wasn't quite sure why.

"Sustained!" His Honor rang out. "Whether the eyes were bloodshot as a result of the imbibing of alcohol calls for a medical conclusion beyond the field of expertise of this witness. The jury is instructed to disregard the trooper's suggestion that drinking alone caused the defendant's eyes to become bloodshot."

I sat down in a heap, exhausted yet exhilarated. This trial work was tough, but rewarding.

"That was fantastic!" Hummel assured me.

And so it was. A surgeon always remembers his first appendectomy, a pilot his first solo flight. I would never forget my first objection, which was, indeed, sustained. Never mind that the favorable ruling came from a judge who was paying closer attention to a set of breasts than to the testimony at hand.

"What that trooper just said about my eyes, it ain't true," Hummel whispered. My eyes wasn't bloodshot. It's the proof I've been tryin' ta tell ya about all mornin', but you had ta go to the toilet."

I was concentrating upon important trial testimony. What was Hummel babbling about now?

The assistant district attorney pushed on. "Trooper, tell the jury what next occurred."

"When I remarked that the defendant's eyes were bloodshot, he responded that my eyes appeared to be glazed, and then asked if I had one too many donuts."

"Now, Trooper, you have testified about your observations of the defendant, the smell of alcohol, the defendant's slurred speech, staggered gait, disheveled clothing, bloodshot eyes, and your field sobriety tests. Were you able to make a determination as to whether the defendant was inebriated to such a degree as to render him incapable of safely operating a motor vehicle?" Ritter inquired.

Judge Porter stopped staring at Ms. Hooters again, and turned to me.

"Mr. Fox — aren't you going to object?"

I jumped to my feet. "I object!"

"On what grounds?" the Court inquired.

"Grounds?" I asked myself. "I need grounds?"

"Overruled. I'll allow it," His Honor proclaimed without so much as a moment's consideration. "The totality of the circumstances permits the witness to formulate an opinion."

I inched back into my chair, dejected and confused.

"Don't take it personal or nothin'," Hummel consoled me. "You're still battin' 500."

The witness advised the Court that the defendant was incapable of safe driving.

"Cross-examine," Ritter announced.

I got the distinct impression that meant I was supposed to do something.

"Do you have any questions of the witness?" Judge Porter coaxed.

Hummel was again tugging at my sleeve. "The cop is lyin'. My eyes wasn't bloodshot!" he whispered in my ear.

"How would you know?" I shot back. "It was dark and you had drunk 15 beers!"

"'Cause this here eye — the left one — is fake. It's made of glass and don't never get bloodshot!"

I looked into Hummel's blue and bluer eyes. A beautiful sight.

"Do you wish to inquire of the witness?" an impatient Porter reiterated.

"Yes, Your Honor," I confirmed. I faced the witness. "Tell me, trooper, how did you determine that my client's eyes were bloodshot? Wasn't it dark at the accident scene?"

"I had a flashlight powered with six fresh batteries. I beamed it in his face."

"And what did you see?"

"Little red veins, lots of them, going in all directions, like what happens when you drink too much."

12

"Were there red veins in the left eye?"

"Yes."

"Were they in the right eye?"

"Yes."

"Your Honor," Ritter complained as he rose to his feet, "this question has been asked and answered several times. The evidence is clear that the defendant's eyes were bloodshot."

"Agreed," Porter confirmed as he looked at his watch and then the clock on the wall. "Might we move on, Mr. Fox?"

"I'm done with this witness," I advised His Honor.

"The Commonwealth rests," Ritter announced.

"Marvelous," Porter gushed. "Will we be putting on a defense today?"

"Put me on the stand!" Hummel begged. "I've been waitin' four months for Justice. I ain't gonna wait no more."

Up to this point in time I had not seen my client walk. He had patiently remained seated at the defense table since the moment I had first been shanghaied into court.

Now he struggled to stand. His balance was shaky at best. He made his unsteady way to the witness stand, where he labored to climb one step prior to being sworn in as a witness. I tried to present my questions in a logical sequence, but Hummel seemed to be in a hurry, a trait the judge found endearing.

"I don't got no 'staggered gait'," he informed Porter and the jury. "What I got is a wooden leg. It makes me walk funny, like I'm gonna fall on my face." Hummel knocked on his left thigh. A hollow wooden sound echoed throughout the courtroom.

"And I wasn't disheveled. The night of the accident, I was wearin' my lucky shirt, just like I am now. This is how I always dress."

Some lucky shirt. Hummel was wearing it when he totaled his wife's new car, and now he was facing possible incarceration.

"And my speech wasn't 'slurred.' On the night of the accident, my head hit the dashboard, and my false teeth shot out of my mouth from the impact. I didn't find em' under the seat until two days later."

"And my eyes wasn't bloodshot neither," Hummel assured those in attendance. "Just the right one gets bloodshot."

"Uh huh, Mr. Hummel. And why is that?"

"The left one is made of glass."

With those dramatic words, Hummel hit himself on the back of his head, causing his left eye to shoot out of its socket with the same velocity as apparently did his teeth at the time of the accident. Hummel deftly caught the glass orb in his outstretched hand, and proudly displayed the unblinking sphere to the startled jury.

I couldn't tell what was unraveling more quickly — Hummel's body or the prosecutor's case. The jury returned in 15 minutes with an acquittal. His Honor would get to his golf game with time to spare. Hummel had found Justice. Ritter hadn't convicted an innocent man. Ms. Hooters accepted a dinner invitation from the tipstaff. And I would complete my title search by 5:00 p.m. I love it when everyone is happy.

"You did a good job," His Honor shouted to me as he clacked down the hallway in his robe and golf shoes. "If ever I need a lawyer to handle another case, I'll certainly keep an eye out for you."

CHAPTER TWO: THE DOG LICENSE

I needed to file some papers at the courthouse — a mundane task I performed daily. Sometimes I'd clock in a landlord-tenant complaint, or maybe a change-of-name application. On a really special day, I might try to petition for habeas corpus, if a client actually wanted his corpus back.

When I was a kid, I watched every episode of Perry Mason. Once a week, Mason would convince some hapless soul to admit from the witness stand that he, not the accused, had committed murder. I decided at a young age that this was really neat, so I went to law school.

Well, it's been more than a quarter of a century since graduation, and not one person has yet admitted, as a result of my brilliant cross-examination, that he or she was guilty of anything. Perry Mason, on the other hand had, during the same period of time, subtracting 30 percent for reruns, obtained 847 confessions from unindicted third parties to murder in the first degree. What was I doing wrong?

Come to think of it, I don't recall Mason ever filing any papers. Maybe that was the problem. I was filing papers, instead of planning the extraction of confessions.

Entering the massive marble lobby area, I spotted a familiar face behind the information desk. There sat Mabel, the telephone/ operator lady, seated at her same perch for the better part of a century. There wasn't a question about the courthouse she hadn't

15

fielded hundreds of times before. Her answers were delivered quickly, clearly, happily, almost as an involuntary reflex. She knew everyone who worked there, and everyone knew her. And in our small county, most everyone was on a first name basis.

"Good morning, Larry," she sang out.

"Good morning, Mabel," I replied, completing the familiar ritual.

Her switchboard buzzed with the day's first telephone inquiry. "Courthouse . . . Yes . . . that hearing will be held in Courtroom No.1 . . . on the second floor . . . well, because Courtroom No. 2 is on the first floor . . . No, Courtroom No. 3 is in the basement . . . because Courtroom No. 4 is on the third floor . . . No, Courtroom No. 5 is on the fourth floor . . . There is no fifth floor. You're welcome."

There had been a movement within the bar association to renumber the courtrooms to coincide with the floor upon which each was situated. It was hoped that by doing so, some of the judges would actually be able to locate their courtrooms without assistance. Each courtroom had been consecutively numbered as it was constructed. Unfortunately, Courtroom No. 1 had been placed on the second floor, giving rise to confusion that only escalated with time. Mabel vetoed the Bar Association's renumbering proposal, claiming that the present system made perfect sense to her. Since she had been around longer than the Bar Association, she carried veto power.

"Could you help me?" asked an older gentleman, who stood with his mother next to me at the information desk.

"Of course," courteous Mabel responded.

"Oh good," the exhausted man sighed. "I've already been to city hall, and them folks sent me to the SPCA. And they sent me here. I need a dog license for my mother's dog, Spot. Is this the right place?"

"No, dog licenses are issued by the Prothonotary. Take the elevator to the second floor, and it's down the hall, the first door on the right."

Since I wasn't Perry Mason, I, too, was going to the Prothonotary to file papers.

The name "Prothonotary" comes from the Old English term meaning, "If you file it here, we will lose it." Rumor has it the Minor Carta was placed in this repository for safekeeping, but was soon lost. Somebody then drafted a bigger copy, the Magna Carta, so it would be harder to misplace. To this office I volunteered to personally guide the dog permit seekers.

"Oh, thank you, sir," Freddie, my newly found friend exclaimed.

"Mom, this nice man will show us where to go."

"What?"

We approached the Prothonotary's office. Freddie suggested to Mom that she sit on the hall bench just outside the office door.

"Ma, sit out here for a minute, OK?"

"What?"

He pointed to the bench, so she, understanding his sign language, gently lowered her frail body onto the wooden seat. Freddie and I entered the Prothonotary's office — I to file papers — Freddie to obtain a dog license for Spot.

"May I help you?" asked Lori the file clerk.

"I need a dog license," Freddie advised the young clerk.

"Very well, sir. You have come to the right place. We have dog license applications right here," Lori said, as she placed a form on top of the counter before her.

"Thank God for that," Freddie sighed with obvious relief. "My mother can hardly walk," he informed Lori with a nod toward Mom who remained hidden from view.

"I've been dragging her all over creation," Freddie continued. Spot needs a dog license so we don't get arrested. It took two hours to find a parking space."

Lori found a pen. "Would you like me to help you fill out the form?" she volunteered with a smile.

"Yes, please," Freddie agreed quickly. "I don't see or hear so good anymore."

"What's the dog's name again?"

"Spot."

"S-P-O-T?"

"Right."

Lori filled in the dog's name.

"The owner?"

"My mother. Today's her 95th birthday. I brought her along, in case there are any questions I can't answer," Freddie explained.

"I'm glad you mentioned that. We have senior citizen dog licenses for those over the age of 65. They cost just three dollars instead of the usual five," Lori volunteered.

"But Spot isn't over 65, unless, of course, you're talkin' dog years," Freddie protested mildly.

"I was talking about your mother," Lori corrected him.

"What?"

Lori reached for another application form.

"YOUR MOTHER, NOT THE DOG," Lori explained.

"OK," Freddie agreed with a nod.

"Hair color?"

"Grey."

"Sex?"

"Female."

"Eye color?"

"Brown, but one eye has a cataract."

"Neutered?"

"I think so."

"Date of operation?"

"Hold on, I'll find out — that's why I brought her along," Freddie said.

"WHEN DID YOU HAVE YOUR HYSTERECTOMY?" Freddie shouted at his mother, who was patiently perched on the bench in the hall.

"AROUND 1945," Mom hollered back.

Freddie returned to the counter, armed with the necessary information.

"1945," Freddie replied without hesitation.

"Wow, Spot is no spring chicken," Lori calculated.

"No, she's a dog," Freddie corrected.

"Breeding?" Lori continued.

"Episcopalian," Freddie responded.

"My, that's unusual," Lori observed.

"Not really," Freddie replied with a shake of his head. "There are more of them around than you might think."

"Very well, sir, that completes the form," Lori confirmed. "Do you have $3.00 with you?"

Freddie produced an ancient leather change purse and with shaking hands withdrew three equally ancient crumpled dollar bills. The purse was connected to Freddie's belt by a long, tarnished silver chain. Freddie's cautious and deliberate counting of the money left me with the impression that most of the joint assets possessed by him and his mother were probably contained in that small pouch. These two individuals, Freddie and Mom, stood as examples why this continues to be a great nation. They worked hard their whole lives, yet had little to show for it, except mutual concern for a dog and a desire to obey the law. Finding the courthouse wasn't easy for them, but they had now complied with the dog-licensing statute.

"That's $3.00 even," Lori said as she completed her receipt and reached for a brass dog tag. "Now put this identification tag around her neck, and she'll be legal again."

"I will," Freddie beamed, "and thanks for everything."

He found Mom waiting on the hallway bench. He took the dog tag, produced a piece of string he had been saving for the occasion, and created a simple necklace which he ceremoniously placed around Mom's neck. Mom looked surprised.

"Now you're legal, Mom," Freddie proudly announced.

"That's a dog tag!" she shouted back. "It belongs on Spot!"

"No, Mom," Freddie corrected. "Lots of people make that mistake. Every soldier I served with in Korea wore a dog tag. The dogs didn't!"

19

"They didn't?"

"Nope. Lots of things like that is backwards, Ma. Like the Humane Society. It's suppose to help animals, but it's named after humanes."

Mom seemed to grasp the concept, as mother and son ambled down the hallway. Freddie continued his lecture. "It's like the word 'hysterectomy.' Them Webster idiots don't know a thing. It should be 'hersterectomy' . . ."

CHAPTER THREE: THE PARKING TICKET

Gofredo Pelaggi was not amused. He had been cited by a City of Bethlehem police officer for parking illegally. As a professor emeritus of English at Lehigh University, Pelaggi took exception to the criminal charge filed against him.

"The sign stated *'Fine for Parking'*," he explained from across my conference room table. "So I parked there. Had the sign read *'You will be fined if you park here'*, I would have obediently honored the directive and left the car elsewhere. I won't pay the $20.00 penalty. I'll go to jail first!"

I waited patiently for the next phrase, knowing that its utterance was as certain as office overhead. His dramatic tone suggested he believed I had never before heard these words:

"It's the principal of the thing!" he yelled, his clenched fist making emphatic contact with the surface of my scratched conference room table. Thousands of fists before had hit the same table in similar proclamation.

The good professor had a valid point. As any student of English would have confirmed, the sign was misleading at best. If, for instance, it had read "*mediocre for parking*," this entire unfortunate incident would have been avoided.

The professor's protestations had not fallen upon deaf ears. I, too, have on occasion chanced upon a sign, the contents of which could be subject to various degrees of interpretation. Within the

21

Commonwealth of Pennsylvania, many signs appear to have been drafted devoid of the one necessary word that would have given them any actual meaning.

"*Construction 3 Miles.*" Does construction commence now, or in three miles? If it commences three miles ahead, over what distance will the construction continue?

"*Bridge Freezes Before Road Surface.*" A mysterious warning. If the bridge freezes in front of the road surface, how far before the bridge does this occur, and why is that information important to a motorist? Similarly incomprehensible is the pronouncement "Adopt A Highway Litter Control."

"*No Littering — $500.00 Fine.*" Apparently if one fails to litter, the offense is punishable to the tune of $500.00.

"*End Road Construction.*" Permanently? If these signs have been approved by the State of Pennsylvania, then why did it sanction the work in the first place?

What is one to do upon approaching a sign that announces "*Falling Rock,*" or "*Slow Children Playing,*" (which isn't politically correct, by the way).

"*Drive-Through Window,*" and "*Deer Crossing,*" are confusing, too. How many deer actually read and follow such signs?

What about signs employing abbreviations, the lettering of which doesn't appear anywhere in the actual word abbreviated, such as "*Ped Xing*"?

"*Push to Talk,*" has proven to be confusing. Last summer I drove several hundred miles in one day without rest. Toward the end of my journey, I entered the Pennsylvania Turnpike, and approached the automated ticket booth, where an outstretched ticket awaited my grasping hand, similar to the brass ring on a merry-go-round. A large black button was positioned just below the ticket, with a sign that said, "*Push to Talk.*" I was tired, lonely, and hadn't spoken to a soul for hours. I decided to give this roadside pleasantry a try. Nothing happened, so I pushed the button a second time.

"What?" came the gruff voice. It was clear I had just disturbed a nap. Startled, I didn't know quite how to begin the conversation.

"Well, whadya want!?" he persisted.

"I just want to talk," I began apologetically. "The button said I could."

"You some sorta nut?" the voice inquired.

Why was this employee hired at taxpayer expense as a roadside conversationalist if he had no intention of actually befriending passing motorists? I drove on, without so much as a goodbye.

The world's most confusing sign exists at the entrance to the Lehigh Valley International Airport in Allentown, Pennsylvania. It is worth the price of an airline ticket from anywhere just to see it. Its gross area approximates that of a tennis court. And to ensure that patrons of the airport don't miss it, it's illuminated at night.

"Arriving Passengers — Turn Left."

"Departing Passengers — Turn Right."

Yogi Berra once said, "When you come to the fork in the road, take it." Would that I could.

I remember the first time I was confronted by this sign. Had its author properly utilized recognized adjectives to modify the noun "passengers," perhaps terms such as "enplaning" and "deplaning," I would have known which way to turn the car. Such was not the case, and so, as I tarried staring at the sign, I unwittingly began to delay anxious motorists behind me.

Still, I couldn't help myself. Was I arriving to depart from the airport, or departing from the airport to arrive at my destination? Did the sign refer to the motorist who was reading it, or rather, someone in an airplane bound for Allentown? Was I, therefore, coming to the airport to fetch a passenger who was departing from the airplane, thereby arriving at the airport, or was I meeting a passenger who was departing with me after arriving by airplane?

The guy behind me beeped his horn, stuck his head out the window and yelled, "Hey Pal, move it or milk it!"

I wondered if he was arriving or departing, or just picking someone up who might be arriving or departing. I decided to follow him as he passed me. He turned to his right while several other vehicles proceeded unhesitatingly to the left.

This motorist, having just made reference to a cow, or the lactation thereof, now pulled into a large parking lot. I parked next to him, and then noticed that the other cars that had turned to the left were now joining us in the same parking area.

"Are you arriving or departing?" I asked him as he sprung from his vehicle.

He shot me a disgusted look, shook his head, and then ran toward the terminal building, luggage in hand. I hoped both his comings and goings would be safe ones.

Obviously, Gofredo Pelaggi and I had something in common — the need for clear unequivocal signage. I took the case.

During the last 35 years, one man alone had served the north side of the City of Bethlehem as the only jurist to hear motor vehicle violations — Magistrate James Collins. Whether there were citations for parking tickets, speeding, dawdling, failing to yield the right-of-way, going the wrong way, or failing to stop, every allegation of vehicular wrongdoing eventually made its way to his courtroom — the courtroom that time had forgotten.

The magistrate sat on a throne at the front of his dingy hearing room, facing six rows of pews, wooden benches scavenged decades ago from some forgotten church. The throne was positioned upon four casters supported by ball bearings, so that it could roll with Collins perched upon it.

Generations of luckless defendants awaiting their fate had, during their brief visits, carved initials and other mementos into the uncomfortable pews. Rumor had it that third- and fourth-generation defendants often sought out the craftsmanship of ancestors long dead, and then continued the family tradition of defacing the courtroom.

Magistrate Collins was a tobacco company's dream come true. No one could recall ever having seen him without a cigarette dangling from his trembling lips. Sometimes he would forget one was there and he'd absentmindedly light a second. Had he been able to introduce more nicotine into his body by cramming cigarettes into his ears, he would have done so.

Collins rarely moved. His ash gray skin and unblinking eyes gave the impression of a lizard sunning itself on a rock. Animation came only with death rattle coughs, from what was left of his emphysema-riddled lungs, as puffs of smoke made the journey up his asthmatic windpipe and past his tar-stained teeth. Each time he coughed, it seemed as though it might well be his last. His wheezing could be heard throughout the courtroom. It was the only proof that he was actually alive, and not just on fire. Smoke filled the stuffy room and a hazy cloud hovered permanently over Collins' head.

The most intriguing conversation piece in this hall of justice stood silently at Collins' left side. There reposed an 8-foot green compressed-oxygen cylinder — complete with 50 feet of clear coiled plastic tubing, starting at the top of the cylinder's valve stem, and ending at Collins' nose, where the tube branched into each nostril to feed his awaiting oxygen-starved lungs. The 50-foot life line permitted Collins to roll himself, throne and all, into a nearby antechamber, where he could relieve himself on yet another throne without dragging the oxygen canister behind him.

Before this august trier of fact, Pelaggi and I appeared, seeking Justice. I opened Collins' office door, allowing my client to enter first. There, in all his splendor, sat Collins, sucking on a cigarette, the remnants of another still smoldering in an overfilled ashtray on his desk. Pelaggi, who apparently possessed some hazardous materials knowledge, knew well the dangers of smoking in proximity to a source of compressed oxygen. He decided to pass this information along to me and the six or seven others seated in the courtroom, most of whom appeared to be busy carving obscenities.

"Holy Moses!" he screamed, "everybody hit the deck! That loony bastard's going to blow us all to hell and back!" With those fateful words, Pelaggi grabbed my shirt collar, and pulled me down next to him on the creaky wooden floor. No one else followed our brace-for-explosion example, so after a minute or two I got back up onto my feet.

"This is no way to endear yourself to the court," I leaned down and whispered to Pelaggi, who couldn't hear me, since his hands were covering his ears, protecting him from the pending explosion.

I tapped him on the ribs. "Please stand up, Professor," I whispered. "I've been coming here for 20 years, and no one has died in an explosion — yet."

Slowly my disbelieving client rose to his feet.

"How . . .do . . .you . . .plead?" Collins inquired between wheezes.

"Not guilty," I proclaimed, as I began my case. Rarely had I ever waxed so eloquently. I discussed the grammatical distinctions between the phrase *"Fine for Parking"* and *"Mediocre for Parking."* I reminded the court of the chilling effect upon commerce and the downtown merchants in particular whenever an improper ticket was issued. Finally, I struck at the very heart of the issue: I demanded *Justice.* As I addressed the court, I positioned myself on one side of the room, and then the other, hoping to maintain the magistrate's attention.

In the closing seconds of my oration I had taken on a rather dramatic pose, and in the last few moments of my summation, turned with outstretched hands to the half-dozen part-time whittlers, and noticed that most of them had stopped their carving. *My*, I thought to myself as I struck a Perry Masonesque pose, *I've captured everyone's attention with my flawless lawyering.*

But I hadn't. It was then that I heard the dull thud from behind me, and pirouetting back to face His Honor, noticed that he had apparently fallen asleep, his forehead having slammed onto his desk.

"You're standing on his goddamned oxygen hose, Counselor!" Pelaggi screamed as he pointed at my feet. And so I was. I had unintentionally rendered Collins unconscious, or maybe that happened upon head-to-desk impact. At any rate, this cranial-forward momentum succeeded in extinguishing the remains of the cigarette hanging from his mouth. It was at that noteworthy moment that smoke stopped pouring from his limp body for the first time in 35 years.

A secretary emerged from the reception area, and ran to her boss's lifeless side. "You've killed him!" she shrieked in a scene reminiscent of the reaction Dorothy received when she inadvertently poured water on the wicked witch in the Land of Oz.

"I didn't mean to," I pleaded, just like Dorothy. Great. I had come to nullify a lousy parking ticket, and now I might be charged with involuntary manslaughter.

The ambulance personnel arrived quickly, quite possibly because they parked illegally right in front of the courtroom door for easy access to the deli across the street. By the time they lifted Collins into the stretcher, his eyes had begun to open, and that familiar ashen gray color was returning to his cheeks. He began to mumble something in the direction of his grieving secretary.

"Where . . . cigarettes?"

Humiliated by the disaster, I tried desperately to apologize to His Honor, but Collins had more pressing concerns on his mind as he was rolled toward the ambulance.

"Hey . . . Pal," he pleaded as he grabbed my sleeve, "have . . . a . . . light?"

Well, all's well that ends well. After a three-week hospital stay, Collins returned to the bench, good as new. He dismissed the charges against Pelaggi, reasoning that since the original hearing had not been continued prior to the court's loss of consciousness, a second hearing for the same offense would violate Pelaggi's constitutional double jeopardy protections. My client was pleased. Justice had been served.

I, too, was about to experience a direct benefit as a result of my client's acquittal. I wondered what fee I should charge now that I had prevailed. After all, it wasn't the money, it was the principal of the thing. My client must have been reading my mind.

"Bill me," Pelaggi advised, after learning of the favorable verdict. "I'll pay it, so long as it doesn't exceed the cost of the parking ticket."

CHAPTER FOUR: THE LIBRARIAN

Traffic Court Judge Collins was feeling much better. After just a couple of weeks' recuperation at Municipal Hospital, the goose egg on his forehead was all but gone, and the familiar smoky haze again filled his beloved courtroom. He even had enough strength to strike and ignite his own matches, and to lift his cigarettes unassisted to his waiting lips. It was good to see him looking so vibrant again.

"Has the judge ever considered quitting smoking?" I asked his secretary in the outer office as I waited with several doomed motorists charged with various vehicular violations.

"I don't think so," she confided. "He once told me that if the first 50 years of butts didn't kill him, the last 20 or 30 years wouldn't either."

I would have to evaluate that logic later. The judge had just gasped out my case heading between asthmatic wheezes: Commonwealth . . .v . . .Libera . . .Dewey. I motioned to my nervous client.

"OK, Ms. Dewey, it's our turn," I said. She nodded reverently, and followed me toward the fumes.

Ms. Dewey. At about 60 years of age, and 4 feet 6 inches tall, she had been our city reference-room librarian for, well, as long as I could remember. She walked with straight posture, the scratching of her skirt slip marking her unhesitating advancement toward His

Honor. She was polite, soft-spoken, well-educated, and a person motivated by her convictions and beliefs. That which was good and true was to be pursued; that which was evil was to be banished. That's why she appeared in court today. She, too, was in search of Truth, Justice, and the American Way. "I didn't do it," she reaffirmed, as the court asked for her plea.

"You . . . may . . . be . . . seated," Collins coughed in the direction of my client.

Ms. Dewey had been accused of failing to come to a full stop at the intersection of Jacksonville Road and Westgate Drive. Her accuser, State Trooper McCarthy, now sat before us, prepared to testify. If I lost the case, the librarian would be subjected to a $25.00 fine.

The trooper, having seen all this before, testified in a neutral, almost disinterested manner.

"As I proceeded southbound on Jacksonville, I rapidly approached a 1954 Cadillac Fleetwood sedan traveling about 15 miles per hour in a 40-mile-per-hour zone . . ."

"Do you always drive an antique classic car?" I whispered in my client's ear.

"What do you mean?" she responded softly. "I bought that car new. It's hardly broken in. I go for the 12,000-mile maintenance visit next month."

The trooper continued. "The operator of the vehicle was a knuckle driver. . ."

"I beg your pardon," I interrupted. "A 'knuckle driver'?"

The officer paused in slight embarrassment. "It's a term we use at the barracks. No disrespect meant to your client, counselor, but it refers to, you know, a car without a driver. No head. No body. Just knuckles clutching the top of the steering wheel, like there's a munchkin in there dangling in midair."

"The seat *is* very soft," Ms. Dewey volunteered. "I tend to sink into it a little."

The cop agreed.

"Yes, ma'am. Driving one of those old classics is luxurious."

The cop turned and whispered to the judge: "It's like sitting in a bucket full of tits."

A most unusual image floated into my mind, but I had no time to cogitate, since the witness was about to continue his testimony.

"The defendant came to the intersection, glided through without coming to a complete stop, then accelerated back up to her 15-mile-per-hour cruising speed."

"How fast was she allegedly going when she failed to stop?" I inquired.

"Maybe 5 or 6 miles per hour."

"And you arrested her for that?" I demanded. "Everyone goes through stop signs at that speed! Did you have some other reason for stopping my client?"

"Well, I was curious to see if anyone was actually driving the car," the trooper admitted.

"And was anyone driving?" I inquired.

"Well, sort of. Ms. Dewey was in the car, for sure. But it would be more accurate to say the car was driving her."

"What do you mean?"

"I don't think she can see over the dashboard, and that's why she went through the stop sign. She couldn't see it."

"I can see perfectly," the defendant asserted. "I just didn't have my usual number of books to return that day, so I wasn't able to sit at my desired elevation."

Soon it was time to present closing arguments.

Don't get . . . up . . . Fox. Stay . . . away . . . air hose," Collins panted.

I gave my closing argument seated at the defense table. The arresting officer outlined his position. Collins appeared to be in a trance, but content, with a cigarette hanging from his mouth.

"Guilty," he coughed. "Twenty . . . five . . . dollar . . . fine." And then there was judicial silence.

Ms. Dewey was stunned. How could our great nation's judicial system have abandoned her in her hour of need?

"Take an appeal," she solemnly instructed me, as we left the courtroom.

"But Ms. Dewey," I tried to reason, "it's only a $25.00 fine. If you don't have the cash on you, I'll gladly loan you the . . . "

"Take an appeal!" she snapped as she headed toward the classic Cadillac. She opened the door, sat down in the driver's seat, shut the door, and descended from view, all before the engine turned over. Two determined sets of knuckles appeared to clutch the wheel as the black sedan pulled away from the curb and cruised down the street at a breakneck speed of 15 miles per hour.

I filed the appeal as directed by my client. It did not matter that I believed such review by a county court judge would be a waste of the court's time and my energy. Certainly, the state trooper would present the same testimony, and the county judge would probably arrive at the same guilty verdict.

On the other hand, lower court decisions have, on occasion, been overturned. I remember during my first year of law school, studying the case of "Anjou vs. Boston Elevated Railway." The poor plaintiff in that litigation had slipped on a banana skin while standing upon a train station platform. She nearly broke her back, and therefore sued the defendant railroad, claiming the defendant maintained a responsibility to keep its passenger waiting areas banana-skin free. Unfortunately, the jury didn't award her any damages, so she sought review before a higher court. And as luck would have it, the jury's findings regarding the banana skin were reversed on a peel.

It was this type of appellate justice that Libera Dewey now sought before the Honorable C. B. Porter, Judge of the Northampton County Court — the very same judge who had presided at my first trial, almost 20 years before, when I represented Joseph Hummel. During the last two decades, Hummel had become a faithful penman of Christmas cards, although I sometimes received them as late as March. Judge Porter and I had also become good friends, especially since we shared a similar sense of humor.

When my client's case made its way to his desk, the judge invited me back to his chambers for a little pre-trial conference. I sat in one of the lumpy office seats as His Honor scanned the entire two-page Libera Dewey lower court record. The judge first appeared confused, but then he smiled slightly as he looked up from his desk.

"I've been on the bench about 30 years, and I've heard lots of motor vehicle appeals for drunken driving, hit and run, speeding, reckless driving — anything involving a potential jail sentence or a serious injury. But I can't recall the last time someone appealed a simple $25.00 stop sign violation. It costs 10 times that amount just to hire a lawyer!"

"My client believes she was unjustly charged," I advised the Court. "I told her I'd pay the fine, but she wouldn't hear of it."

"Then we better give the accused her day in court," Judge Porter proclaimed as he stood up and reached for his black robe. "Be ready to proceed in 10 minutes," His Honor advised.

I might have been mistaken, but I thought I noticed a sparkle in the judge's eye as I began to leave the court chambers. I returned to my client.

"Don't be nervous," I assured her. "Judge Porter is a very gentle man."

"I can't help it," she confided. "This courtroom is so daunting." Her wide eyes surveyed the huge cathedral of justice. Judge Porter called the proceedings to order. Trooper McCarthy took the witness stand. His testimony paralleled that of his previous statement recited before Magistrate Collins. Libera then testified in her own defense, but to no avail.

"Guilty!" Judge Porter announced.

Libera's shaking hands searched in her purse for a handkerchief to dab her tear-stained cheeks. I had failed her a second time. His Honor didn't seem to care.

"Is there a need for a pre-sentence report?" the judge called out to me from his elevated bench at the front of the courtroom.

This inquiry caught my attention. It was Porter's intention that it would. After all, such reports were used by the court only in major criminal cases where significant periods of incarceration might be imposed. The reports, compiled by the county probation office, reviewed the convicted party's family background, education, vocational prospects, community contacts, previous convictions, dependents in need of support, etc. This information hardly seemed necessary for a $25.00 traffic fine.

"Counselor," he repeated, "do you wish to have the Court order a written pre-sentence report prior to the imposition of sentence? If not, I believe I am ready to begin the sentencing stage of the proceedings."

"I don't believe a formal report is required," I responded in disbelief.

"Good," Porter confirmed. "That will save the county a lot of time, money, and effort. Now let's see here, where did I put the Sentencing Book?"

With those words, the judge turned his high-backed swivel chair, and faced an ancient bookcase positioned behind him. The disintegrating leather volumes entombed within this ceremonial courtroom furniture had surely not been touched in the last century. Porter delicately opened the cut crystal glass door of the mahogany bookcase, blew away the dust on the shelf, and began to search for a specific treatise. Although I stood below the judge's elevated bench, I could nonetheless still see the book he ultimately chose — "Ladner on Conveyancing" — a famous work dealing with the law of real estate.

"Ah, yes, here it is," Judge Porter sighed with a smile, as he swiveled his massive chair back toward us. "The Sentencing Code!"

He delicately placed the large volume before him, affixed his reading glasses to his face, and began to page backward and forward, scanning several chapters of the book.

"Bear with me," he apologized to Ms. Dewey. "I know the precise sentence I want is in here . . . somewhere."

By now, the attention of the other 15 or 20 attorneys in the courtroom had been captured by the actions of Judge Porter. Porter stopped paging, coming to rest at an outdated chapter on mortgages and liens.

"I think I've found it," he proudly announced. "Are you ready, Ms. Dewey?"

"Ready for what?" my client reverently inquired.

"Why, to be sentenced, of course," Porter advised.

Ms. Dewey had strength to utter but three or four words.

"Well, I suppose so," she said.

"Good," Porter continued. He placed his second finger upon the page before him, and spoke, as if reading directly from the ancient book.

"It is the sentence of this Court that you pay the costs of prosecution, pay a fine of $25.00, and that you . . . pardon me, Ms. Dewey . . . I appear to have lost my place . . . oh yes, here it is . . . and that you undergo imprisonment in the Northampton County Prison at hard labor for the rest of your natural life, to be sustained only by bread and water."

The judge looked up from his reading material and removed his glasses.

"Do you have any questions regarding the sentence of the Court?" he asked of my trembling client.

Dewey, stunned by the severity of the pronouncement, struggled to regain her equilibrium. She spoke as if she were in a trance. "If only someone had told me before this hearing that I could get life in prison, I would have gladly paid the original fine, and not taken an appeal."

"Well, it's too late now, lady!" the judge said as he sat in silence, scoffing at Ms. Dewey. Then he cracked a huge smile, advised Dewey, much to her relief and mine, that on second thought, the sentence of incarceration was, under the circumstances, too harsh, and that she could go home.

"Oh, thank heaven," the librarian sighed. "Where do I pay the $25.00 fine?"

"Don't worry about that, either," Porter proclaimed. "It's on the house."

Ms. Dewey was so glad to leave the courthouse, she made a mad dash for her car, revved up the engine, and peeled out of the parking lot in a cloud of dust at nearly 23 miles per hour. I wondered if either she or her classic Cadillac would ever be quite the same.

CHAPTER FIVE: ANTLERS AWAY

I can't image a more stressful job than working as a security guard at the National Portrait Museum. Each oil canvas — Washington, Jefferson, Monroe, and Lincoln, just to name a few — has one striking thing in common: the eyes. No matter where you stand in this ornate gallery, no matter which room you visit, the founders stare at you. Sullenly. Intensely. Move right or left, they don't miss a trick. Look away and suddenly look back, they haven't so much as blinked.

"Washington is the creepiest," one guard confided. "If I stand in this room too long, his eyes begin to pierce right through my skull. It gives me the willies."

Wendel and Elsie Smidlap decided to buy the Cape Cod residence at 1242 Roselawn Drive.

"It has everything!" Elsie sighed as she described to me her dream home. "Self-cleaning oven, central air, a fireplace, and a sun room."

"It sounds delightful," I said as I studied the agreement of sale.

"What's more, there's a garbage disposal," Wendel chimed in.

They had been searching for more than six months. I was pleased they had finally found a house in their price range. I completed a title search, helped them coordinate mortgage financing with the bank, and attended settlement on the day the formal deed finally passed hands from the sellers, Ruben and Gloria Proboski, to the buyers. As was custom, my clients toured the house the night before settlement to confirm that everything was still in working order. As usual, I had never entered the house. That was the realtor's job.

Elsie beamed, as she and Wendel began to sign the mortgage documents. Attorney Hoover Repash accompanied his clients, the Proboskis, to my office and presented us with the new deed. Everyone agreed to the arithmetic computations and tax prorations, so the settlement went through without a hitch. I gave the sellers their check, congratulated my ecstatic clients on their new purchase, and then proceeded to the courthouse to record their deed. The Smidlaps now officially owned the house. I drove back to my office, another job well done.

"It's Mrs. Smidlap on the phone," my secretary announced before I took my coat off. "She's crying."

My heart stopped momentarily. I remembered back just a few years ago when I got a call right after settlement from another distressed client. On that prior occasion, the residence had just burned to the ground. The new buyers wondered if the check they had given me to pay for house insurance had been mailed to the insurance company — a timely question, given the circumstances.

I reached for the telephone. "Mrs. Smidlap, is everything . . .?"

"No," came the choked, desperate response. "The moosehead is gone!"

"Moosehead?"

Wendel joined the conversation on his upstairs extension. "The one that use to hang above our new fireplace," Wendel explained. "Eugene is gone."

"The moose has a name?"

"Yes. We decided on Eugene when we signed the agreement of sale," Wendel explained.

Why not, I thought to myself. As mooseheads go, "Eugene" was as good a name as any.

"I don't remember mention of a moosehead," I thought out loud.

"Well, Eugene was what attracted us to the house in the first place," Elsie explained. "Even during last night's inspection, he was there above the mantle. Now he's gone. Those Proboskis must have taken him just before settlement. All that's left is a whopper of a hole in the wall."

"They tried to cover it with some stupid stuffed fish," Wendel interjected, "A scrod. I could have gotten scrod anywhere!"

"You just got to get Eugene back," Elsie blurted out. "He came with the house!"

I had worked on this transaction for more than two months, from review of the agreement of sale, to recordation of the deed. Not once had anyone ever bothered to mention Eugene. I'd have to call Attorney Repash and see if he knew the whereabouts of the missing moose. This required that I be able to describe and identify Eugene, lest I happened upon the wrong stuffed head.

"What does Eugene look like?" I asked with a shake of my head.

"He's a moose," Wendel proclaimed.

"I understand," I assured him. "Does he . . . Eugene . . . have any distinguishing characteristics that would set him apart from other moose . . . mooses . . . I mean moosi?"

"Well . . ." Elsie chimed in, "he has sort of a moose-tache, you know."

"Yeah," Wendel agreed, "some hair on his upper lip. And when you look at him from anywhere in the living room, no matter where you are, it's like his eyes are following you! He paid attention to us."

"Like the portrait of Washington on a one dollar bill?" I suggested.

"Yes," Wendel concurred. "Exactly!"

Why would any rational human being want something like Eugene displayed in his home? As a conversation piece? Wouldn't more conversation be generated if the other end of Eugene were so mounted?

"He had those things sticking out of his ears," Elsie continued.

"Earrings?" I blurted out, trying to be helpful in a difficult moment.

"No, antlers," Wendel explained. "He was full grown."

"He had a pleasant smile, too," Elsie concluded, "just like the Mona Lisa."

"Yeah," Wendel sighed, "like the Mona Lisa."

I now had a clear description of the missing moose. I was ready to contact Attorney Repash.

But what if the sellers declined to return Eugene? What sum of money might I demand in damages? What's a moosehead with Washingtonian eyes and a Mona Lisa smile accompanied by a moose-tache worth? Personally, I'd have paid my garbage man whatever he quoted just to haul it away. Whether visiting the National Portrait Museum or lying around the living room in my jammies, I prefer not to be stared at.

My clients, however, didn't share my mooseaphobia, and so I began to research Eugene's replacement cost. Obviously, no amount of money would suffice if, perchance, you were a moose, grazing in the woods. You'd want to keep your head, no matter what the price, even if it were to appear above a mantlepiece.

I decided to call a taxidermist. Egbert's Taxidermy had a listing in the yellow pages.

"Hello, is this Egbert's?"

"At your service," the animal embalmer responded.

"Do you have any mooseheads for sale? I'm looking specifically for one that smiles like the Mona Lisa, stares at everyone, has antlers, and sports some hair on its upper lip."

"Hey Mister," a sarcastic Egbert suggested, "we don't carry a supply of mooseheads — you're supposed to bring them to us. There ain't no spares lying around!"

Egbert had reiterated the golden rule of making rabbit stew: first, you have to catch a rabbit. Replacing Eugene with a suitable substitute wasn't going to be easy. Neither the L.L. Bean nor Lands' End catalogs inventoried a single moosehead. I decided I better just call Repash and demand Eugene's timely return.

Repash was attentive and polite. I explained who Eugene was, and where he was last seen. Good to his word, I heard from Repash the next day, after he spoke with his clients. Unfortunately, Eugene was as much loved and revered by the Proboski clan as appeared to be the case with the Smidlaps. Apparently Mr. Proboski drank a beer with Eugene's picture right smack on the bottle. As a result, he had developed an unshakable kinship with the moose.

"My clients believe the moosehead, now known as 'Eugene,' to be an object of art, similar to a portrait hanging on a wall, and therefore, a removable piece of personal property," Repash proclaimed. "Nowhere in the agreement of sale did my clients suggest that this . . . Eugene . . . was a permanent resident of the home. He has, in fact, migrated with the Proboskis to greener pastures."

What was I to do? There was only one possibility left — formal court action to recover the purloined cranium and accompanying antlers. I diligently researched the law, hopeful that some past precedent would suggest that my clients had been wronged. There wasn't much case law on point. Eugene, like Gideon and Miranda before him, might make new law.

In desperation, I reviewed all available ancient remedies and equitable petitions. Most of the esoteric procedures were titled in Latin. My eyes fell upon the phrase "Amicus Curiae" — "Friend of the Court." That was catchy. Perhaps I could borrow from that. Why not plead "Moosus Curius"?

I filed the petition the following day, and scheduled an informal conference with the court for the next Thursday. I sent Repash notice of the meeting, and he agreed to attend in Judge McBride's chambers.

"I see someone's missing a moose. How did the moose get on the loose?" Her Honor inquired without so much as a smirk.

I explained about the fish over the mantle, Proboski's brand of beer, and the lack of moosehead inventory at the taxidermy shop.

"Has any thought been given to shared visitation?" the learned jurist inquired. "As an example, the Proboskis could love and nurture the moose . . ."

"Eugene," I interjected, "Your Honor."

"Whatever . . . say, from Wednesday through Saturday. Then the Smidlaps would welcome what's-his-name into their home Sunday through Tuesday."

Judges always try to compromise everything, even that which is incapable of being compromised. The proposal was just too complex. What would happen on Eugene's birthday, or at Christmas time when everyone would want to accentuate the moose with decorative antler balls and holiday garlands? Who would transport him back and forth? In what? He couldn't hitchhike. He didn't have a thumb.

Her Honor listened attentively to all these insurmountable problems as she leaned back in her red leather chair, a judicial expression engulfing her facial features.

"I suppose there's only one thing left to do," she confirmed as she rummaged through her purse for a quarter.

"I'll flip this coin," she advised me. "If it comes up heads, you get it. If it comes up tails, start looking for Eugene's other end to hang above the mantle."

I held my breath as the coin was launched into the air.

CHAPTER SIX: IT'S AN EMERGENCY

Some professions are fraught with emergencies, which Webster defines as "a sudden unforeseen occurrence." That's why, as an example, in the medical profession, there are emergency rooms — special places specifically designed to accept such situations.

In the legal profession, thankfully, the exact opposite is true. There are no emergencies, not even little ones, because with proper planning, nothing is ever unforeseen. As a result, there are no emergency rooms in any courthouses or law offices. There are, however, signs over some of the doors reading "Emergency Exit" — meaning, if you think you have an emergency, then perhaps you ought to leave now.

There are those few skeptics who might, under the most unusual of circumstances, disagree with me. Despicable Romanoff comes to mind. I represented him at his murder trial, after which his luck began to take a dramatic turn for the worse. One day, quite some time after his conviction, I received a call at my office.

"This is Graterford Prison with a collect call for attorney Fox. Are you attorney Fox?"

"Are you actually named Graterford Prison?" I inquired.

"No, I'm the operator at the prison. Will you accept a collect call from Despicable Romanoff?"

I had to think for a moment. Wasn't he on death row? If I accepted the charges, there was no guarantee I'd actually ever get my money back. On the other hand, Despicable wasn't much of a talker — the cops never got him to say anything — so I figured the conversation would be short.

"I'll accept," I told Ms. Graterford.

"OK. Please hold for the electric-chair room, and have a nice day."

As I was waiting, an uncomfortable thought began to take hold: Wasn't today the very day that the judge had sentenced Despicable to be . . .

"Hello . . . death chambers . . . prison guard Switcher speaking. May I help you?"

"Hi there. I hope so. This is attorney Larry Fox. I was wondering, is Despicable Romanoff still there by chance?"

"Hold on." (Mumble, mumble) "Yeah, he's right here. Let me unstrap one of his hands."

"Thank you," I responded.

Soon Romanoff's unique and unmistakable voice came through the wires, all the way from Graterford.

"Lawyer Larry, is that you?"

"Why, yes, Romanoff. You sound like you have a cold."

"No, I feel fine. It's this dang . . . Hey, Switcher, could you take this hood off for just a minute? Great. Thanks. Fox, can you hear me?"

"Yes, you sound much clearer. How are you?"

"OK, for the moment, and thanks for taking my call, 'cause I wouldn't have bothered you unless this was a real emergency."

Despicable then went into as much detail about his concerns as his abbreviated schedule would permit. Now, at first blush, one might think that Romanoff's present situation rose to the level of an emergency. However, after a moment's calm reflection, it is obvious that wasn't the case.

Despicable had received a fair, perhaps even above average trial. He had taken advantage of every conceivable appeal I could think of, and some he had dreamed up himself. And look at it from the prison's point of view. In all probability, the writ of execution had been properly signed and witnessed. The model and type of electric chair had been certified by the Commonwealth as safe for human use. The executioner had, in all likelihood, taken the requisite number of hours of advanced electrocution courses.

Quite frankly, what Romanoff described to me did not rise to the level of an emergency, since he wasn't actually dealing with a "sudden, unforeseen occurrence." He knew it was coming. It couldn't have been that much of a shock. Why did he wait until the last minute to call? Had he contacted me yesterday, I would have, at the very least, advised him not to sit down.

"Emergencies" can sometimes take a more subtle form. I had spent two arduous days at the office of my close friend, attorney Robert Thorndike. We were serving as co-counsel in complex litigation scheduled to be heard at trial in a week. Thorndike's secretary, Janice, had strict orders not to disturb us. It was during our review of the proposed cross-examination of the fifth witness that Bob was interrupted by the intercom. He was visibly displeased, but responded in a pleasant manner.

"Janice, I told you I didn't want to be disturbed."

Janice's apologetic voice returned through the speaker. She had been Thorndike's loyal secretary for more years than either cared to admit.

"I know, Bob, but this lady keeps calling, saying it's an emergency."

"Who is she?"

"A Mrs. Wesson."

"Who?"

"Mrs. Wesson."

"I don't represent anyone by that name, do I?"

"No, she's a new client."

"What's the emergency?"

"She won't tell me. She refuses to speak with anyone but a lawyer."

"Well then tell her I'll call her back."

We returned to our trial preparation exercise, an effort that proved to be short-lived. It was Janice at the conference room door.

"Is this about that Wesson woman, again?" Thorndike demanded.

"She appears to be quite distressed."

"OK. All right. I'll take the call," my vanquished friend conceded. "Otherwise, we won't have a moment's peace." Bob activated the speakerphone.

"Mrs. Wesson, this is Robert Thorndike. How may I help you?"

"Oh, thank heaven I got through. You see, this is an emergency!"

"What is the problem, ma'am?"

"Every day about this time, my neighbor's cat waltzes into my back yard to take a dump. What can I do legally to stop this trespassing on my property?"

From my vantage point, it appeared that Thorndike had, upon hearing the words "cat" and "dump" concluded that this was not an emergency situation.

"You have repeatedly called my office about cat poop?"

"Oh my God!" Wesson interrupted. "Here comes that damned cat right now! He's doing it again! What should I do?"

In retrospect, Thorndike should have disconnected the call, and returned to our arithmetic calculations.

"Lady — there's only one thing to do — shoot the damn cat," he proposed.

With those words, the caller hung up, her voice replaced by a dial tone. She hadn't so much as said "thank you."

"You don't think she took you seriously?" I pondered out loud.

"No, of course not," Thorndike assured me. But he, too, looked slightly hesitant. "Maybe I better have Janice call her back." "Janice, get that Wesson lady back on the line," Thorndike requested over the office intercom.

"She didn't leave a number," his secretary responded.

I picked up a telephone book, hoping to find the caller's strange last name. Thorndike did the same, with a similar lack of success. Somewhere out there I couldn't help but fear that a feline friend might, as we spoke, be taking its last dump.

Luckily, Mrs. Wesson proved to be a poor markswoman. Only one pellet from the shotgun blast hit its target. As a result, little Snowball received just a superficial laceration to the tip of her tail, a wound that healed in about two days.

Mrs. Wesson, on the other hand, did not fare quite as well. After the cops arrived, they relieved her of the shotgun, and then committed her to the local mental hospital for observation. She, in turn, told the cops she was merely following instructions from Thorndike.

Snowball's owner, Mrs. Osgood, was not amused. As a result of its narrow escape from death, the cat's personality allegedly took a turn for the worse. Snowball refused to take a dump in any yard but her own. She would sit and stare at the tip of her tail for hours at a time. Nor was the injured feline again able to watch any gunplay depicted on television. A cat psychologist failed to bring Snowball out of her depression, so Osgood decided to sue. Thorndike asked me out to lunch after he was served with the legal papers.

"Why did Osgood sue you, if Wesson was the actual triggerwoman?" I asked over soup and sandwiches at the local diner.

"Because Wesson, it turns out, is penniless, and probably mentally ill. Osgood figures I'll pay to avoid the litigation," Thorndike theorized.

"How much are Snowball's damages?" I inquired.

Thorndike produced the formal complaint from his briefcase, and read verbatim from the document: "Let's see . . . $240.00 for veterinarian bills and overnight observation; $650.00 for a feline psychologist; $1,000.00 for permanent scaring to the cat's tail; $1,500.00 for the mental distress suffered by both Snowball and Osgood; plus legal fees and court costs of $2,000.00."

"That adds up to about $5,400.00," I blurted out.

"$5,390.00 to be exact," Thorndike corrected. "I won't pay it. Not for some broken down trespassing cat. Osgood can get a new one for $5.00 at any animal shelter. We've got to fight this."

The *we've* caught my attention. Was Thorndike suggesting that I had some mutual interest in this litigation?"

"Of course, I'll want you to represent me at trial, Larry," Thorndike confirmed.

My diplomatic suggestions to Thorndike that he might want to tender a moderate settlement offer to Osgood were unwelcome and summarily dismissed.

"It's a $5.00 cat that hardly got scratched. If I offer anything, it suggests I did something wrong, which I didn't," Thorndike asserted.

I decided I better prepare for the hearing scheduled before Magistrate Gombocz.

In Pennsylvania, magistrates are elected to hear minor disputes; judges are elected to preside over major litigation involving large sums of money. Magistrates play an essential role in the judicial system, for without them, the courts would be overburdened and chaotic. Anyone can seek to be elected magistrate. Formal legal training is not required — just a modicum of common sense. If a litigant is unhappy with the decision rendered by a magistrate, an appeal can be taken to a board of arbitrators composed of three attorneys, and a further appeal can be pursued thereafter before a judge and jury.

Gombocz had been a magistrate for more than 40 years. He had been re-elected again and again because he had a well-deserved reputation for compassion and fairness. He would patiently preside over each case, no matter how insignificant, aware that the litigants standing before him had come seeking justice and fair play. Gombocz was part magistrate, part psychologist, part priest, and part father figure.

Mrs. Osgood hired attorney Roland Livingstone to represent her. Livingstone was the only person I had ever met who could strut while seated. He was composed of nine-parts hot air to every one-part ego. He had a flare for the dramatic, and used the courtroom as a stage for his emotional presentations. He enjoyed interrupting opponents and their witnesses at will with his deep baritone voice. At 6 foot 3 inches, he towered before the bench like the Colossus of Rhodes.

The first witness called to testify on behalf of the plaintiff was Dr. Humphrey Vernutten, the veterinarian who had attended to Snowball's injuries. He confirmed that his patient had been a victim of a shotgun blast, and that one centimeter of the cat's tail was now missing. After treating the cat, he noted a possible residual psychosis that necessitated consultation with a feline psychologist, Dr. Marie Blunderhosen.

Blunderhosen testified that Snowball would never be the same again. She suffered from nightmares and depression. She had developed acute hairballitis, and not even catnip could make her happy.

Osgood advised the magistrate that she, too, was seeing a psychiatrist as a result of emotional distress. In the midst of her testimony, she broke down and cried. The magistrate handed her an extra-strength tissue as he valiantly attempted to fight back a tear of his own. It was about this time that I noticed among the clutter on Gombocz's desk a picture of a kitten cradled in his loving arms.

The magistrate didn't appreciate attorney Roland's theatrical stunts, so he refused to award him any legal fees. But he did find in favor of Snowball in the amount of $4,000.00. Thorndike was livid. "Take an appeal!" he ordered in my direction.

"You know, Bob," I said as I tried to calm him down, "an appeal could be dangerous. A board of arbitrators might come back with an even higher verdict. I don't think you're looking at this from a neutral and detached perspective."

Thorndike didn't hear a word I said. I filed the appeal.

The three arbitrators proved to be more emotional than Magistrate Gombocz. After personally offering condolences to Mrs. Osgood, they left the hearing room with tissues of their own. In addition, they awarded Snowball $8,000.00 in damages.

"It's an outrage!" Thorndike protested. "Take an appeal!"

"Do you really think a jury trial is a good idea?" I questioned. "What if one of the jurors owns a cat?"

Thorndike could not be dissuaded. I took the appeal.

"What?" Thorndike screamed. "How could a jury have awarded $20,000.00 in damages? The cat was hardly scratched! Take an appeal!" he ordered.

Civil appeals from a jury trial may be filed with the Superior Court of Pennsylvania. It is a complex process in which the appellant must pay for and reproduce the entire trial transcript, and then file a brief reflecting the legal basis for challenging the trial court's adjudication. No testimony is heard by the Justices of the State Superior Court. Rather, the Justices review the trial transcript and legal briefs, after which legal counsel are scheduled to appear before the Justices to submit oral argument in favor of their respective positions.

Argument of cases arising within the eastern portion of Pennsylvania is usually scheduled in Philadelphia in the ornate courtroom of the Superior Court. Oral argument by legal counsel is a formal affair, since only a limited number of days is set aside each year for such presentations. Counsel are given exactly 15 minutes to argue their points of law, since as many as 30 separate arguments are heard each day during these appellate proceedings.

About half an hour before court commences, all of the attorneys scheduled to argue appear, and are assigned a number, designating their place on the argument list. As a result, some attorneys will be heard almost immediately, while others must remain the better part of the day. Despite the fact that only 15 minutes are allotted to each attorney, the journey to Philadelphia, appearance in court, and the return home usually consume the entire day.

Thorndike decided to accompany me, even though I would be the only one permitted to address the Justices. We were assigned to be the 16th argument on the list. Since 30 arguments were scheduled that day, we might conceivably be heard before the lunch break. We sat in the fifth row watching as teams of attorneys addressed the panel of three black-robed Justices. I counted about 100 attorneys and their clients patiently awaiting their 15 minutes of stardom.

The Justices kept a tight schedule. If an attorney attempted to take just five seconds beyond his or her allotted 15 minutes, counsel would be cut off in mid-sentence by an abrupt reprimand from the court. As a result, the case assigned prior to mine, No. 15, was reached during the morning session.

Case No. 15 dealt with a defendant who had been convicted of murdering two individuals during an armed robbery of a grocery store. The murderer was scheduled to die by lethal injection, and since this sentence was viewed with displeasure by the defendant, his public defender counsel, Irving Abrams, was directed by the condemned felon to take an appeal.

Abrams had been waiting nearly three hours to be heard. He nervously assembled his final notes as he sensed he was about to be called to the podium positioned before the Justices. The life of Abram's client literally rested in his ability within the next 15 minutes to convince the three omnipotent Justices that the death sentence should not be carried out. In all likelihood, Abrams had been preparing for this moment for weeks.

The court clerk addressed the assembled attorneys: "Case No. 15, Commonwealth vs. Griffith. Attorney Abrams, please come forward." In a scene similar to when Dorothy, the scarecrow, tin man, and cowardly lion approached the Wizard of Oz with justifiable fear and trepidation, poor Abrams took a few cautious steps forward, toward the great and powerful Justices. He was about to say something, when the Chief Justice interrupted.

"Counselor, my brethren of the Court and I have read your learned brief, and commend you for a job well done. Your references to the applicable law are on point and incisive. You are a credit to the Office of the Public Defender, and are to be applauded for your labors on behalf of your client."

"Why . . . thank you, Mr. Justice," was all the astonished Abrams could think to say. Up until that point, the Justices had consistently maintained an air of self-righteous agitation, as they fired smoke-and-brimstone-laden questions at the miserable attorneys trembling at their feet. Now, without explanation, they had bestowed kindness and compliments upon an attorney representing a murderer. As is often the case, everything happens for a reason. The Chief Justice continued his remarks.

"The Court wonders, Mr. Abrams, if you would be kind enough this morning to extend a courtesy to the Court, a courtesy for which the Court would consider itself truly in your debt."

Poor Abrams was at a loss. He did nothing other than nod his head up and down in respectful silence. The favor to which he was about to agree remained unexplained. But with the life of his client hanging in the balance, now did not appear the time to decline the Court's unexpected request.

"Thank you for your assistance, counselor," the Chief Justice continued. "Because of the high quality of your brief, there is simply no need for oral argument. You have already touched upon every conceivable issue. As a result, my brethren and I wonder if you would agree to give up your 15 minutes to an attorney from Bethlehem, Pennsylvania, who is here to argue that his client, who conspired to murder an innocent cat in cold blood, should be shown mercy by this Court. We want to question this attorney for at least half an hour, to review all the facts in this heinous crime."

This last statement by the court caught my attention, and that of Thorndike, as well. Apparently the court was predisposed toward the safety of felines, and had found little merit in my client's appeal. After hastily conferring with Thorndike, I approached the podium, and announced that the appeal had just been withdrawn, and that the jury verdict would be honored by my client.

"A wise move, counselor," the Chief Justice noted, as he turned to the other Justices and proclaimed, "Justice has been served. Let us pray that Snowball makes a speedy recovery. Court stands recessed for lunch."

CHAPTER SEVEN: I'M FROM THE IRS, AND I'M HERE TO HELP YOU

You'll have days like this. I represented the estate of Mildred Kleppelmyer. She had departed this life more than a year ago last July. I had successfully shepherded her estate through the multitude of high hurdles and pitfalls designed to turn an attorney's hair gray. We had sold the widow's house, appraised her jewelry, paid the estimated inheritance tax, found the lost insurance policy, paid the decedent's debts, including the overdue water bill, and mediated three arguments arising among the bereaved beneficiaries. All I needed was a written confirmation from the Internal Revenue Service that the decedent's personal income tax return had been approved, and that a refund would be forthcoming. Upon receipt of this document, I could then distribute the remaining estate assets to the dearly departed's beneficiaries — those grieving second cousins twice removed, all of whom had already picked out new cars.

I called the IRS to see when I might receive the confirmation on IRS Form 235A.

"Welcome to the Internal Revenue Service automated hotline," the robotistic voice announced. "For your convenience, please listen to the following menu before making your selection. These instructions will be repeated in Spanish."

For my convenience! There isn't a voice messaging system on the face of this earth that exists for *my* convenience. Such systems are convenient for those who install them. Period. If I had one at my law office, I'd be out of business in a week.

"If you are calling to order a 1040 Short Form, press one. If you are calling about an audit, press two. If you are calling to ask for a filing extension, press three . . ."

Twenty-four selections later, I still hadn't heard anything remotely applicable to what I needed. Do you suppose the family members of the bureaucrats working for the IRS face this automated hell each time they call to remind Mom or Dad to bring home cat litter? Of course not! They have direct-dial numbers, and I'd have bled out of my eyeballs to get my refund-grasping hands on just one of them.

"And now, Señor e Señorita, the same menu in Spanish . . ."

I had been suspended on the telephone for 12 minutes. Was I entitled to interest on the refund computed from the first minute I began this call?"

This telephonic limbo reminded me momentarily of Old Judge Baker, who use to take about two hours in court just to accept a simple guilty plea. Other jurists accomplished this task in less than 15 minutes. I remember representing Edwina Filbert who had more shoplifting convictions than Bill Clinton had affairs. Since the TV set she stole was found by the store security guard under her sweater, she decided to save the Commonwealth the cost of a trial. Actually, it was the antennae poking through her hair that first caught the guard's attention.

"I plead guilty," Edwina advised His Honor, who proceeded to outline in agonizing detail every appellate right known to mankind. After a two-hour lecture, the judge finally came up for air.

"Now, do you have any questions regarding your rights?" he inquired of Edwina.

"Yeah," my client proclaimed, as her glazed eyes slowly began to focus upon the judge. "Does my sentence begin now, or two hours ago when you started your damned yammering?"

The IRS phone robot was now concluding its bilingual instructions. I had been on the telephone for no less than 20 minutes and hadn't spoken to a soul.

". . . Buenos dias. If you are calling from a rotary phone, or need further assistance, please remain on the line, and an IRS representative will be with you shortly. Your call is important to us, and will be answered in the order it was received. For your protection, your conversation is being recorded."

Ethnically correct music began to filter into my ear. The "elevator" version of LaBamba. I began to drift off.

"May I help you?" a voice startled me back to consciousness.

"Are you human, or machine?" I questioned.

"Human," the voice assured me.

"That's wonderful," I responded. "I'm Larry Fox, and I serve as legal counsel to the estate of Mildred Kleppelmyer. The IRS reference number is R-12-747622BQ79A-73268.

"One moment please . . ."

Back with the music. It had taken me 20 minutes to get this far. I decided I better control myself. I wouldn't want to be disconnected at this point because some human government employee thought I had a bad attitude.

"Your reference number is valid. How may I assist you?"

"I need confirmation that the decedent's personal income tax return for last year was approved as submitted, and that a refund of $2,462.00 is forthcoming."

"One moment please."

Back alone in limbo land. I sharpened three pencils, but after a few minutes of grinding, similar to my new IRS friend, they, too, were gone. I tried sharpening a fourth, but after three inches of the writing instrument had disappeared into the electric sharpener, it made a strange noise, and I realized I was clutching half of what use to be a pen.

"Thank you for holding," the voice began. "We will be pleased to send that information to Mrs. Kleppelmyer within the next three weeks."

"Excuse me, Ma'am. Mrs. Kleppelmyer died last year. I represent her estate."

"Well, this is privileged IRS information which, pursuant to the Privacy Act can only be sent directly to Mrs. Kleppelmyer. Does she still live at 528 Maple Street in Bethlehem, Pennsylvania?"

"No, she's dead, and I sold her house."

"Before she got her refund? You really shouldn't have done that. The confirmation and check can be sent only to her. I'm sure you and Mrs. Kleppelmyer both understand."

"Mrs. Kleppelmyer doesn't understand a thing," I said. "She's dead. And she doesn't live there — or anywhere — anymore."

"Very well. I'll send the check to her as soon as possible. Have a nice day." Click. Like Mrs. Kleppelmyer, the line was now dead.

I phoned the people who bought the Kleppelmyer house, and asked if they would forward any mail addressed to the decedent. They answered on the second ring, in English, without voicemail, or a menu. They agreed to help. It felt good to be among the living again.

I am always amazed by those who eagerly boast that they are in the process of defrauding the government by failing to pay their fair share of taxes. These felons miss the point. By stealing from the government, they steal from the rest of us whose taxes would be lower if each of us paid the piper.

Who among us hasn't heard some shirker proudly volunteer "I'm working under the table"? Now, I'm the first to admit Washington makes a profession of squandering money, but the remedy is to vote the fiscally irresponsible out of office and institute budgetary controls. Tax cheats are no different from those criminals who drive motor vehicles without insurance. Because of them, insurance costs for the rest of us are astronomical.

There was unmistakable urgency in Ramona Ogilvee's voice as she begged me to come to her house.

"The IRS just got here, and they're takin' away my stuff," she sobbed over the telephone. "You're my lawyer. DO something!"

It had been at least two years since my last contact with Ramona, but I needed no prompting from my secretary to recall who she was. Ramona was the only client I had ever represented who purchased a house with cash. On the day of settlement, she showed up with three suitcases filled with $1.00 bills totaling $150,000.00. It took two-and-a-half hours to count the money, and lug it to the bank. Ramona and her two daughters moved into the house next day in an upscale neighborhood near the edge of town.

There's nothing illegal about purchasing goods or services with cash. After all, each $1.00 note specifically says it may be used as legal tender, both for debts public and private. So I never asked where she got the money, and she never offered to tell. Apparently, it was against her belief system to transfer funds through a checking account.

"I'll be right over," I promised. Remember, there are no emergencies in the legal business — just clients who think they have an emergency. In all honesty, I had never actually seen an IRS raid, and like a doctor who personally places himself in harm's way to view the ravages of a rare infectious disease, I wanted to witness this most dreaded of governmental procedures firsthand.

I had to park my car on the street, since Ramona's driveway was occupied by two large yellow rental trucks, each painted with the phrase "An Adventure In Moving." Several men were busy loading furniture, a refrigerator, a collection of rugs, and other personal belongings.

I waited at the front door as four men carried out part of a grand piano. Inside, Ramona was sitting on the last chair in the kitchen, close to where the breakfast table used to be.

"They're taking everything!" she blurted out.

"How unfortunate. Why?" I asked.

"They claim I owe them money. They're taking the house, and the cars, too!" Ramona cried as she buried her face in a handkerchief.

I located the agent in charge. There he was in the empty living room — the only person standing around, not lifting a finger. We introduced ourselves.

"Agent Herbert Snatcher, IRS Special Collections Division."

"Larry Fox, attorney for the grabee," I responded.

He produced a legal document — a federal court order both for the seizure of Ramona's personal property and home, and for the removal of Ramona and any dependents therefrom.

"We took her bank account, too," Snatcher confided to me out of the corner of his mouth.

"Will I receive an inventory of what was taken today?"

"Right down to the fried pretzel dough ovens," Snatcher assured me.

"The what?"

"Pretzel dough. That's what got her in trouble in the first place."

I would soon learn, as I began to piece together Ramona's story, that Special Agent Snatcher was the master of understatement.

Fried pretzel dough is a Pennsylvania Dutch delicacy composed of ingredients similar to waffle or pancake batter. When poured from the small end of a funnel into deep vats of hot cooking oil, the mixture quickly takes on the appearance of a large pretzel afflicted with the mumps. This cooked concoction is complemented with white powdered sugar, or other toppings to taste.

People have been known to stand in line 100 deep at county fairs or stock car races just to sink their teeth into this tender taste sensation. Most fried dough eaters have two things in common: they are overweight, and if you listen closely, you can hear their arteries hardening — even above the roar of the car engines. It has been said that cottage cheese was invented to prove there is no accounting for taste. Fried pretzel dough was invented to prove that some people will actually pay money to stick just about anything into their mouths.

The cost of the ingredients per serving is about 5 cents. Ramona sold the finished product, after two minutes' cooking time, for $1.75 a piece. Each weekend during the spring, summer, and fall, she would haul her portable fried dough stand to another horse show, car race, flea market or similar assembly, and set up shop with her deep frying ovens and batter mixers. During the winter, she vacationed in Florida at her oceanfront villa, which was also purchased with cash. After paying the fairgrounds or race track a weekend rental fee, she was free to keep what she made. Business was brisk so earnings quickly piled up.

Ramona didn't believe in cash registers or receipts. She put the money in cigar boxes. When one filled up, she'd reach for another. During a typical weekend, she would average about $10,000.00 in cash. Her gross for nine months' work approached $350,000.00. After paying her two daughters $5.00 per hour to help out, and after deducting the cost of materials and rental fees, Ramona netted about $300,000.00 clear each fried dough season. She failed to report *any* of this income to the IRS.

"Why should I?" she told me. "I earned that money under the table!"

Within five years, she had bought a house in Pennsylvania and a villa in Florida, furnished them, and managed to deposit another $750,000.00 in a savings account at the local bank. It was the interest generated by this account, an account that had mysteriously grown without a confirmed source of income, that finally caught the attention of the IRS.

Agents decided to monitor Ramona's movements. They began to frequent the same county fairs and race tracks where she sold her delicacies. With the assistance of high-powered binoculars, they began counting the number of servings sold. Then they seized her bank account, the house, the villa, the fried pretzel dough wagon, and the two Mercedes convertibles, one parked in the garage, the other at the villa.

"I want my stuff back!" Ramona demanded as we sat in my office a week after the IRS raid.

"I don't think that's possible, Mrs. Ogilvee," I advised. "You see, no federal or state taxes were paid on your earnings, and as a result, the IRS claims you owe them money, as well as five years' compounded interest penalties. There's also the possibility of a jail sentence."

"I don't understand," Ogilvee protested. "I was just working under the table. Everyone does it."

"I don't, Ms. Ogilvee," I corrected her. "It's a felony if you fail to pay your proper share of taxes. Ask Pete Rose."

Ramona left my office in a huff, apparently in search of an attorney with advice more to her liking. The last I heard, she was paying off the government's fines by working in a fried dough stand she rented from the IRS, a stand equipped with a cash register that magically produced receipts with every $1.75 sale.

CHAPTER EIGHT: THE ZONING HEARING

Who would have expected such vociferous opposition. I certainly had no advance warning. Yet, there we stood, in the midst of an angry mob. I truly feared they might try to lynch my client, which would have been unfortunate, since he had not yet paid me in full. I looked about nervously for a potential escape route, but the old township municipal hall had just one door at the rear. We wouldn't make it out alive.

Shoe repairmen never seem to have time to fix their own shoes; auto mechanics drive cars that need work. The thought now flashed through my mind that I hadn't quite finished my own Last Will and Testament, even though I had been working on it for the past 20 years. "If I live through tonight, I'm going to . . ."

"You stinkin' bum!" a man barked as he pointed his pudgy finger in my face. He was dressed entirely in black, his hair slicked back into a ponytail, and he was carrying a protest sign.

I wouldn't have taken this case, had I thought for one moment that it would have generated such controversy or emotion. I leave the high-profile confrontations to those attorneys who thrive on being interviewed by TV persona for the 6:00 o'clock news. Obviously, this ruckus would be one of the lead stories for the local media. I always try to avoid the eye of a hurricane, but now I was stuck. For a split second, I thought back to how it all began, just two short months ago . . .

A Mr. Zipperfel contacted my office, wanting me to review a zoning issue, and to represent him at the township zoning hearing.

As an aside, the physical appearance of a new client is of great significance to me, and often determines whether or not I'll represent the individual. If, for instance, the client is carrying a briefcase larger than mine, I never take the case.

If the client is wearing a bow tie, I'll pass, too. Shifty are those who intentionally choose to look ridiculous and at the same time take themselves so seriously.

Mr. Zipperfel wasn't carrying a briefcase or wearing a bow tie. He showed up on time, dressed in a clean polo shirt. A good risk.

"I want to open a retail business in the township," he explained. "I already have two similar stores within a 50-mile radius. This one will be located equidistant between the other two at Broad and Center."

"How can I help?" I asked.

"The zoning officer says I must attend a municipal hearing to obtain a special exception before he will issue a business permit."

I quickly located the township zoning ordinance and its accompanying zoning map. Sure enough, retail uses were conditionally permitted, if the applicant could demonstrate that the proposed business did not constitute a danger to the community's health, safety or welfare.

"What are you planning to sell?" I asked in passing.

"Condoms," came the response.

"Prophylactics?" I gasped. Zipperfel didn't bat an eyelash.

"Every type manufactured in the free world," he boasted. "Some glow in the dark, some have sequins. We can even print them up with personal messages or campaign slogans."

Zipperfel was obviously proud of his wares, and in a single stretch, so to speak, went on for 10 minutes to describe a multitude of interesting products, most of which I didn't know existed. It sure put a fresh spin on displaying political catch phrases. Our conversation brought to mind one of my favorite jokes: This duck waddles into a drug store, and asks the pharmacist for a condom.

"Shall I put that on your bill?" the clerk inquires.

"What type of a duck do you think I am?" the offended bird asks.

Zipperfel and I discussed the concept of a *special exception* as it pertains to the law of zoning. Special exceptions are similar to the well-known cereal "Post Grape Nuts" — one of the strangest names in breakfast food. No posts. No grapes. No nuts. Just odd-shaped micro-pellets that get stuck in your teeth.

It's the same with special exceptions: they are neither special nor exceptional. If the applicant can show that he will comply with the zoning ordinance, he'll most likely get a permit. Therefore, my job was simple. All I had to do was prove that Zipperfel's business would not violate the health, safety, or welfare of the community.

"I'll take the case," I advised Zipperfel. He shook my hand and wrote out a retainer check.

"Don't worry," he assured me. "It won't bounce. It ain't rubber."

I drafted the zoning petition, filed it with the township zoning officer, and waited the statutory period for public advertisement of the hearing. On the evening of the hearing, Zipperfel and I drove together to the township meeting hall.

"Must be something big goin' on tonight," Zipperfel mused about the lack of parking.

"Funny," I responded, "we're the only zoning hearing on the agenda."

We walked through the hearing room's only door. The place was packed. The only remaining seats were at the applicant's table. I slowly made my way through the narrow aisle to the front of the room; my arms cradled prepared notes of testimony, drawings of the store's proposed location, and the zoning ordinance. Zipperfel followed closely behind.

"That's them!" some old lady called out, an initial proclamation that proved to be the catalyst for a chain reaction of verbal assaults.

"You stinkin' bum," said the man with his finger in my face. Honestly. I was offended by that remark alone. But he wasn't finished. He reached deep within his insult arsenal, and dropped . . .

63

THE BIG ONE: "You . . . You . . . ATTORNEY!" Gosh. Being called a 'bum' is one thing . . .

Just then, something hit the back of my head. I spun around in the midst of a sea of protest signs now bouncing above the crowd. The TV camera lights beamed in my face, just as the synchronized and accurate hurling of condoms began.

"I hope they bought these at one of my shops," Zipperfel confided as he shamelessly stooped to collect as many prophylactic projectiles as possible. "Some of these are top quality." He stuffed them into his overcoat pockets.

Soon the cops showed up, and Zipperfel was finally able to testify. A week later, I received official notice that the special exception had been granted. Zipperfel would open his third store.

"I knew you'd come through for me!" Zipperfel said as he wrote out a check in final payment for my services. "And how about that front page spread we got the next day in the papers? And the local TV coverage!"

"I'm pleased for you. Still, there's something that's been confusing me since we left the hearing. I nearly soiled myself that night. You, on the other hand, didn't even flinch."

I studied his face. He didn't respond. He wouldn't even look at me. I may be a sissy, but I'm not stupid.

"Zipperfel," I coaxed, "no one's that cool under pressure, not even you. What gives?"

"Well, counselor, it's like this . . ." Zipperfel began. "Publicity like that would have cost me a fortune. It's just not in our budget right now. So I swapped a little controversy for some free airtime. So what? No one got hurt."

"You mean to tell me all those protesters . . ."

"Friends of mine. The guy with the ponytail dressed in black who got in your face is one of my store managers. He still busts a gut just thinking about it."

"Do I even want to ask why you didn't tell me?"

"You would have jumped ship. Besides, I needed you to put on a good face. Make it real and all. It gave the hearing authenticity."

He was right about everything. I'm sure I looked like I could have used a diaper that night. And his new store did well, since everyone knew about it almost overnight. His second check didn't bounce either. Quite a businessman, that Zipperfel.

I can still remember when Aunt Freda had her first barium enema. She was out of sorts for about three days afterward. The nurses at the hospital felt so sorry for her, they gave her a copy of her X-ray as a memento of her visit. The picture outlined in vivid detail most of her lower intestinal tract. Aunt Freda was particularly proud of the location at which her large and small intestines joined together.

"That barium stuff is radioactive," she advised me as she pointed to the place where they found the blockage. "They can see right into your body and everything."

The two men who were now seated in my conference room had been referred to me by a client for whom I had previously obtained some rather complex zoning remedies.

"We heard you're pretty knowledgeable about zoning, counselor," the smaller guy with the photosensitive glasses began. He introduced himself as Irving Thermo, and his partner, Harvey Cleare.

I shook Cleare's hand first, or was that Thermo — no, it was Cleare, the one with the bad rug. Anyway, it's funny how new clients find their way into a lawyer's office. Not once in 25 years has a single litigant ever asked me what law school I attended, or what my grade-point average was. After you hang a shingle to practice law, nobody cares if you were on dean's list or academic probation. Clients only want to know if you can win their case, and how much it will cost.

Thermo's cell phone rang. "Pardon me," he apologized. Irritation spread over his face. "If they are on strike, then get another courier! I don't care how you handle it, but the shipment must arrive today!"

As Thermo folded the telephone back into his pocket, Cleare explained the reason for their visit.

"We're in the medical supply business. We transport and sell low-level radioactive medicine for use in hospitals. The Nuclear Regulatory Commission oversees our operations that cover most of the United States. We'd like to set up an overnight distribution center here in the Lehigh Valley, so we can better service all your local hospitals," he explained.

"It's really quite safe," Thermo interjected. "Our products have a shelf life of approximately 24 hours. We transport the materials in lead-lined containers, using an overnight carrier, assemble the product as required by the doctor, and transport it directly to the hospital for immediate use."

"We'd like to stress at the zoning hearing how safe our operation is," Cleare chimed in. "Nothing can go wrong."

It all made perfect sense to me, so I filed the zoning application, and scheduled a hearing at the municipal building. Thermo and Cleare appeared as witnesses. Their testimony was succinct, professional, and convincing. For 25 minutes, Cleare addressed the board members, outlining the numerous safety precautions exercised by his company. He had obviously given this lecture scores of times before. The zoning hearing board found the evidence to be acceptable, and unanimously approved all the variances we had requested.

Thermo and Cleare had to catch a late-night flight back to California. They thanked me for my assistance, and quickly departed. So did everyone else, including the stenographer, the members of the zoning hearing board, and a few dozen interested spectators. That left just me and Joe, the night janitor, who began to lock up the municipal building. Joe had known my father years before when they both worked at the steel plant.

"It's good to see you again, Joe," I said with a wave of my hand. "Good to see you too, Larry," Joe replied as he turned out lights in the hearing room. For a split second we stood in the dark together as he opened the door to let me out.

That's when we both saw it — the eerie green glow emanating from the two chairs where Thermo and Cleare had only moments before been sitting. Green glowing footprints marched out the door, and into the dark parking lot next to the building. The footprints stopped where their car, now gone, had been parked.

CHAPTER NINE: THE NON-CUSTODIAL PARENT

"How are you, Larry?" It was the "P.J." — the President Judge — calling on my office telephone. I felt fine.

"I feel fine, Your Honor," I said as I hid my worst suspicions.

"And your family — how are they?"

"They're well too, Your Honor."

The P.J. and my draft board had something in common. When either governmental entity asked about my state of health, it was cause for concern. There was a pregnant pause, so the P.J. decided to cut to the chase.

"I was wondering if you might do the Court a small favor?"

How could I refuse? After all, it wasn't as if the P.J. were asking for himself. This was for "The Court," a noble cause. More important, if I said "yes," the Court might react with favor when next I appeared before it. Alternatively, if I were prone toward suicide and chose to decline this kind invitation, the chances were excellent my next 30 clients would end up in the slammer.

"I'm so pleased you're able to help," His Honor gushed. "I would like you to represent a gentleman pro bono who has been named as a defendant in a 'termination of parental rights' case initiated by the County Office of Children and Youth."

Now let's cast some light on what His Honor actually said:

I would like you to represent . . . You are hereby ordered to serve as legal counsel. If you refuse, life as you know it will end.

A gentleman . . . some indigent, sleazy bum who has petitioned for court-appointed legal assistance.

Pro bono . . . for free, i.e. you will spend more than 100 hours preparing for a week-long trial, but don't bother to send anyone a bill. Your sole reward shall be knowing that you have served the court in its time of need.

Who has been named as a defendant in a termination of parental rights case . . . Your client is a scumbag who has failed to provide even the slightest parental care or interest in his children. So the county office tasked with overseeing the welfare of children has petitioned the court to end this bum's rights to his children, and to place the children in a home where they will be loved and nurtured.

His Honor was patiently waiting for my response, and so similar to being an unwilling participant at a shotgun wedding, I answered the only way I could:

"I am humbled that the court is inclined to entrust me with this matter, and hope that I will fulfill my duties to both the court and the client." Roughly translated: "Judge, I may not be a Rhodes Scholar, but even I know when someone is dumping a 5-pound shovel-load of crap on my desk."

"The court thanks you, attorney Fox. You may pick up the file at the court clerk's office. Good day." And with those parting words, His Honor returned me to the solitude of my office overhead, now enhanced with yet another non-income producing file.

I once saw a cowboy movie in which a lynch mob made the condemned cowpoke dig his own grave before they hung him. Similarly, I had to hike to the courthouse to acquire the bum's file, due to some undisclosed county budgetary postage restriction.

"How can you represent such a stinkin' low life?" the court clerk demanded, as she shoved the thick file into my chest. Don't you have better things to do?"

It was Friday afternoon, and I was tired. "You're right, Joyce," I confirmed. "Lawyers? We're all bloodsuckers."

I reviewed my client's file over the weekend. His children's county reports, medical histories, and counseling records were voluminous. This man, this "father," William Jordan, was scheduled to appear at my office first thing Monday morning.

The file reflected that William had fathered five children — perhaps six — he wasn't sure. The two latest arrivals were the objects of the county's petition to terminate his rights. Baby girl Shelly was now six months old, and baby boy David first made his appearance one-and-a-half years prior in time. Their mother, Donna, my client's on-and-off-again girlfriend, was a heavy cocaine user. As a result, David was born three months premature, suffering from severe cardiac problems and a deformed right arm. Although he weighed just 2 pounds at birth, he was subjected during his first three months of life to two open-heart surgeries. His heart was the size of a golf ball.

Shelly had not fared much better. Born blind and severely retarded, she would never be able to talk. Since the mother was presently in prison on drug charges and my client had failed to take any responsibility for his children, the county placed them in a foster home, pending disposition of the case. Despite all of the problems burdening these infants, their new foster parents had already petitioned to adopt them.

It was 11:00 a.m. Monday morning. To my great surprise, Mr. Jordan was late for his appointment. Apparently he was better at fathering children than telling time. I secretly hoped he was a no-show. I sure didn't need another free case, and I wasn't particularly jazzed about representing a scumbag who neglected his kids. Unfortunately, as I looked through my back office window, an unfamiliar white Jaguar swerved into the parking lot, coming to a stop right next to my 10-year-old dented Dodge. Last week an errant shopping cart had slammed into my car at the mall, but who could tell?

A tall, lanky man deftly extricated himself from the contoured front driver's seat, and walked toward the door.

"This better not be William Jordon," I fumed to myself as I backed away from the window.

"Mr. Jordan is here to see you," my receptionist advised. My blood pressure escalated as I headed to the conference room to meet my newest client.

"I'm pleased to make your acquaintance," I lied as we shook hands. He lied in return. Now we could get down to business.

The initial interview was unremarkable. Yes, he loved his children, but he just hadn't found the time to be with them because he was so busy. But he was planning to change all that once he got a job and could pay something toward child support. I told him a pre-trial hearing had been scheduled before Judge McMurtry next week to discuss the multitude of procedural issues requiring clarification prior to the actual trial. William said he would *try* to make it. I told him to cancel his other pressing engagements, since his presence in court was mandatory.

The pre-trial conference took place in Courtroom No. 1, the large ceremonial chamber serviced by four separate entrance doors — one at each corner of the huge rectangular chamber. I stood before Judge McMurtry. My client, who stunned us all by showing up, was at my left side. Attorney Agnes Lipshutz, representing the Office of Children and Youth, stood at my right. Agnes had a self-righteous air about her. She quickly made it clear that she was well aware what was best for these two children, and that she had no intention of stipulating to anything I might request on my client's behalf.

I petitioned for psychological studies of both the children and parents, since I wanted an expert to testify at trial regarding the children's need to be raised by their father. Agnes thought the initial evaluation outlined in the file was sufficient.

I wanted to meet the children personally to better understand their present interaction with the couple who was raising them. Agnes thought this would unduly disturb the children.

I sought to visit where the children were living. Agnes suggested that this would constitute an unnecessary invasion of privacy.

"Your Honor," Agnes sighed, "the file we gave Mr. Fox is

voluminous, and contains everything he needs to prepare for trial. The medical records alone exceed 500 pages!"

Agnes was right about the medical records. These two innocent infants had spent most of their short existence in hospitals. They would probably need continued assistance throughout their lives. The medical bills paid by the county during the last year to keep them alive exceeded $1.5 million. My client hadn't paid a cent of this.

Things didn't go that well for William. His Honor appeared inclined to side with Agnes. "If your client wants a new psychological evaluation, he'll have to pay for it," Judge McMurtry said from the bench. The Court's other unsympathetic pronouncements took the same fiscal and philosophical approaches. It was about at this time that I first noticed the pairs of sheriff's deputies positioning themselves at each door. "Eight deputies for a civil proceeding," I mumbled to myself. "Some important criminal case must be up next."

"Does that conclude the pre-trial?" Judge McMurtry inquired.

"I believe so," I said.

The Northampton County Sheriff appeared out of nowhere — his job required he be able to do so — and positioned himself directly behind my client who was none the wiser. In a heartbeat Jordan's arms were drawn behind him, and handcuffs snapped on his wrists.

"Hey, what the hell is this?" Jordan protested.

"Justice," the deputy shot back.

His Honor didn't seem very surprised. Over the years, he had seen the various forms Justice can take. He barely looked up as he asked the sheriff for an explanation. Apparently, this wasn't the first time he had witnessed this type of shackling pursued in his courtroom.

The sheriff began to read from a formal looking document. "We have reason to believe, Your Honor, that this perpetrator is the same William Jordon who owes $18,474.00 in back support for five children."

Fantastic. Now I was representing a perpetrator.

"I'm flabbergasted and amazed," Judge McMurtry mumbled in the midst of a yawn. "Tell me it just isn't so, Mr. Jordan," his judicial hand propping his judicial chin.

Jordan looked in my direction. I got the distinct impression he was waiting for me to do something, like come to his defense. What legal argument should counsel advance at a time like this on behalf of someone who probably has all of $3.00 in his Gucci wallet? Judge McMurtry came to my rescue.

"Don't look at Mr. Fox, Jordan. He only represents you in the termination-of-parental-rights proceedings. Now we're talking child support — a whole different ball of wax."

I studied Judge McMurtry's face for an instant. He wasn't such a sinister-looking guy after all.

"Do you owe the county domestic relations office child support?"

The perpetrator paused pensively. "It's possible."

"Don't play with me, Jordan. Is or isn't there an outstanding order for child support with your name on it?"

"Sorta."

"Well, wouldn't it be nice if you *sorta* supported your own children?"

"It's like this, Your Judgeship . . ."

Apparently the Court had lost interest. "How much of the back support can you pay this morning?"

Jordan thought for a moment. "Eight dollars."

"That leaves you $18,466.00 short. How did you get to court today?"

Jordan stared at the judge as if he didn't understand the question.

"Come, come Mr. Jordan. Did you drive here today?"

"Uh huh."

"And what, pray tell, did you drive?"

"A car?"

"Good. Now we're getting somewhere. What type of car?"

74

"A Ja . . ." Jordan's voice trailed off to an inaudible whisper.

The judge leaned over to better hear. "A what?"

"A Jaguar," came the whisper again.

"A Jaguar?" Judge McMurtry echoed in disbelief. "Wonderful. And where might we find this jalopy now?"

"Why?" Jordan inquired.

Now, had I been in Jordan's handcuffs, I'm not sure I would have cross-examined the judge, for he was clearly in no mood.

"Hand over the keys."

"To my Jaguar?"

"Trust me on this one, Jordan — where you're going, you won't need it."

"My Jaguar?"

"The County's Jaguar."

The judge was, of course, correct. Jordan would have never been able to fit that big hunk of metal in a small jail cell, and he wasn't going to need a ride home — just a toothbrush and some jammies.

"Search him for the keys," the judge ordered the sheriff, who quickly found them in Jordan's left pants pocket.

"You better not scratch it!" Jordan sputtered in the direction of the sheriff.

"You better hope it fetches $18,466.00 at auction, son," the Court admonished Jordan, "or you may not be kissing another woman or walking on green grass for a long time."

Jordan was starting to get the big picture. And so it was on this sunny day that the judge wasn't quite finished. He spoke as he thumbed through Jordan's bulging file.

"I note that Mr. Fox was appointed to represent you free of charge since you claimed on your legal aid application that you had no assets."

"Only $8.00, Your Judgeship."

"And a Jaguar touring car," the Court reminded my soon to be former client. "I'm guessing, if you can afford a Jaguar, you can retain private counsel."

Judge McMurtry turned to me. "You are relieved from further

responsibility in this case, with the thanks of the Court."

I smiled, nodded in respect, and darted out sideways past two deputies still standing at the side door.

I don't know what ever happened to Jordan or his Jaguar. I drove my beat-up Dodge back to the office, enjoying every squeaky, uncomfortable mile.

CHAPTER TEN: THE PRACTICE OF ECCLESIASTICAL LAW

My wife, Teresa, is a devout Catholic, and her religious devotion is almost as strong as her affection for her two cats. I don't possess the same burning passion for these two lazy, fur-ball-regurgitating felines. However, they make my wife happy, and that's good enough for me and very lucky for them.

Around the time we began settling into married life, "Catholic Things" started happening without warning. For one, I began to receive home delivery of the parish newspaper, *The Sainthood*. I have since become an avid reader of this publication, for I was amazed at the plethora of information contained within: bingo schedules, church bazaars, retreats and the like.

Once in a while Teresa would convince me to accompany her to Mass. There I learned about the "blessing of throats," the need to carry extra cash, for there was always a second collection for the ministries in Africa, and the need to eat a full breakfast, lest your empty stomach gurgle during the silent intentions.

One night, about three months after our wedding, I was relaxing after dinner with the latest issue of *The Sainthood*. I made it half way through last week's bingo scores when, without warning, there came a knock at the door, precisely at 8:00 p.m.

". . . Oh, and by the way," Teresa sang out, "tonight is parish visitation." Another Catholic thing.

Parish visitation is a misnomer, for one does not visit a parish. The parish, in the form of a priest, visits you. Thus, the knock at the door.

"Parish what?" I inquired of my wife.

"Let the priest in, dear."

"The who?"

"The priest — for parish visitation. Didn't I tell you he was coming?"

No, she hadn't, but it was too late. This wasn't like trick-or-treat night where the knockee has the option of refusing entry to the knocker. If I didn't open the door immediately, we could easily descend into the burning depths of hell for all eternity.

I opened the door. There in the spring night stillness stood the Rev. Mahn — a Bible in one hand and church-related paraphernalia in the other.

"Good evening, Father," Teresa warmly began as she approached my side. "We've been expecting you." It was easy for her to call him "Father." Not me. Especially since he was 10 years my junior. And "we" had not been expecting him at all. But now Teresa, having lied to a priest, had a legitimate reason to go to confession.

The soft-spoken Mahn, a recent graduate of the seminary, extended a delicate hand to each of us as he entered our home.

"Good evening, my children," he said.

We began to discuss important Catholic things for what seemed an eternity — but that was appropriate, since eternity is what Catholicism is all about. Finally, the good Father appeared ready to leave.

"Would you like me to bless your home?" he inquired solemnly.

"Please," Teresa affirmed.

The young seminary graduate reached into the depths of his overcoat, and located a small silver ball that dangled from an ornate chain and handle. Lifting his hand above his shoulder, he deftly projected a few drops of holy water onto my newly painted living room walls.

"Do you have any questions before I leave?" he asked.

I wondered if holy water stains paint, but Teresa had other, more pressing concerns.

"Yes, Father," she quietly petitioned. "When I die, will my cats ultimately join me in heaven?"

This question intrigued me, since I noted that my wife was not as concerned about my heavenly reunion with her as she was with that of her cats.

The Father was noticeably caught off guard. Apparently he had yet to be backed into the animals-and-souls corner. He paused a priestly pause.

Now, I've been to enough boring bar association seminars and rubber-chicken lunch lectures to know that in order to book a return engagement the guest speaker must play to the audience. This should have been a no-brainer for young Mahn. But I could see he was getting lost in hesitation.

Finally he spoke. "My child," he began, "animals don't possess souls, and therefore cannot enter the kingdom of heaven. In point of fact, the cat is not mentioned once in the entire Bible." With those words, the holy visitor took his leave of us. Teresa watched from behind the curtains in the front window as the priest walked down our porch steps. She turned to me, sullen and upset.

"It isn't fair," she sighed. "Those cats have the same right as anyone else to go to heaven!"

Teresa was seeking "Justice" albeit for her cats. They were her best friends. Her confidants. When I did something stupid, which was pretty often, she turned to them. For the church to forbid feline entry past the pearly gates just because they had fur and tails seemed unfair and discriminatory. I tried to console my wife by assuring her that all cats go to heaven, but she remained despondent.

"You're not a priest, you're a lawyer. You couldn't possibly know about such things!"

She went upstairs to comfort her cats, who had already retired in our bed for the evening, unaware they had just been denied eternal life.

"That man will never set foot in this house again," she cried out from the bedroom. Indeed, Father Mahn never again darkened our doorstep.

About a year later, after finishing our dinner, I decided to relax with the latest issue of *The Sainthood*, but was interrupted by a knock at the door.

"And by the way," Teresa advised me, "tonight is parish visitation!"

"Any reason why you can't tell me these things in advance?"

"Later, dear, you're keeping the Monsignor waiting."

"Monsignor?"

"Later, dear, he's waiting."

I opened the door. There stood Monsignor McFall — complete with Bible and other church paraphernalia.

"Welcome, Father," I announced without hesitation. He was at least 20 years my senior. I didn't even mind if he called me "my child," since he had more gray hair than did I.

"We've been expecting you," I confirmed. Now I, too, had a reason, besides choosing to practice law, to go to confession.

McFall turned out to be an OK guy. We talked about lighthearted Catholic things, like Vatican II, and then he, too, blessed the house. The paint was now a year old, so the holy water splashes didn't bother me a bit. As he was about to leave, he asked if we had any questions.

"Monsignor, when I die, will my cats join me in heaven?" Teresa asked.

The good Monsignor was about to retire after 40 years of service. Surely he had been asked this question before, and surely he had enough sense to . . .

"I'm not sure, my child. There's very little written on the subject."

I couldn't believe my ears. Great Casey had struck out with the bases loaded! Who cared if there were a scarcity of church dogma, or for that matter, catma, on the topic. Would it have killed him to give this desperate woman the answer she wanted? One that, by the way, would have driven her to faithful weekly Mass attendance? She cried herself to sleep that night, her limbo-bound cats snoring beside her.

About a year later, Teresa and I were just finishing dinner. Let's move ahead to where I open the door. What a surprise, it was a priest, with Bible, and other religious paraphernalia in hand. Father Benedict had recently returned from a two-year tour of duty at the Vatican. Father was our age, and had known Teresa for years. They had attended parochial school together, and their parents were good friends.

After discussing old times, Father blessed our house and asked if we had any questions. Teresa had just one.

"Father, when I die, will my cats join me in heaven?"

In less time than it takes to douse a wall with holy water, Benedict unhesitatingly responded: "Teresa, there is no doubt in my mind that you and your cats will reunite in Heaven."

As Teresa sighed in relief, I noted that *my* eternal fate still remained a mystery.

That night Teresa slept soundly for the first time in two years, a look of contentment on her docile face. The cats appeared to grin, too, as they purred.

Unlike the confused clergy before him, Benedict was an adept and insightful student of ecclesiastical law, the law which ordains, among other things, who to expect to find in heaven, should you be blessed enough to arrive there one day. Benedict was a practitioner of church law; I of worldly civil law. Yet despite the difference in our reference books, we both knew without hesitation there is sufficient room among the heaven-bound for a few extra cats.

CHAPTER ELEVEN: BASEBALL - A GAME OF INCHES

I dislike highway billboards. They are unsightly and intrusive. They detract from the passing scenery, and serve little or no purpose. As a result, I have trained myself to ignore them lest my attention be diverted from the road.

I have not always been successful in this endeavor. Some of the advertisements are so artfully designed, so colorfully alluring, that I can't help but take a peek.

A few months ago, somebody dismantled the old Lehigh Valley Diner sign on Route 22 at the last Bethlehem exit. The sign had been there since the '60s, and had gradually fallen into disrepair. The cherubic boy pictured above the flow of traffic had originally flashed a toothy grin as he stuffed blueberry pancakes into his fat face. Time had been unkind, however, and his cheeks had lost their rosy glow. Most of his teeth had faded away. The written message had suffered, as well, from the passing of the seasons. "*Best Food in the Valley*" now read "*Best oo ley*". Only long-time local residents understood the cryptic words.

And so they removed the decrepit structure — the kid, his faded fat cheeks and the pancakes. The victory for highway beautification was, unfortunately, short-lived. Almost overnight, a new billboard stood in its place — larger than its predecessor. It sported 40 high-intensity lights to capture the attention of all motorists, even those, so common in Pennsylvania, who were trying to take a nap.

Sure enough, everyone noticed it. Depicted high above Route 22 was a blond, angelic, tender, twenty-something, scantily-clad masseuse — the type of masseuse from which dreams are made — not the type who works you over at the YMCA. And in her caring, delicate hands, lying prone, was her male client, naked but for a miniature glittering wash cloth strategically placed upon his buttocks. Naturally, his smile was wider than that of his pancake-eating predecessor.

And the billboard's written message left little doubt as to the type of services provided: "The Body Factory: We Don't Miss A Muscle."

Apparently, the Factory's staff of young ladies, indeed, didn't miss much of anything, and the news of their remarkable services spread far and wide.

Nonetheless, the huge sign gave rise to several complaints that made their way to the local district attorney. Oddly enough, not one of those complaints came from a disgruntled customer. Rather, it was noise from the politically influential president of the local chapter of No Illegal Titillation (NIT) that moved the district attorney into action. The chief prosecutor decided to investigate the allegations of criminal wrongdoing by sending an undercover detective for a personal massage.

Rumor has it, shortly thereafter, a fistfight broke out among the five county detectives, each claiming some noteworthy malady requiring a massage. Senior county detective Alphonse Fortunelli stepped in to break up the ruckus.

"Shut the hell up you guys," he scolded. "I'll tell you what. I'm going, and if you don't like it, tough shit."

That's why Fortunelli was in charge — he knew how to make decisions.

Two days later, Fortunelli, driving a trash hauling truck he seized during another daring county sting, appeared at the Body Factory, disguised as a garbage man. He ordered and received the most expensive deluxe massage. Just like President Nixon and the Watergate tapes, 18 minutes of the session seemed to have left

84

Fortunelli's recollection. The mysterious hot pink Velcro bandage affixed to his unmentionables may never be adequately explained. Nonetheless, after recuperating from this treatment, Fortunelli, known affectionately thereafter as "the county dick," arrested the young lady who had administered the treatment. A long line of loyal customers booed as the exhausted detective escorted the prisoner to a waiting paddy wagon.

"It's an outrage," Darlene MacMillan, also known as "Hannah the Hands," asserted as she slammed both fists upon my office conference table.

"Whatever happened to free enterprise?" she barked. "I demand Justice."

Ms. MacMillan seemed to take issue with the wording of the criminal indictment charging her with prostitution. Allegedly, she massaged a lot more than Detective Fortunelli's muscles, and in Pennsylvania that arguably rose to the level of a felony.

"I want a trial," MacMillan persisted. "What'll it cost?"

I quoted her a fee. She didn't blink. Most of my clients do. The massage business must be good.

"You want cash, or some gift certificates instead?"

"Gift certificates?"

"Sure. Maybe you have a sore muscle or two that need relaxing. Hell, I made bail. I'll be operational by tonight."

As a matter of fact, my left arm was kind of sore from yesterday's tennis match . . . the bad Larry began thinking.

"I don't believe so," the good Larry blurted out. So Hannah slapped a wad of bills on the table, and I was officially retained as legal counsel for a floozy.

Word of the charges and pending criminal proceeding spread through the county. At the trial, a bevy of interested citizens filled every seat in the courtroom. The assistant district attorney assigned to the case, Maurice Fabian, was competent and capable, but had one fatal flaw. He had a habit of asking excessively vague questions.

Trial got under way on a Tuesday in Courtroom No. 2, with Judge Thaddeus Rinehold presiding. He had served on the bench for 30 years. He had nine grandchildren. He taught Sunday school. Hannah's goose was cooked.

"You may want to consider wearing something a little more conservative," I advised Hannah in a pre-trial strategy session.

"Like what?"

"Like, oh, I don't know . . . clothes that fit come to mind."

Hannah took my advice, and on the opening day of court, she had hidden most of what had given rise to her burgeoning business. She appeared resplendent in a dowdy, brown-plaid, below-the-knee dress that came straight from the fashion pages of *Librarian Monthly.*

Interested, vocal citizens of the community filled every seat of the vast courtroom. NIT, its board of directors, and members got floor seats up front.

"Hang the bitch," an unbiased spectator mumbled as we made our way down the aisle — eyes straight ahead.

"Yeah, hang her, and her stinkin' lawyer," another added. Guilt by association. That was a new one.

Not everyone, however, was so uptight. The courtroom balcony was populated predominantly by Hannah's supporters. One such pleasant looking fellow — a Pagan warlord-type generally seen about 2:00 a.m. lounging in a back-road diner eating six eggs and a rare steak — yelled out "Hey hot stuff!" and blew her a kiss through the gap in his front teeth. My client, recognizing a friendly face, caught the kiss and rubbed it on her right butt cheek.

Judge Rinehold, upon ascending the bench, took immediate control of his courtroom, cautioning all in attendance that any further interruption in the proceedings would not be tolerated. Fearful of being ejected, the admonished crowd, in giddy anticipation of the colorful testimony, patiently heard introductory instructions and opening statements of counsel.

The district attorney advised the jury of eight women and four men that a disguised detective Fortunelli, ordered the "World Series" massage, and that after having paid a fee, received services during which every square inch of his body was handled.

The district attorney left little to the jury's imagination as he described, with uncharacteristic animation, the lurid details giving rise to the downfall of my client.

Detective Fortunelli took the witness stand. Harrison Ford he was not. He had a pot belly that swayed as he walked, bifocal glasses which repeatedly sought to fall off his nose, a large bald spot lurking in the midst of his combed-over gray hair, and a face colored bright red from years of searching for a properly dry martini. At 5 feet 6 inches, all of his 180 pounds were spread unevenly on his 58-year-old body that lacked any evidence of exercise. Fortunelli projected the image of an unsuccessful used-car salesman working the night shift in a bad neighborhood. *This* was the prosecution's star witness.

"Yup!" was his answer to the stenographer's inquiry as to whether he planned to tell the truth and nothing but the truth.

"You may be seated," the district attorney announced, as he began his direct examination.

"What is your name?"

"Who, me?"

"Yes, you."

"Detective Fortunelli."

"Is 'Detective' your first name?" Judge Rinehold dryly inquired.

Fortunelli had to think for a moment. "Why, no, Your Honor. It's Alphonse."

"Then why don't we tell the jury your full given name, just in case they might be wondering," Judge Rinehold suggested.

"OK," the county investigator agreed. "I'm Alphonse Fortunelli."

The district attorney took a deep breath, and began his long awaited direct examination.

"In June of this year, were you working undercover at the Body Factory offices?"

"Yes, I was," Fortunelli confirmed in his most official voice.

"That's a lie!" Hannah whispered in my ear. "By the time I saw him, he was on top of the covers."

87

"I'll be sure to follow up on that during cross-examination," I whispered back.

"Tell the jury what happened," the district attorney continued.

Fortunelli, now happily the center of attention, didn't need much prodding from the prosecutor.

"Well, it was like this," the witness mused as he settled back comfortably into his chair. "I got a tip about the defendant and went in for closer surveillance."

"Were you alone?"

"Yes. But I was willing to face any potential danger single-handedly."

"Go on."

"No, really, it's true."

"I meant 'go on with your story,'" Fabian sighed.

"Oh! Right. Well, I go inside, and size up the menu."

"Menu?"

"Uh huh, the different specials and their costs. The 15-minute 'Batter Up' massage is $30.00. Next is 'The Home Run' — it costs $40.00. Then 'The Grand Slam' for 50 bucks, and finally 'The World Series' at $60.00."

"And you chose . . .?"

"The World Series. Could have been dangerous, but, hey, that's my job."

Tell us what happened next," Fabian instructed.

"Well, this lady appears from behind a curtain, and she's wearing sort of a bikini. She takes me by the hand and says 'OK, slugger, you're up to bat!' "

"Is that woman in this courtroom today?" Fabian inquired.

"I think so," Fortunelli hesitated. "It wasn't exactly her face I was looking at."

"Go on."

"The next thing I know, I'm lying on this massage table, surrounded by burning incense and candles. The lady began rubbing my back with warm scented oil."

"What were you wearing?"

"Not much — just a towel. And before I can say swing batter she rolls me on my back and applies oil on my genital area."

The jury was riveted by the testimony. An older juror inched to the edge of his seat and turned on his hearing aid.

"Did she then massage your genital area?"

Fortunelli, who had spent $60.00 of taxpayer revenue to take part in the World Series, could not tell a lie.

"Yes," he confirmed with a look of contentment.

The district attorney pressed on — trying to extract over what length of time the alleged immoral act had actually taken place. "How long was it?" he questioned.

Fortunelli, not the sharpest tool in the shed, assumed Fabian meant an anatomical measurement. After all, the line of questioning up to this point had centered upon genitalia, not grandfather clocks. Fortunelli raised his right hand, and placing his thumb and second finger about an inch apart, he turned to address the jury.

"Well, initially, it was about this big, but after the warm oil was applied . . ."

His Honor had had enough. Rising from his high-backed seat towering over the courtroom, in less time than it may have taken Hannah to pop open a bottle of honeysuckle essential oil, the judge grabbed his gavel, banged it twice and yelled at the top of his lungs: "I OBJECT!" The room fell silent.

"He can't do that, can he?" my client elbowed me in the ribs. "Judges can't object, can they?"

She was a learned student of prime time TV law drama. And Judge Rinehold, who now stood red-faced with gavel in hand, immediately realized the error he had committed. He may well have caused a mistrial.

The jurors felt cheated. Now they might never hear the rest of the lurid details. And Fortunelli was most unhappy. Without further clarification, the official court record would forever reflect that one inch was all he had.

"I'm paying you good money to defend me!" MacMillan barked. "Do something!"

Right on. I stood up and approached the bench. "Your objection is overruled," I quietly advised His Honor, outside the earshot of the jury.

"You can't rule on an objection," His Honor whispered at me, as he sat back down in disbelief.

"Why not?" I pondered. "You can't object! Only lawyers may!"

"In my chambers!" was all he could muster.

As I followed the judge to chambers, my client grabbed my sleeve.

"When you talk to Judge Stick-in-the-Mud, tell him I am willing to get out of Dodge by high noon — *if* he drops all the charges."

Once in chambers, the district attorney accepted Hannah's offer — the flawless wisdom of which the judge quickly recognized. That afternoon, the Body Factory closed its doors for the last time in Pennsylvania to the delight of the membership of NIT. Within a week, my client had opened a new office 10 miles away in New Jersey and had been invited to join the local Chamber of Commerce. As for Fortunelli, he had had his 15 minutes of fame, and would never star in another World Series.

CHAPTER TWELVE: THE
FUNERAL BILL

There are "rights" and there are "privileges." A right is a God-given empowerment which cannot be taken away. As an example, in Pennsylvania, every trucker has the right to drive 75 MPH on the interstate. Those of us who can't keep up should just get in line behind them, turn off our engines, place our cars in neutral, and let the after-draft suck us along until we get to the next tollbooth.

A privilege, on the other hand, is a revocable benefit, retained only as long as the privileged party meets certain conditions. In Pennsylvania, for example, a person may drop dead, but only if he or she pays a tax for the privilege of doing so. It's called an "inheritance tax." That's why so many people retire to Florida. Without that tax, it's much cheaper to kick the bucket in the Sunshine State.

The term "inheritance tax" is misleading at best, since the decedent, sadly, doesn't inherit a thing. I didn't propose this tax, and I make no money from it. Nonetheless, some of my clients blame me for its existence, since I am required to collect the money on behalf of the Commonwealth, and then dutifully transmit the proceeds.

Some of my living clients mistakenly believe they pay this tax when they inherit from a decedent's estate. Not true — only the dead pay. Here's how it works:

People work like dogs their entire lives. Some may actually, as a result, acquire modest personal wealth. After the lights go out, so to speak, loved ones, friends, and other anticipatory relatives stand in line for the collective bounty. This is where a Last Will and Testament comes in.

It is best to execute a Last Will before death occurs, since with the onset of rigor mortis, it is more difficult to take pen in hand to sign legally binding documents. It has happened though, that creative, previously forgotten beneficiaries have appeared at the courthouse with alleged authentic "Last Wills" that were ultimately found to have been signed after their loved one's untimely passing. The courts generally discourage this form of post-mortem estate planning.

Among the beneficiaries reflected in any Last Will and Testament lurk several silent, unintended recipients. The Commonwealth of Pennsylvania comes to mind. It gets 6 percent of the estate's value if bequests are made to direct family members; and 15 percent if bequests are granted otherwise. If the estate is substantial, the federal government confiscates an even larger tax. The lawyer, unsuccessful attending physician, executor, funeral director, etc., must also be paid. In other words, while surviving beneficiaries don't pay taxes, funeral bills, or other fees, they do receive less in the end, because of the debts incurred by the estate.

I so advised Edgar Kent when he came to my office requesting that I represent him in the probate and accounting of his beloved mother-in-law's estate.

Kent produced the usual large grocery bag stuffed with insurance policies, funeral bills, bank accounts, IRS returns, medical statements, a Last Will, a paid bank loan receipt, a safe deposit box key, car title with attached lifetime muffler guarantee, two boxes of costume jewelry, a social security check, and a myriad of other papers reflective of the long and recently ended life of Anna Feuerbach, his mother-in-law.

Kent was 72-years-old, a widower, his wife of 50 years having predeceased him just a year earlier. They fell in love when he, as a

19-year-old U.S. Army private serving in post-war Germany, met her in a suburb of Berlin. They soon married and returned to America after he was discharged.

Kent obviously loved his wife and cherished the family they had raised. Unfortunately, he didn't share the same warmth for his dear mother-in-law. They apparently got off on the wrong foot when he expressed notable surprise upon meeting his fiancée <u>and</u> her mother at the port of entry. The chasm of alienation grew ever more wide during the next half century.

"Old bag," Kent muttered to himself as he sorted through her mess of papers now lying in a heap on my conference room table.

"About six months ago, after my dear wife passed away, I came home and found her mom, the decrepit hag, spread eagle on my kitchen floor. She wasn't breathing. After saying a prayer of thanks, a momentary lapse of sanity caused me to kneel down and give the decaying carcass mouth-to-mouth resuscitation. I shudder to think about it . . . Anyway . . . suffice it to say just as her dentures came loose she starts huffing and puffing again. The medics arrived, and after a week in the hospital, she's back home good as new. Yep. And she couldn't have been more grateful.

"She says to me in that German accent of hers 'Dey tells me dat you saved my life.'

" 'It was nothing, Mama Feuerbach,' I said in case my wife was listening from up there.

" 'Better dat I had died on de kitchen floor, den dat devil lips de likes of yourn had touched mine,' she said and then spat on my feet.

" 'No wonder you're still here. Even hell wouldn't take you, you old gas bag,' I snapped back.

"Well as luck would have it, several months later, she dropped dead again; this time for good. I buried her ass last week."

"I'm sorry for your loss?" was all that seemed appropriate to say.

Back to business. I explained we could deduct the cost of the decedent's last medical bills, and funeral expenses from the gross value of her estate. By doing so, we'd decrease the net inheritance tax due.

"Whatever," Kent agreed. "She was too damn cheap to pre-plan her funeral. She thought she'd live forever. The bitch almost did."

The funeral bill, reflecting all services rendered, caught my eye.

"Mr. Kent," I began, "it appears the funeral director missed a zero. This bill is for just $250.00. Even at $2,500.00, that would be an unusually inexpensive funeral."

"Nope. No mistake. It cost me $250.00 to plant her alright, and that was about $245.00 too much."

"You buried your mother-in-law for $250.00?"

"Well, not exactly 'buried.' 'Disposed of' is more like it."

I had to ask. "How'd you manage that?"

"Well, see after she dropped dead the second time in the kitchen, I loaded her bones in the car and took her to an undertaker down the street."

"You drove the decedent there?"

"Well, every time I called for help before, there were ambulance bills and the like. I figured I'd just cut out the middle man," Kent explained matter-of-factly.

"Fascinating," I admitted.

"Anyway, I had driven her everywhere with her bitching and moaning for the last 30 years. What was one more trip? For once she sat in the back seat, and kept her trap shut. I didn't even check to see if her seat belt was fastened.

"So, we get to the funeral parlor, and the guy says he has to put her in refrigeration. 'Why,' I ask. 'Where she's going she ought to start getting use to the heat.' He says 'cause it's the law,' until he gets a death certificate. He can store her for $75.00 a day. 'Nothing doing,' I says. I could have left her sitting in the air conditioning at home for that. So I take her to the next grave digger down the street . . ."

"You put her back in your car?" I stammered.

"Yep! The next mortician wasn't as greedy as the first. He agrees to keep her on ice at no additional fee. But then he started the hard-sell.

"Did I want a coffin? Embalming? Nice clothes? 'No. No. No. Just cremate her,' I said.

"He adds up the bill.

" 'That will be *$250.00*,' he advised me."

" 'Why so much?' I inquired.

" 'Well, *we have to transport her to the crematorium and . . .*'

" 'I can do that. I drove her *here*, didn't I?'

"He ignored my offer.

" *'How will the ashes be interred?'*

" 'Just give 'em to me.'

" *'In what receptacle shall they be deposited? We have beautiful boxes with individual gold locks . . .'*

" 'Locks?' I said. Who the hell would steal her? I'll put her in an old cigar box . . .' "

I sat in stunned silence.

" *'Would you like an engraved name plate for the box?'* he asks me.

" 'How much?'

" '$35.00.'

"Hell, no, I thought. So, I drove over to a bowling supply store. I picked out the cheapest trophy they sold and had 'em engrave her name, date of birth and death on it. I peeled the plate off, threw the trophy in the garbage, and stuck the plate on the box and shipped her back to Germany, by third class mail. I've been waiting years to do that. Well, a week goes by and don't I get a letter, half in German, half in English from the old lady's second cousin thanking me for the remains. Apparently they buried the box in the family plot.

"They wondered why she never mentioned in all those years that she was a champion bowler. They wanted to know if she bowled into her later years.

"I didn't get it 'til I was at the bowling shop and again saw the name plate I pried off the $5.00 trophy. The words 'CHAMPION BOWLER' appeared at the bottom.

"So I wrote back to the German relatives that she had been rolling strikes and spares until her last breath."

CHAPTER THIRTEEN: THE LAW OF SUPPLY AND DEMAND

My best friend, Kirby, is something of a "motorhead" — all he really cares about are cars and car parts.

It was Saturday morning, and time for me to head over to the office to gather the mail and listen to phone messages. A full moon shone in a cloudless sky the night before. I couldn't begin to imagine the disasters awaiting my attention.

My home phone rang — it was Kirby, bearing an invitation.

"Want to go to an auction with me this morning?"

"I can't," I explained. "There was a full moon last night. I probably have four or five clients in jail as we speak — each clamoring for a bail-reduction hearing."

"They'll still be in jail when we get back. Take a two-hour vacation. It'll do you good."

Kirby had a point. Anyway, the sooner my clients were released, the sooner they'd be back on the streets. Safer for everyone if they stayed put.

"What type of auction?" I inquired.

"Car parts — they're selling really great stuff over at the Zionsville Auction House, like bumpers and rear-view mirrors."

The excitement in Kirby's voice was infectious. This might be my chance to find a distributor cap or a muffler bracket real cheap. Similar to a loose exhaust system, opportunity only knocks once.

The auction house parking lot was jammed with hundreds of cars, not one of which looked like it had arrived there under its own power. We drove in Kirby's '84 Chrysler, the one missing both a headlight, rear left door handle, and a current state inspection sticker. It was the pride of the fleet that particular day.

The auction house was filled to capacity with motorheads. I stood out like an Edsel. I was the only one there without grease under my fingernails, the only one there not fondling the gear boxes and clutch plates on display. A pretender.

"What do I hear for this Chevy Nova side window?" the auctioneer called out.

The bidding was fierce, and quickly rose from a quarter to $.50, stopping finally at the dizzying sum of $.75. The new owner flashed a toothless victory grin.

The bidding moved from radiator caps to gearshift knobs. And then it happened. They brought out a large cardboard box containing 350 fan belts designed for a 1956 Plymouth sedan.

"Wow," Kirby sighed, as his eyes grew wild with excitement. Kirby was a collector of sorts, and kept all the treasures he bought, traded, or acquired over the years in every room in his house. His three-car garage wasn't spared, and so he was forced to now park his cars outside.

"You're not going to actually bid on that, are you?"

Kirby had no time to respond. The auctioneer had already initiated the bidding.

"What do I hear for this box of 350 1956 Plymouth fan belts? There's over 40 pounds of unused fan belts here, folks! Where on earth you gonna get another deal like this?"

I wasn't thinking "where," but "why?" when Kirby suddenly opened his mouth.

"One dollar," Kirby blurted out.

There was dead silence.

"Damn!" Kirby whispered. "Too much!"

"Sold to the man with the sideways baseball cap for a buck," the auctioneer decreed.

"What the hell are you going to do with 350 '56 Plymouth fan belts?" I demanded.

"I dunno," Kirby admitted. "They gotta be worth something."

"But you don't even own a '56 Plymouth," I continued.

"Not at the moment," Kirby conceded. "But this sure gives incentive to start looking, don't it?"

True, I wasn't being very supportive. "Do you own any type of Plymouth?"

"Just a back bumper, but someday I might find the rest of the car."

A pale, long-haired teenager approached with the oversized box of belts. Kirby gave him $1.00 as the box hit the concrete floor with a thud.

What a useless container of junk.

"Hey, Mister." Some other motorhead called out before Kirby had a chance to survey his cache. "You wanna sell one of them fan belts? I have a '56 Plymouth, but didn't need the whole stinkin' box."

"They're a $1.00 a piece," Kirby confirmed.

"Come to think of it, maybe I should buy two more, just in case this one breaks," said the man.

Kirby thought for a moment, debating whether he could part with such a significant portion of his inventory. Finally he produced two more fan belts as two more dollars came his direction.

Kirby had now recovered his initial investment three-fold in the span of one minute, and still retained another 347 fan belts. No longer could I consider his recent acquisition a bad investment.

I got a dinner invitation from Kirby about a week later. His wife, bless her heart, is a gem — a fantastic cook, but better than that, she never complains when Kirby brings home more stuff. I lived nearby, so I opted to walk to their place for what promised to be a great meal.

It was springtime, and everyone in Kirby's neighborhood had begun to cultivate backyard gardens. I could see garden after garden, with row after row of young tomato plants rising to meet the sun. They were growing straight and proud, supported by dozens of wooden polls affixed to fan belts gently encircling the green, leafy stems.

In this day of big business, consolidation, mergers, and acquisitions, the Bethlehem Ice Cream Company (BICC) was a notable exception. The company enjoyed success due in large part to a loyal, local clientele, and competent management by four generations of Sprinklemans. Great Grandpa Sprinkleman started the business back in 1935, before the advent of modern refrigeration. He personally sold his product from house-to-house by use of a truck cooled with blocks of ice. His son, Grandpa Sprinkleman II, expressed his creativity during the 1950s when he introduced several new flavors of ice cream and three types of sherbet.

Sprinkleman III automated the factory in the '70s, and established quality control testing. Sprinkleman IV was responsible for the computerization of operations. Despite these improvements, however, the entire family intentionally sought to keep business small and manageable. There were just 30 employees; sales were limited to a 100-mile radius of the company's one and only factory, located since its inception, in Bethlehem, Pennsylvania.

Great Grandpa was a 94-year-old whipper-snapper. His secret to a long and healthy life? "Eat a big bowl of Sprinkleman ice cream every day!" Perhaps Great Grandpa had stumbled upon something, for amazing as it was, he worked each and every day, just as he had since 1935.

"I ain't ready for no rest home yet," he once told me as he licked a chocolate ice cream cone.

Not everyone agreed. Sprinkelman III had confided in me that no one actually knew for sure what Great Grandpa did when he roamed unattended through the plant. Some employees had expressed concern that he might fall into one of the 5,000-gallon vats, and end up as part of a distribution of pistachio frozen yogurt. When the plant security guard began to tail him, Great Grandpa told him in no uncertain terms to "bug off."

"I'm at my wits' end!" Sprinkleman III complained to me in the privacy of my law office. "Great Grandpa has been acting very strange lately. Sometimes he tries to mix the ice cream himself, even though every process is computer controlled, and has been for years."

A problem, indeed. Great Grandpa was the biggest stockholder in the corporation. Strange though he may have become, he was still very aware of his position in the company, and he wouldn't be ordered about. He had the ability to fire the other three generations of Sprinklemans at will, if he so chose, and everyone knew it.

It's never easy to determine at what point someone's mental abilities may have deteriorated, thereby warranting intervention by well-meaning third parties. As far as Great Grandpa was concerned, he was as right as rain.

And he wasn't going down without a fight. Great Grandpa had both the keys and security code to the factory's front door. One night, for reasons that still aren't clear, Great Grandpa entered the plant alone at about 2:00 a.m. After locating his favorite 5,000-gallon vat, he began to dump a complex mixture of flavors and materials into 3,500 pounds of waiting vanilla ice cream. By daybreak, 30 gallons of maraschino cherries were missing, as were 50 pounds of walnuts, and all of the company's licorice, peppermint, and almond extract. Also unaccounted for were supplies of butterscotch syrup, concentrated lemon juice, and peanut butter. Two hours after activating the automatic mixers, Great Grandpa's newest flavor sensation was reality, and ready for distribution.

Sprinkleman III called me in the morning, after he discovered 5,000 gallons of mystery ice cream oozing from vat No.3.

"What am I going to do?"

"With the ice cream, or Great Grandpa?" I asked.

"Both!"

The easier question first. "Is Great Grandpa's concoction edible?"

"As a matter of fact, it's not bad," Sprinkleman III admitted. "It's sort of a marshmallow-peppermint-lemon-licorice-peanut-butter jubilee, with 15 or 16 other things floating about. Great

Grandpa has always had a natural gift for mixing, kind of like a brewmaster."

I thought for a moment. "Is it safe to eat?"

"I think so," Sprinkleman III confirmed. "I had some two hours ago and I'm still kicking."

"Then let's donate the whole batch to the state hospital. You can take a tax write-off for the cost of the goods."

The next day, BICC shipped 3,500 pounds of mystery-flavored ice cream to the local state hospital.

The gift was an instant hit. Two patients who hadn't said a word in more than two years asked for seconds. A week later, Sprinkleman III got a call from the hospital dietician asking for another shipment. "We'll be glad to pay full price," she said.

"Unfortunately we're not expecting a new shipment for some time," Sprinkleman III lamented.

He spent that afternoon with Great Grandpa trying to recreate the mystery formula, hopeful that the old man's mental capacity wasn't as diminished as everyone had thought.

CHAPTER FOURTEEN: VEETZ

I was assigned to represent Ramon Rodriguez, an unsuccessful part-time crook, who, more often than not, as a result of serious flaws in his burglary plans, found himself incarcerated. During such periods of confinement, he became a full-time jailhouse lawyer.

Spanish was his primary language, but he could, to a limited degree, converse in English. We first met on a Tuesday afternoon after he had been booked for yet another felonious break-in, this time at the Murphy residence.

"Is you my pubic suspender?" he inquired through the bars of his jail cell.

"Yes," I confirmed. "Would you like an interpreter?"

"No," Rodriguez assured me. "I don't need no interpeter. And listen up, Four Eyes, here's what I want you to do . . ."

And with that introduction, he began to issue orders, the most important of which included calling his mother to determine if she would post his bail. He also sought confirmation that the prison warden would let him order an extra large pizza with anchovies and black olives for delivery to his cell. Next, I was to suppress the evidence the cops found in his car, including his burglary tools and the silverware he had removed from Mrs. Murphy's house. Oh, yes, he also wanted a change of venue. In a manner of speaking, he, too, sought Justice.

Rodriguez was no amateur, for he knew exactly how to manipulate the system to his advantage. Change of venue. This last instruction was rather sophisticated. And I *had* to do his bidding, for if I didn't, after the inevitable guilty verdict, he would petition to have it set aside, claiming he had been inadequately represented by incompetent counsel who had failed to pursue his venue request.

The research required to prepare the change-of-venue pre-trial petition was time-consuming and arduous. I had to locate every newspaper article and radio and television newscast that focused upon Rodriguez's many criminal exploits, and present them in chronological order to the court. I also had to provide detailed legal argument as to why my client could not possibly receive a fair trial within the county where he was arrested.

I presented my findings to the court, and after arguing the legal issues before Judge Bossert, awaited His Honor's inevitable conclusion — that my labors were in vain, and that Rodriguez would be tried in this county. Naturally, no one was more surprised than I when the formal court opinion arrived in the mail, directing that the trial be removed from our local jurisdiction, due to unfavorable pre-trial publicity. I raced over to the prison to tell Rodriguez the good news. His mother had actually declined to post bail, so he had been sitting in jail for almost a month.

The jubilant look on my face announced the reason for my visit, even before our cumbersome English-Spanish exchange began.

"Your request was approved by the court!"

"You do good, Avogado," Rodriguez offered up, as a glimmer of satisfaction projected from his dark eyes.

The sincerity of emotion in his voice touched me, and convinced me, despite the language barrier, that all of my effort on his behalf was at least appreciated. No other public defender client had ever expressed such gratitude.

"Muchas gracias! Muchas gracias!" Rodriguez added. "Now for my first choice, I want extra cheese, anchovies, and black olives!"

I was confused. What did pizza have to do with a change of venue?

Rodriguez looked confused, too.

"Change of venue? What's that? I told you I wanted a 'Change of Menu.' The food in here stinks, man, and they won't let Pizza Palace deliver!"

The Pennsylvania Dutch aren't Dutch, and they don't come from Pennsylvania. And there are other peculiar things about them. They backwards talk. They say things like, "Down the stairs throw me my hat." To add to the confusion, they sometimes utilize the letter "V" as if it were a "W," and vice versa. My Pennsylvania Dutch accountant refers to "inwestments" and "inwentory." It's enough to down the stairs throw him sometimes I wish.

Of course, it could be worse. I have a friend from Boston who pronounces every word ending with the letter "R" as if it ended with the letter "A," and vice versa. He never ignores these letters, mind you, he just transposes them. Last week he asked me just as serious as you please if I wanted to join him for "a pizzr and a beea." As we sat down, he told me he had just visited a sick relative recovering from the effects of a "comr."

Aaron Shingeldecker was 92 years of age, and still worked his 60-acre farm in Heidelberg Township. I don't know what was thicker: his Pennsylvania Dutch accent, or his skull. As his attorney, I had suggested to him for more than 20 years that he draft a Last Will and Testament.

"Vhat duh I need dat fer?" he responded. "I don't plan on dyin' jurst yet."

Each day he arose at 4:30 a.m. to milk the cows. Jacob, his elder son, lived on a neighboring farm. Jacob would often help since his father had been a widower residing alone for almost 30 years. The younger son, Chester, rarely helped, even though he, too, resided nearby.

"Chester don't deserve to git de same as Jacob vhen I die," Shingeldecker once confided to me.

I received a telephone call from the cardiac unit of the local hospital. The nurse advised me that Aaron had just been admitted to the intensive care unit, and was asking for me. I grabbed my note pad and rushed to his bedside.

Shingeldecker lay near death, yet was still as cantankerous and stubborn as hell.

"Vhat took you so long?" he gasped, as he struggled to speak, tubes branching into his nostrils. "I'm twice your age, and I gut here fust."

I took the hand that was free of IV needles gently into mine. I hoped there was something I could do to comfort my dying friend.

"Now look, maybe it's de time to vite my vill. I vant dat my two sons git de farm. Jacob gits de land, and de fermhouse, OK?" he whispered, as a nurse tried to convince him to save his strength. "Chester gits vhats left."

Shingeldecker might die any moment. He picked this occasion for me to complete a subdivision plan of the farm, and incorporate its terms into a coherent legally binding document, including a land survey, engineering plans, subdivision approvals, soil and erosion studies, wetlands delineations, and drafting of deeds. Shingeldecker saw the hesitation on my face.

"Gimme dat," he gasped, as he reached for my note pad. "You lawvers know too much, and do too little. I don't gut de time fer jabber. I'll vite my own damn Vill!"

I didn't dare stop him — this might well be his last dying act. With a shaky hand, Aaron wrote a two-sentence Will with a resolve and sense of purpose not even a failing heart could deny:

MY LAST VILL

I give to my son, Jacob, all de land ver de veetz is growin, and de fermhouse. I give Chester vhat's left.

Signed: Aaron Shingeldecker

My client handed me the pad and pen. I silently witnessed the Will, which seemed to bring peace to Aaron. He laid back in his bed, closed his eyes, and died.

After the funeral, I took the two-sentence testamentary devise to the courthouse for probate. It was accepted as the valid and binding Last Will and Testament of Aaron Shingeldecker, deceased. Unfortunately, Jacob and Chester maintained contradictory interpretations of what each beneficiary was to receive. Each brother retained separate legal counsel, and the matter proceeded to trial.

Jacob thought "veetz" signified all the fields where "wheat" was cultivated.

Chester thought "veetz" meant the land where his father had planted "beets."

The trial judge wondered if "veetz" might have referred to "weeds."

Both parties took an appeal to the Superior Court. No decision has yet been received from that appellate tribunal.

CHAPTER FIFTEEN: THE PAY TOILET

There's the old gag about the farmer who threw a $20.00 gold piece down the hole in his outhouse. When asked by a neighbor why he had done so, the farmer replied that he had, while previously utilizing the commode, inadvertently dropped a quarter into the abyss, and he didn't plan to go after it unless there was sufficient incentive.

The City of Bethlehem is serviced by its own municipal sewage system. Hundreds of miles of underground piping connect thousands of homes and businesses to a municipal sewage filtration plant in which human and other wastes are rendered environmentally safe. The plant is staffed around-the-clock by city sanitation employees who work long hours under admittedly adverse conditions. It is because of these unsung heroes that the act of flushing a toilet in our fair city can be done without a second thought.

The filtration plant is engineered to break down effluent through a complex series of filters and aeration equipment. When foreign objects not designed for disposal in a toilet make their way to the plant, difficulties can, and often do, arise.

Early last spring, at the beginning of a Tuesday morning shift, the filtration plant control panel began to signal an alarm. A flashing red light indicated that matter incapable of biological decomposition was clogging a filtration screen. Freddy Lipschutz and Hubert Eastwick were dispatched by their supervisor, Irving Gross, to ascertain why sludge had stopped oozing through the screens at filtration tank No. 6.

Freddy climbed down the ladder, a difficult task in his hip boots, hard hat, rubber gloves and dangling 15-pound tool kit. Hubert stood above, with flashlight and walkie-talkie, ready to radio back any findings to their supervisor. Freddy loosened the sludge screen, and began to inspect it, expecting to find the usual toothpaste tubes or diapers at the root of the problem. The screen, however, appeared to be clogged with cardboard, or plastic, and lots of it. Freddy scraped the mess from the screen, placed it in the portable waste can and ascended back to ground level, can in hand.

"Who the hell would throw all this damn cardboard down a toilet?" Freddy complained to Hubert, as sweat continued to drip from beneath his hard hat down his temples. Both men knew better than to wipe their faces. They would inspect the suspect material after coffee break.

It was Hubert who ultimately washed down the waste can and its contents with a hose and brush. That's when the first $20.00 bill floated to the surface. At first, Hubert thought it was play money from a child's board game. But Freddy wasn't so sure.

"That's a pretty good likeness of Andrew Jackson," he said as he examined the note.

"Who?"

"Hello? The guy on the $20.00 bill?" Freddy lectured.

"Oh, then what's he doin' in the sludge bucket?"

It was a question several others would ask before week's end.

An inspection of the reverse side of the note found a picture of "The White House." However, because of the note's recent journey from commode to filtration plant, it might have been more aptly designated "The Brown House," a color which slowly turned to green as Hubert delicately continued to clean the soggy legal tender. It was an authentic $20.00 bill, as were the hundreds of other bills they found compressed like cardboard into one large federal reserve glob.

Freddy and Hubert decided to skip lunch that day, as they gingerly and lovingly separated each bill, gently washing the notes in a waiting bucket of soap bubbles. They tenderly laid the currecy, each a $20.00 bill, upon the locker room floor to dry.

"Two hundred and fifty-two, two hundred and fifty-three, two hundred fifty-four . . ." Freddy counted, as he pointed at each bill now quietly reposing in dry dock, again green and growing crisper and more spendable by the moment.

"That's a lot of cash," Hubert surmised. "How much is 254 $20.00 bills?"

Freddy found a pencil, and, after some figuring and erasing, completed a few calculations on the back of one of the dryer notes.

"$5,080.00!" he announced, a John D. Rockefeller glow radiating from his face.

"We're rich!" Hubert exclaimed, as he surveyed the down payment for a new Trans Am right there on the locker room floor. Suddenly, he hesitated. "Maybe we ought to tell the supervisor."

Freddy, who was not inclined to hazard a three-way split of the booty, protested.

"No way. I don't want old man Gross involved. He'd take it all faster than you could flush a crapper."

Unfortunately, Irving Gross and the other 16 sanitation plant workers were not inclined to agree. That afternoon, just before the day shift ended, the alarm signaled yet another blockage. Freddy and Hubert raced to the sludge filtration screen and Hubert, this time, descended into the darkness of the tunnel's walkway. He unfastened the screen and quickly located another mass of coagulated cardboard. By now, the second shift had arrived. Angelo and Bennie agreed to take over the clean-up duties.

"No need," Hubert said. "Me and Freddy got everything under control."

"Have you idiots gone mental?" Bennie questioned. "It's 10 minutes past your shift! Do you like working in this shit, or what?"

It was impossible for Freddy and Hubert to hide the fiscal facts from the arriving second shift. By nightfall, another $7,000.00 had been recovered. The 11:00 p.m. to 7:00 a.m. third shift located approximately $4,000.00 more. Just about everyone remained at the plant around the clock, as coffee and donuts were delivered on the hour. One employee even went home, located an iron from his laundry, and returned to press the creases from the dried bills.

By sunrise, approximately $16,000.00 lay drying on Irving Gross's desk. "We're rich," he said. Three shifts of sanitation workers' heads simultaneously nodded up and down.

Benjamin Franklin once said, "Three can keep a secret, if two of them are dead." And so it was that news of the bounty quickly made its way to city hall, where His Honor, the Mayor, had been trying unsuccessfully to balance the municipal budget.

Before Irving could divvy up the spoils of the day's labors, the Mayor had already phoned me. I was one of the assistant city solicitors, and it was my lucky day to be on call. The Mayor explained to me that a large amount of money had been fished out of the sewage treatment plant, and that the sanitation workers were planning to divide it among themselves.

"Doesn't that money belong to the city?" His Honor inquired. "It's the city's treatment plant. They get a weekly wage. That should be enough."

I had never taken a course in "Hopper Law," so I didn't know, at first flush, how to respond. After all, most of the laws pertaining to toilets are unwritten, as confirmed by my friend who worked as in-house counsel to an outhouse company.

Come to think of it, the mayor was also paying part of my weekly wage. "It is yours, Mayor," I proclaimed without hesittion.

"I thought so," His Honor confirmed. "Now you go over to the treatment plant, and bring that cash back to city hall."

Have you ever attempted to extricate $16,000.00 in ironed $20.00 bills from three shifts of sleep-starved sanitation workers? Suffice it to say, I will never again feel entirely safe sitting on a toilet seat, lest one of the workers makes good on his threat to "get me when I least expect it." At any rate, I returned with the cash — in a plastic bag — to city hall.

The Mayor's new found budgetary surplus was short-lived. Within a week, several third party claims had been received at city hall. The Mayor put copies of the written demands on my desk. The sanitation workers had hired an attorney to reclaim their money, plus interest at the current commercial bank rate. The city police laid claim to the money, theorizing it must have been the illegal gains of criminal activity. They wanted it — apparently as evidence. The IRS placed notice of a federal lien on the money, claiming somebody out there owed taxes on it. And the Attorney General of the Commonwealth of Pennsylvania asserted that if the original owner of the money did not step forward, the funds should then escheat to the state after seven years, the statutory waiting period for reclamation of lost goods.

The Attorney General had an interesting point. Who was the real owner of the money — you know, the guy who accidentally flushed $16,000.00 down the toilet? I could just imagine his telephone call to my city hall office.

"Hello, is this the assistant city solicitor, Larry Fox?"

"Why, yes it is. May I help you?"

"Yes. You might find this humorous, but indulge me for a moment, won't you? Last week I was taking a crap and didn't realize that when I pulled my pants back up, $16,000.00 must have dropped out of my back pocket into the toilet. I hate when that happens - don't you? Anyway, I was wondering if I might come by and pick it up?"

That call never came, so I did what any other confused city solicitor would do: I petitioned the County President Judge to place the money in an interest-bearing account, after which I advised all parties of record to pursue their respective claims before the court.

There's a moral to the story — don't keep loose cash in your back pocket; it could create a sludgefest.

CHAPTER SIXTEEN: TAKE MY WIFE, PLEASE

One client of mine who recently completed a three-year war in the pursuit of a divorce decree explained to me that his perception of love had undergone refinement. "Love," he announced, "is finding any single woman at least 75 years of age, who has a chronic, hopefully fatal heart condition, and who possesses a 30-year assignable, vested pension."

In the practice of law, there is one common principle: that peaceful adversarial confrontation is to occur through the use of procedural rules known and agreed to by the parties. There is, however, one exception — matrimonial law. There are no rules in matrimonial law, especially if another woman represents the wife. There is, as the old saying goes, a difference between a female domestic relations attorney and a pit bull: you can reason with a pit bull and sooner or later it will release its grip. Given the option of engaging in a knife fight or facing protracted battle with an indignant wife, the choice is clear: with a knife fight one faces a mercifully quick death. With a domestic relations case, death, while certain, will be painful and slow.

Albert Slobofski retained me to obtain a divorce. It was the same story I had heard a hundred times before. He and his wife had drifted apart, and now he had found someone new. This did not particularly please Mrs. Slobofski — who felt she had given the best years of her life to this 30-year marriage, and until death she didn't plan to part, unless it was with all his money, and then only after she had tortured him mercilessly.

Actually 30 years is an incredibly long time to be married. When the concepts of monogamy and marriage were first invented thousands of years ago people married at the age of 15, lived to the ripe old age of 24, then lost all their teeth, and died. It was almost unheard of for spouses to live together more than 10 or 11 years. There was no need back then for divorce, or for divorce lawyers, because just about the time couples started getting sick of one another, one or the other, or both, would drop dead.

Today, divorce is more common, and in modern-day marital schisms, everything is usually split in half, 50-50. She gets the house; he gets the mortgage. She gets the kids; he pays child support. She gets the car; he gets the loan book. She gets the furniture; he gets an army cot.

There are some exceptions to this rule of distribution. As an example, there's the China and Crystal Doctrine. China is amassed from well-intentioned wealthy aunts and bridal shower invitees who reluctantly ban together to buy the blushing couple the obligatory fine china and crystal in the lovebirds' must-have pattern. After the wedding, these pricey treasures are carefully placed in a china cabinet no one will ever open. At divorce time, the wife fights tooth and nail for these irreplaceable necessities, so that when she dies, her children and their spouses can place the valuables where they won't be touched, before again arguing over who gets them.

I reviewed with Albert the above outline of equitable distribution of marital property, and it seemed fair enough to him, provided he didn't have to look at Gladys anymore. Unfortunately, Gladys and her attorney, Ethel "I-was-divorced-once-myself-and-we'll-take-that-son-of-a-bitch-for-everything-he's worth" Brownzweig didn't feel the proposal was quite acceptable.

There was, for instance, the matter of his pension at the steel plant where he worked as a welder, and his company stock option plan. They also wanted his insurance policy to irrevocably reflect

Gladys and the next three generations of her offspring as sole beneficiaries. Albert balked. His new girlfriend might need the money someday. And so we, Albert, Gladys, Ethel, and I were locked in stalemated matrimonial discord.

Gladys wouldn't let any grass grow under her feet, however. She had Albert thrown out of their house by court order, claiming his continued presence jeopardized her future well-being. She had his bank account frozen and then petitioned for spousal support. She convinced a doctor to draft a medical evaluation confirming that because of the stress related to their divorce proceeding, she was unable to work. She threw his "stuff" (at some point in time in every divorce the litigants discuss the present location and sanctity of their "stuff") in the garbage, like his hunting boots, fishing poles, and his comfortable old underwear. And she invited her mother to live with her rent-free. These unilateral actions by Gladys, pre-approved by attorney Brownzweig, were intended to, and did in fact, send my client into a tail-spin.

"She had the locks on my house changed. I can't even get in to see my dog," he moaned. "Can't you do something?"

At some point in every divorce, that question is asked. There is, of course, no answer, because there are no recognized rules of engagement in matrimonial litigation. However, one rule of physics is applicable: for every action, there is an equal and opposite reaction. In Albert and Gladys' case, for instance, as his blood pressure increased, hers decreased. As his days grew dark, hers became bright with sunshine. She was enjoying his slow and painful demise.

And then, it happened. One day, almost two years to the day after Albert had been unceremoniously tossed out of his house, his previously forlorn appearance displayed an unmistakable rejuvenation. For the first time in recent memory, there was color back in his cheeks, a spring in his step, and a glowing smile. He was truly the picture of vitality and mental health. This seemingly overnight metamorphosis caught my attention. What new vitamin had he discovered?

"Nope, there's no mysterious elixir," he confided. "I simply decided finally to take your advice. Just now, while Gladys and the mother-in-law-from-hell were out shopping in my car, I went over to my house and divided everything equally, just as you had been suggesting for the last two years."

"And Mrs. Slobofski agreed to this distribution?" I naively inquired.

"I don't know. She's not back from the mall yet. She still has all my credit cards, so she often makes a day of it."

Before he and I could begin our meeting in my office that fateful morning, the phone rang. The police. They were at the Slobofski residence with Mrs. Slobofski, attorney Brownzweig, and Mrs. Slobofski's mother. They were calling to see if Mr. Slobofski might be available to drop by the house — or more precisely, what was left of it. We drove over together.

Mr. Slobofski had, as we say in the law business, embarked upon a program of "self-help." You may recall he was a welder by trade. So with the assistance of some rather sophisticated welding equipment, he successfully cut in half just about everything they jointly owned.

I took a short tour of the battle zone, as did Brownzweig and the cops. Albert certainly had been thorough. The kitchen combination freezer-refrigerator, which consisted of a freezer above, and a refrigerator below, had been cut longitudinally. The grandfather clock, washer, dryer, living room sofa, and dining room table had met similar fates. And it didn't appear as if anyone could ever again refer to their piano as an *upright*. Nothing, it seemed, had escaped the welder's torch, including the house itself. Each room, from the floor to the ceiling, had been cut in half. I could see skylight as I walked about, as if I were standing in a planetarium.

Spared was the family car. "I would have divided that in two as well," he bragged to the investigating officer, "but she was still in it. Maybe she'll let me finish the job tomorrow. She can have the trunk — she always did carry more luggage." Albert started to laugh; something I now urged him to refrain from doing.

Brownzweig was not amused. "Your client's dead meat — dead meat — do you understand?" she stammered red-faced, as she waved a finger about two inches from my nose. "I'm having him arrested. How do you like that?"

"On what charge?" Albert interjected. "Littering? I'll clean the mess as soon as you and Gladys get off my property. Mother-in-law can stay if she wishes. Then when I'm finished, I'll toss her out with the rest of the garbage!"

Brownzweig, who was never at a loss for words, stood strangely silent for a peaceful moment. Apparently Albert had raised a rather interesting point.

"I'm kind of wondering why you called us here, too, ma'am," one of the policemen said, addressing the befuddled attorney. The cop began pointing fingers of his own. "If this husband damaged this wife's property, then she can sue him," the officer concluded as he turned to walk back to his patrol car. "This here's a domestic dispute. You all have a nice day."

The police drove away, leaving the four of us, plus mother-in-law, standing in the midst of the rubble. I could sense Brownzweig was about to wax brilliant again. I debated whether Albert and I should simply ignore her and leave too, but Albert appeared willing to peaceably review the next procedures. At last it appeared that rules of engagement were about to be outlined in this long-standing battle to the death. Brownzweig began the discussion.

"I'll sue you, you son of a bitch, for everything you have!" She was again waving fingers at my client, but he just stood tall and smiled.

"I don't have anything anymore," he calmly reminded her as he slowly surveyed the damaged possessions strewn about us. "It's all been divided up." This calm in the eye of the storm only served to enflame Brownzweig more.

"I'll attach your pension, insurance, and company stock plan!"

"Not likely," Albert corrected her. "Last week I was laid off permanently. That's when I decided it was time to finalize things and move on with my life. My pension never vested, there's no

119

more insurance, and the stock plan is worth about $800.00 — just enough to buy some more welding rods. Listen, Brownzweig, there's nothing you can take, 'cause you took it all. If you and your client hadn't been such pigs, we could have settled this divorce two years ago without paying a fortune in legal fees that you artificially generated. Gladys would have gotten enough to start a new life, and none of this would have happened. Now get out of my house, and don't let that half-of-a-door hit you in the ass on your way out!"

Brownzweig's jaw was moving, but no sounds were emerging. Soon she, Gladys, and mother-in-law left, probably to find substitute housing. I located Albert in what use to be the kitchen. He had a look of contentment on his face.

"I don't agree with what you did," I admonished him. "It was pretty stupid, and someone might have gotten hurt."

"You just don't get it, do you counselor?"

"Get what?"

"You can't put a value on good health. I haven't felt this calm in two years. Today I heard the birds chirping for the first time in years. And I still have enough money to pay your last bill."

He sent me a check the next day with a small note that read: "Thanks for the good advice."

Sometimes it's the wife who decides to leave. Recently, Francis Fuller, a dairy farmer, stopped by my office to review his legal rights. It seemed his wife, Matilda, was threatening to leave both him and the farm for greener pastures — California to be exact. After 32 years of milking cows, she had had enough.

She petitioned the court for spousal support, so she could amass enough money for a one-way train ticket to Hollywood. Francis didn't want to pay her a dime. "She's got a bed and roof back at the farm," he solemnly pronounced.

So off we went to "Happy Court," the local bar's slang term for spousal support court, to determine if Matilda was legally entitled

120

to any of the buttermilk money Francis had been methodically stashing away for three decades.

Happy Court and an orthodox Jewish synagogue service possess striking similarities. By unspoken choice, all of the men sit on one side of the room, and all of the women sit on the other. Sometimes they stare at each other in prayerful silence. Those officiating over the assembled multitude, whether Judge or Rabbi, wear black robes, and often refer to one or more of the Ten Commandments. After a while, a participant leaves so destitute the only thing he can thereafter afford to eat is unleavened bread.

Into this macabre setting I strode with client in tow, wondering if a more apt picture of purgatory could ever have been painted. The judge, numbed by years of witnessing domestic blisters, rather than bliss, yawned while calling out the next case, "Jones versus Jones, No. 87."

Two nondescript losers stood up from opposite sides of the courtroom, tripped over the myriad bodies strewn about the creaky pews, all former lovers now waiting for a turn to destroy each other, and slowly proceeded to the bench. There they were met by their attorneys who turned to face the judge who presided over these marriage ceremonies in reverse.

For some unusual reason, rather than working on another file as I waited my turn, I actually listened to this case — case No. 87. The poor lady testified that she had met the defendant about a year ago. They took a moonlight excursion alone on a small lake in a rowboat, romantic inclinations occurred, and nine months later she gave birth. She now sought child support from this rowboat Romeo.

"The case should be dismissed," the defendant's attorney interjected, a statement which seemed to startle the somber judge.

"Why?" His Honor questioned.

"Well obviously, Judge, if this happened in a rowboat, it's a simple case of canoe-bial bliss."

This bad pun at the expense of the court didn't seem to impress His Honor, who dumped an extra $5.00 a week on the child support order, just so everyone would remember who was actually in charge.

"Case No. 88 — Fuller versus Fuller," His Honor called out. I looked around for a second, then realized I was the one up to bat. I stepped over two babies crawling in the aisle, passed by a woman who was crying softly, and approached the Bench with my client. Mrs. Fuller also made her way forward, accompanied by her attorney, Orville Center. Judge Rendell, as usual, took charge of the proceedings.

"Now, what's the problem here?" he politely asked my client. Francis Fuller addressed the Court above the din of whining children and bickering spouses.

"This here's my wife, Your Honor," Francis acknowledged as he pointed toward his bride, Matilda.

"Nice to make your acquaintance," Judge Rendell announced with a nod of his head.

"She says she's gonna leave me, Judge. If she does, who will milk the cows? She says she wants my money, so she can run off to Hollywood, to be with the stars."

The judge, his face now reflecting some life, turned to Mrs. Fuller. "Is this true, Mrs. Fuller?"

"Yes, it is," Matilda candidly responded. After all, she had just sworn to tell the truth and nothing but the truth.

"Why California, ma'am?" the judge questioned.

"Because 32 years with him and the cows is enough — that's why," Mrs. Fuller pronounced as she pointed at her dejected husband.

"Do you have a job?" the Court inquired.

"Wouldn't you call milking cows and taking care of a stinkin' house for 32 years 'a job'?"

Mr. Fuller interrupted. "If you give her any money, she'll head west, you just wait and see." A tear began to form in Francis' eye, a tear the judge astutely noticed.

And then it happened. The judge asked one too many questions.

"Ma'am, if you don't get any money, are you still going to California?"

"Yes."

"But how will you get there?"

"If need be, I'll fuck my way there, Your Honor!"

Judge Rendell had presided over Happy Court for more than 30 years. At this point in his career, little if anything surprised him. Without blinking an eye, he made one further inquiry. "Lady, have you any idea how far it is to California?"

Judge Rendell took that case under advisement; a formal Order of Court would follow within two weeks. Before I could move away from the Bench, the tipstaff tipped his staff as the court crier cried out the next case, "Number 89 — Perrywinkel versus Perrywinkel." I quickly located my briefcase, and stepped aside, so that the new litigants might proceed. I sensed, however, without even looking up, that a strange aura was overtaking the courtroom. Similar to a scene in a John Wayne western movie where the saloon piano player knows instinctively when to hide for cover, the courtroom, just seconds before abuzz with the mayhem of bickering spouses, now grew as quiet as a social security office on a Saturday. All present, including the babies, were caught in suspended animation, staring drop-mouthed in the same direction.

It was then that I saw them. From the bowels of the rear of the courtroom emerged two people slowly progressing toward the bench as if in a death march. Introducing the Perrywinkels. Frank and Georgia.

Mr. Perrywinkel stood at least 7-foot, 2-inches or taller, with black eyes sunken so deep into his skull that if he were hit in the face with a baseball bat, his eyes would have escaped injury. He had a jagged scar that started at his right ear, half of which was missing, then proceeded across his cheek and face over his lips, and disappeared down his neck. His lopsided black handlebar mustache accentuated his long drawn face. His black motorcycle jacket boasted a large emblem proudly displayed on the back that read "Dust Devils." The earrings dangling from his healthy intact ear were partially covered by long, stringy, black hair. He appeared to be a blushing 30 years of age, although the tattoo of a naked woman discreetly positioned on his right wrist seemed to have weathered far more than three decades of storms.

Mrs. Perrywinkel also advanced toward the waiting judge. She was a cover girl — for *Body Piercing Monthly*. Miniature silver barbells, the type a small chipmunk might use for weight training, protruded from her cheeks, chin, and tongue. Each eyebrow was skewered with golden sewing needles. At least a dozen metal studs ran up and down the length of each ear. There was a metal ball protruding from the tip of her nose. It was safe to assume that other piercings existed elsewhere upon her body, the locations of which were limited only by the imagination. It was a miracle that she passed through the courthouse security system. The baubles nearly drew my attention from her short, spikey, bleached hair and the two-tone rattlesnake tattooed around her neck.

Judge Rendell struggled to keep his composure, as little children, fearful that either Mr. Perrywinkel or Mrs. Perrywinkel might eat them, scurried to safety behind their nervous mothers. The litigants, neither of whom appeared with legal counsel, now stood before the judge. He carefully studied the parties before him, and then decided to work some judicial magic. He uttered a single sentence meant to right wrongs, mend fences, and re-ignite flames.

"How can two lovely people, such as yourselves, obviously meant for each other from the dawn of time, be quarreling?" The Judge sat silently, waiting, gazing knowingly into the two faces before him.

Mr. Perrywinkel began to bawl. He reached for the red bandanna tied to his upper arm, and blew his nose. People ducked. Mrs. Perrywinkel's eyes began to well, a tear falling from the ring in her lower lid.

Mr. Perrywinkel slowly extended his hand to the emotional Mrs. Perrywinkel, who willingly accepted it. "I love you, Doll Face," he softly whispered.

"I love you, too, Cookie Puss." They turned back to the waiting judge.

"Can we go, Your Honorship?" Mr. Perrywinkel inquired.

"That sounds like a good idea," Rendell agreed as he smiled goodbye.

The renewed lovers, still holding hands, strolled blissfully down the courtroom aisle, out the door and down the street to their favorite piercing parlor.

Not all marital disputes become confrontational or require formal court review. Sometimes the parties resolve their differences amicably.

"John and I have an agreement," Aphelia Albert advised me during an initial conference call. "I just need you to put it in writing." Mrs. Albert then made an appointment to memorialize the understanding in written form. Apparently, my client and her husband had amicably worked out all the details regarding the visitation and custody of their two small children.

Mrs. Albert was on time. However, there was one surprise — she brought Mr. Albert with her. I joined them in my conference room.

"Mr. Albert . . ." I began.

"Just call me 'John' . . ."

"Nice to make your acquaintance, John. I wasn't expecting you, today — just your wife. I hope you understand I can only represent one party in a custody matter. It's a conflict of interest for me to act as legal counsel for both individuals."

"I know — I know. It's OK. I don't need a lawyer. We've worked everything out concerning the kids."

"Fair enough, but before you sign any formal written agreement, I urge you to have independent counsel review it."

With that caveat, we began the discussion. She wanted the kids during the week. He agreed to take them on the weekends, starting Fridays at 6:00 p.m. He would pick them up at her new apartment, and return them each Sunday at 8:00 p.m. That made sense, since the little ones had to get up early the next day for school.

"And he has to use car safety seats when he transports them," Aphelia chimed in.

"Of course," amicable John affirmed.

"He gets them during the summer," Aphelia continued, "but if they need medical treatment while they're away, I have to approve first."

John shook his head. "Agreed."

"During the holidays, I get them on Mother's Day; he gets them on Father's Day; we can alternate the others, except Christmas Day. We'll share them half a day each, because we both like to watch them play under the Christmas tree. And since they are twins, we each get one on their birthday," Aphelia dictated.

It was, indeed, refreshing to see two parents working together for the common good of their children. They were, despite the situation, to be commended for that.

"They must be bathed at least once a week, and they go to obedience classes every Tuesday evening, even in the summer," Aphelia pointed out as she carefully scanned the rushed notes I was scribbling on a legal pad.

"They were the pick of the litter," John advised me.

I was thunderstruck. "Are we talking about kids or pets?" I finally asked.

"Our Siamese cats!" Mrs. Albert replied. "I thought you knew."

"Well, I guess we do refer to them as our 'kids,' since they are the only dependents we have," John explained.

Mrs. Albert was paying me more than $100.00 an hour to draft a feline visitation agreement. She could have acquired two new cats at the animal shelter for free. I wondered what other details there were. After all, we had now reviewed schooling, medical care, shared holidays, and transportation. What about religious upbringing?

"Ours is a mixed marriage," Aphelia confessed with a weak smile. "He wants them raised pres-cat-erian. I want them to remain Catlick. I suppose we'll let them decide when they're old enough," Aphelia suggested.

Would that occur before or after catechism classes, I wondered.

SEVENTEEN: TRUE LOVE

When I was growing up, there were guys who seemed, even as teenagers, to have effortlessly mastered the art of meeting and dating the opposite sex. Unlike me, they seldom experienced awkward or embarrassing moments, much less the pain of rejection. How much simpler it would have been if the young ladies who were the proposed objects of my intended affections had been equipped with the simple indicators now included as standard options on my office computer and laser printer.

Social relationships would have been far less complicated had each blushing lass been equipped with an indicator panel that read "warming up," "ready," or "num lock." I would have known instantly whether I stood a chance, was about to get lucky, or whether, in the alternative, the object of my desire had temporarily experienced mental shut down, and as a result, anything I might say or do would be misconstrued. Needless to say, the latter happened to me without warning and with frightening regularity.

Elwood Beamstorfer had been assigned to me as my next public defender client. He, too, had over the years apparently experienced some difficulties pursuing the fairer gender, but unlike most other males with similar disheartening experiences, he had, according to the allegations of the indictment filed against him, found a less complex solution to his social ineptitude. He was accused of dating a cow — a crime in Pennsylvania.

"I really love her, and I know in my heart she loves me, too," he quietly confessed as he stared at me from behind prison bars.

The fact that he might love her or vice versa was, in the eyes of the law, irrelevant, and I told him so. It was unlawful for him to date a cow. For one thing, she wasn't old enough to knowingly consent, and I doubted that her parents would have ever approved.

Law school had not prepared me adequately for this assigment. I didn't recall studying a single case on the subject, nor could I now locate any precedent as a guide. The approaching criminal trial might possibly enter into uncharted legal waters.

My interviews of the defendant gradually produced a history of how this bovine romance blossomed.

"It wasn't my idea," Elwood protested, the din of jailhouse background noise filling his narrow cell. "She's the one who started it."

Naturally I believed him. He had been a dairy farmer his entire life, and he had plenty of his own cows from which to choose, had he been inclined to pursue such an affair. Daisybell, on the other hand, lived two barnyards away, a member of a neighbor's herd. There was no reason for Elwood to have independently sought her out.

"She use to blink them eyelashes at me when I'd drive by," Elwood confided. "After that . . . well . . . you know . . . (no, I did not) . . . one thing led to another."

Elwood probably would never have been caught, had it not been for that indiscreet moonlit liaison in the Bahamas. The rumor floating about the courthouse was that he had taken the alleged victim, Daisybell, with him under a double occupancy travel plan. He tried to pass her off as his wife, but by the third day, her true identity as a Guernsey cow was suspected despite some rather clever disguises and use of deodorant.

"She always wanted to see Nassau," Elwood confessed.

Whether Daisybell was the type of cow who kissed and told, or whether the love-in-the-pasture rumors caught the ear of the district attorney by some other means, the fact is the whole barnyard began to gossip, somebody squealed, and eventually Elwood was arrested.

"What's your defense?" Harry Packweed, a fellow public defender, inquired of me as I reviewed the file in the law library, searching in vain for any case law on the subject.

"I plan to call other cows from the nearby bovine community, to testify, under oath, that the alleged victim, Daisybell, did not enjoy a reputation for proper moral character, and that my client was not the first farmer she had enticed over the barnyard fence."

Packweed appeared impressed. "Wow, I never came across that particular legal theory before," he admitted. Actually, neither had I.

About a week before the trial was scheduled to start, I began to experience the same recurring nightmare — or maybe it was a nightcow.

The dream, like countless others I've had just before trial, was in vivid color. Daisybell had taken the witness stand, sporting one of those frilly head bonnets all the farm girls wear. Her black and white spots stood as a dramatic backdrop for her expansive, yet delicate pink nose. She appeared to be engaged now. Her betrothed was obviously well off — the ring in her nose was quite large. She sat stoically, her witness chair positioned below the sign that read "Positively No Cow Pies In The Courtroom."

The stenographer, schooled in steno-cowophy transcription, swore her in.

"Raise your right hoof — no, your right hoof."

Daisybell appeared to be nervous as she switched legs. This obvious ploy would, however, make the jury even more sympathetic toward her side of the story. The jury already appeared to be prosecution oriented. I had only been able to get six men and women on the panel. The rest were Daisy's peers — three Holsteins and three Guernseys.

The courtroom grew silent as Daisybell prepared to udder her tail. The district attorney began his direct examination:

"How old are you?"

"Moo . . . uh . . . mooo."

"See, she's lying already," Elwood whispered as Daisybell quickly decided to add a few more years to her answer, her eyes darting back and forth behind what were obviously false eyelashes. I made a mental note to cross-examine her about that later.

The district attorney continued. "I draw your attention to the encudder in question."

"Moo."

"Now, Daisybell . . ."

"Moo," the witness protested.

"I beg your pardon," the admonished district attorney apologized. "I didn't mean to be so informal. Now, Miss Cow, do you recognize the defendant? Is he in the courtroom?"

Daisybell, alias "Miss Cow," slowly raised her hoof, the one clutching a handkerchief in the event of an emotional moment, and directed it toward the defense table where Elwood and I sat.

"My God!" I thought. "Is she pointing at me or my client?" Apparently the district attorney was confused, too. After all, the witness had no fingers, (now I realized why the ring had been placed in her nose) and most of her hoof was covered by the handkerchief. He attempted to clarify the issue.

"Who, exactly, are you pointing at?"

"Moo."

"But they both have sinister expressions!" the district attorney suggested, as he turned to view my face and that of my client.

"I object!" I exclaimed as I struggled to my feet.

"Me, too!" Elwood added, it apparently being my client's position that my expression was more sinister than was his.

The judge didn't seem to be in a hurry to rule on the multiple objections, since he, too, appeared to be having trouble making up his mind as to who truly appeared to be more sinister. The district attorney decided to rephrase the question.

"Is it the guy on the left or the guy on the right?"

"Moo."

Well, at least I was off the hook, although some jurors, especially the cows, continued to peer at me in suspicion.

"Who began this relationship?" the district attorney continued.

"Moo."

"That's not true, either" Elwood whispered to me. "It's obvious she's been coached."

My client had a point. Daisybell was too polished in her delivery, with that enticing bovine body language, and the discrete placement of her tail across her udder as she sat in the witness box. And there was her undeniable appeal, if you were another cow, or perhaps my client.

"Now on the day in question, did the defendant do anything against your wishes?" the district attorney inquired.

Daisybell's eyes began to fill with tears as she slowly shook her head up and down, the cowbell around her neck giving the only audible response. She blew her nose in the handkerchief, not an easy exercise given the size of her ring.

"You must answer 'yes' or 'no' so the stenocowapher can take down what you say. What did he do?"

Daisybell sighed, hesitated and took a bovine breath. The courtroom grew so silent you could hear one of the jurors chewing her cud. The spectators strained to capture this next crucial response. Daisybell finally spoke:

"Moo."

Some of the cows on the jury gasped, due to the explicit nature of the response.

"Moo?" the district attorney echoed, as if hearing such testimony once wasn't enough.

"Moo," the witness confirmed.

Such graphic evidence would certainly be hard to refute.

"I have nothing further," the district attorney triumphantly announced. "The Commonwealth rests its case."

"You may proceed, Mr. Fox," the judge solemnly proclaimed. I slowly rose to address the court, wondering if it might be a mistake questioning Daisybell at all.

Law school was so esoteric, so impractical. Few classes dealt with subjects the student would surely face in the everyday practice of law. Here was just another example: proper cow cross-examination. Most of my professors had hardly touched upon the subject. Yet now I was faced with that very challenge. A sympathetic approach might imply that I believed Daisybell, rather than Elwood. An aggressive inquiry, however, might alienate the jury. What about the socratic approach? What to do?

I tossed and turned, struggling to find an answer. Mercifully, it was at this point that I awoke, the answer to this riddle remaining a mystery.

There is, of course, some limited legal precedent regarding in-court testimony and cross-examination of animals subpoenaed to tell their side of the story. *Parade Magazine* described in its January 2, 1994, issue the legal dilemma swirling about a parrot that had apparently witnessed its owner's murder.

The decedent, a young lady, was found smothered to death in her California apartment. Her death had occurred several days prior to the discovery of her body. Her faithful parrot, Max, emaciated due to lack of food and water, was taken from the murder scene to a local veterinarian, so that with proper attention the bird might regain its health.

All evidence of wrongdoing pointed toward a suspicious character named George, whom the police promptly arrested on homicide charges. George denied any guilt and retained learned legal counsel for his defense, attorney Harold Farbus.

As hoped, Max ultimately recovered his equilibrium, and was again able to perch unassisted on the upper bar of his cage. As he surveyed his new surroundings, he announced "Oh my God — don't do it, Robert!"

Naturally, upon learning of this statement, attorney Farbus conjectured that such a phrase might well have constituted the victim's last anguished words, obviously overheard by Max. Somebody named "Robert," rather than his client, clearly was the killer. So Farbus subpoenaed Max to testify on behalf of the accused.

The trial judge, Orpheus Rosenblum, had the unenviable task of determining whether this "birdsay" evidence should be admitted. Would the court likewise permit cross-examination of this bird-brained witness?

"How do we know the bird isn't repeating something it heard at the Veterinarian during its recovery period?" the judge inquired of the prosecutor and defense counsel during pre-trial legal argument on the issue.

"How do we know the bird isn't a chronic liar, who concocted the phrase by himself? What if someone purposely put those words in his beak?"

Attorney Farbus was no fool. He realized that Max's testimony would be crucial to the outcome of the trial, and that the bird's safety as a witness in a capital case was of concern. As a precautionary measure, the attorney requested that the parrot be placed in the state's witness protection program disguised as a macaw.

The court agreed, issuing Max a new social sebirdity number, and a new cage at a secret address. Max would have none of this, however, and flew the coop. Trial has been delayed indefinitely.

Of course, the most famous precedent concerning testimony elicited from the animal kingdom arises from the O.J. Simpson trial. Canine "barksay" was introduced without so much as an appearance by the canine in question.

During the trial, a neighbor living near Nicole Simpson's house testified he was walking his dog just about the time the two victims were murdered. The witness swore that he had heard another doggie, not his own pooch, render a "plaintive wail". It was a moaning sound so mellon-collie it unquestionably signified to those, animal and/or human alike, who heard it, that the wailing dog, having sensed the murder of two innocent people, could no longer contain its grief.

Simpson's defense team had, without objection, allowed the state to introduce doggie barksay into evidence, despite the fact the dog that allegedly made the statement wasn't in court to be cross-examined. No foundation had been laid to establish that the pooch had actually witnessed the murders, or had been saddened by them. Nor was there any proof the doggie-walker-witness knew how to interpret doggie barksay.

Apparently, I'm the only one who questioned these technicalities. Simpson's legal counsel won a case I would have lost; the assistant district attorney has probably retired on book royalties, and I'm still defending speeding ticket cases.

But I digress. You're probably wondering what happened to the farmer and the cow. As with most criminal charges, the case never came to trial. Elwood pled to a lesser charge of "following too closely," and received a probationary sentence. Rumor has it he and Daisybell reconciled, and soon thereafter left the country together.

"I always wanted to see Bombay," she was heard to say.

CHAPTER EIGHTEEN: A QUESTION OF PRIVACY

Last week a salesman showed up at my office with a portable computer. He began to explain why my law library and its hundreds of books were now obsolete. He plugged his little gadet into the wall socket, pushed a button, typed my name, and instantly printed out a list of every appellate case I ever argued before the Superior and Supreme Courts of Pennsylvania. He flashed a triumphant smile, certain that he had impressed me.

"Why do I need that information?" I asked him in disgust. "And why, for that matter, would I want anyone else to have access to such information about me? It's an invasion of my privacy!"

The deflated salesman didn't have any answers, and didn't make a sale. I walked into the law library, and joyously paged through one of my favorite books, a dictionary I've owned for 30 years. I don't fear computers and I don't dislike them. But they have their place. A good book may be passed from one generation to the next as a family heirloom. In three years, I'll have to pay the garbage man to haul away my soon-to-be obsolete computer.

My dictating machine needed new batteries, so I stopped at the local "Radio Hut" on the way home. Radio Hut is one of those retail outlets that sells just about anything through which an electron might travel. I made my way past the various racks of light bulbs, home burglar alarm systems, and remote control race cars. Locating the battery display, I chose four double-A cells and proceeded to the cash register.

"Cash register" is such an antiquated term. The more appropriate description is "computer inventory control system." Irving stood poised to "ring up" (another antiquated term) my purchase. He was already showing the classic signs — glazed look, slow speech — indicating he spent too much time on the Internet. Had he ever heard a Mozart quartet? To top it off, poor Irving was trying, without much success, to grow a mustache.

"May I help you?" he murmured.

"I'd like to buy these four batteries," I declared.

"Will that be MasterCard, Visa, or Radio Hut Credit?"

"Cash."

"Cash?"

"Cash."

"Cash . . ." Irving mumbled shaking his head.

"Is there a problem?" I inquired.

"Are you going to give me . . . like . . . dollar bills?"

"Yes, legal . . . like . . . tender, currency of the realm, dude." I produced four $1.00 bills; an amount I had calculated would slightly exceed the total cost of the purchase. I expected about $.35 change at the conclusion of the transaction.

Irving studied his computer inventory control system, certain that by applying himself, he would be able to overcome the Herculean difficulty created when I tendered such an unorthodox form of payment. His eyes now darted back and forth between computer screen and computer manual with the speed of a hummingbird's wings. Manual. Computer. Computer. Manual. He began to type a vast array of numbers into the system, as the battery's "best if used by" date drew closer and closer.

A line of impatient customers began to form behind me as Irving continued his input of boundless numerical data. He looked up from his toil long enough to apologize to those individuals gathering behind me who were now shifting their weight from foot to foot to promote blood flow. He pointed to me and rolled his eyes as he advised the assembled multitude of the reason for the temporary delay.

"He's paying with what?" they asked collectively.

"Cash!" The lady behind me announced.

"Probably an illegal alien," someone else volunteered.

"Hard to get a credit card, if your credit's no good," some octogenarian theorized. Several onlookers nodded in agreement.

I began to debate what might be my best course of action: return the batteries to the location from whence I had originally procured same; pay by credit card; or stand my ground. Irving interrupted my thoughts.

"OK, I think I did it. I think it'll take regular money now. I need the last four digits of your telephone number."

"I beg your pardon?" I responded.

"He probably don't have a phone," the lady behind me surmised. "Ya know, the bad credit."

"Oh great!" the octogenarian joined in. "We'll be here all damned day!"

"The last four digits of your telephone number, please."

"I never give out that information."

"And I'll also need your name and mailing address."

"I don't wish to give you that data, either. I just want to give you $4.00, get $.35 in change, and leave with my batteries."

"I can't access the computer without that information. If you had just used a credit card, all the data would have been relayed automatically."

"I don't necessarily want you, or anyone else behind me to know my name, my telephone number, or where I live. It's a question of privacy." As that last phrase passed from my lips, I began to fondly recall back when cash registers actually took cash. Was it that long ago that merchants actually took dollar bills and that privacy was a thing of great respect? I decided to take a stand for Truth, Justice, and the American Way. I refused to give personal stats, and I wasn't leaving without my batteries.

"Here's $4.00. Give me my change and a receipt."

"Can't do it without the data."

I decided to go on the offense. I spotted his first name on his identification tag. "Irving," I began, "how long have you worked here?"

"Six, maybe seven months."

"During that time period, how many people have you asked for this information?"

"Quite a few. About once a week, somebody still tries to pay with cash."

"How many of those cash-paying customers have refused to answer your questions?"

"You're the first!"

"Well, Irving . . . may I address you by your first name?"

"Uh . . . OK."

"Well, Irving, you have just met an alien from another solar system, here on sabbatical, and so I would prefer if no one knew I bought these four batteries. Space aliens never leave a paper trail of their inter-galactic activities."

Irving stared in awe. As a likely devotee of Star Wars, old and new, he understood the need for space alien privacy. "I'll get the manager."

A Mr. Hobbs soon appeared. How can someone become a manager of anything, and yet possess an uncanny resemblance to an anchovy staring up at me with dead eyes from its vantage point on a slice of pizza?

"May I help you?" he asked.

"Yes, Mr. Hobbs, I'd like to purchase these four batteries."

"Very well, please step over to our other counter." The crowd behind me let out a collective sigh of thanks.

"Will this be credit card or Radio Hut Credit Line?"

"Cash."

"Cash?"

"Cash."

"Hmmmm."

Mr. Hobbs began to study the batteries carefully as he deftly inputted significant numerical data into the computer.

"The last four digits of your telephone number, please."

"I'd prefer not to dispense that information. I just want to buy some batteries."

Hobbs wouldn't hear me. "And I'll need your name and mailing address."

"I don't give that information to strangers."

He stopped typing momentarily, and looked me in the face for the first time. Big lifeless anchovian eyes. "I beg your pardon?"

"That information is private."

"I can't access the computer without it. What's the big secret anyway?"

"It's an invasion of my privacy. I also don't plan on giving you my mother's maiden name, my blood type, or my shirt size."

"I see," Hobbs said.

I doubted that he did.

"This creates a slight glitch," he mused. "But I think we can get around it."

I was beginning to warm up to Hobbs, and could see, perhaps, how he had advanced to the rank of store manager. He might have possessed some characteristics similar to a fishy pizza topping, but he knew how to get the job done.

"WHAT IS YOUR NAME?" he coaxed rather intently.

"Uhhh . . . Hothouse, Ezekial Hothouse?" I confirmed, spelling both names carefully.

"That's a rather unusual name 'Ezekial,'" Hobbs noted.

"Yeah, the kids use to razz me in school all the time."

"Your mailing address?"

"Igloo #2, Antarctica."

"Zip code?"

"00300."

"Last four digits of the phone at the igloo?"

"1234."

The computer made a whirling noise, and spit out a receipt.

"Your batteries, and change, Mr. Hothouse," said Hobbs as he handed me the bag, a quarter, and a dime. "Have a nice day."

I remained elated through the first two intersections on the way out of the parking lot, until it suddenly occurred that I had, for the first time in my life, utilized an alias in a business transaction. One of the standard questions on the job application for Common Pleas Judge inquires if the applicant has ever utilized an alias. If ever I ran for judge, I would now have to explain why some postman froze to death trying to deliver catalogs in the far north to Igloo No.2.

Actually, the use of an alias in pursuit of privacy has been a cherished family trait, handed down for generations among my relatives. My father, an ardent believer in privacy, was an engineer who devoted his life to the pursuit of logical behavior. He felt that when you bought "more," you should pay "more," and when you bought "less," you should pay "less." Therefore, a pound of meat, under his theory of economics, should cost more than half a pound of meat.

He was surprised to learn that such was not the case when he tried to order an unlisted telephone number from the phone company to protect his privacy.

"Now, you understand, Mr. Fox, that an unlisted number costs slightly more than a listed number," the representative told my father.

"Why? You don't have to print my name in the telephone book. It should cost less. I want less service, not more. Who pays more for less?"

"Lots of people," she explained. "I just bought a car without a roof, and it cost me more."

My father decided further debate was useless.

"Then list my number under the name 'Ezekial Hothouse,' " he snapped as he spelled the name slowly. My father received the lower billing rate. He also received several calls each month for Ezekial. Dad reasoned it was a small price to pay for his privacy.

"I'll see that Zeke gets the message," he assured each caller.

CHAPTER NINETEEN: THE WEATHER CHANNEL

One day, they put a satellite in the sky, and everything changed overnight. It was as if we had collectively eaten the forbidden fruit, and now, possessed knowledge to which we should never have become privy.

It was only a matter of time after the first successful satellite launch that something as bizarre as the Weather "All Weather All The Time" Channel would come along. So much for "anything in moderation." In pre-weather-channel "storm's-a-brewin'-Ma" days, if it snowed, it snowed. Period. Somehow little kids miraculously found their way to school and home again with minimal fanfare.

Deciphering the information derived from satellites is not a science; it's an art. I'm not sure the staff at the Weather Channel has mastered it yet. Similar to when the president of the "Earth is Flat" society was shown the first pictures of the earth, having studied the photographs, he proudly proclaimed: "Looks flat to me!"

The smiling plastic-faced prognosticators of doom employed by the Weather Channel utilize five progressive cataclysmic degrees of impending apocalyptic catastrophe, designed to strike terror into their faithful viewers. There are "alerts," "watches," "advisories," "warnings," and "emergencies," depending upon the proximity, velocity, and size of the approaching threat. The terms can apply to anything — fog, snow, hail, typhoons, tidal waves, earthquakes, even sand storms. Had the Pharaoh of Egypt been watching the television prior to the arrival of Moses at the palace, he would have known about a potential "frog" alert before Moses had even opened his mouth.

How did the human race manage to exist before the Weather Channel anyway? Why is a frost advisory important? In truth, many times threatened dangers never materialize, and tomatoes vine-ripen, as intended. With few exceptions, almost nothing in life is certain, and the Weather Channel has, without apology, consistently proven that. (On second thought, there are two exceptions: 1. If a local political candidate running for office asks me for a contribution, and I give him money, he will lose. 2. The long-distance call I've been waiting for at the office will buzz in only at the precise moment I take a seat in the men's room.)

It was Mrs. Doppler calling. She wished to cancel her appointment again. "I have to reschedule," she apologized. "Apparently, the pain index is on the rise, so I'll be indoors until I hear otherwise."

It appears the good folks at the Weather Channel have concocted yet another means by which to scare anyone who doesn't own a satellite. Now daily prognostications regarding radiation (the sunburn index), pollen count (the asthma index), and changes in moisture content (the arthritic pain index) are displayed periodically on a map of the United States. Doomed is the viewer who resides in an area where all three of these artificial danger zones exist simultaneously.

My aged mother, like most octogenarians, became hooked on the Weather Channel. Once in a while, I'd have dinner at her house, and stay until it was time for her to retire.

"OK, Mom, it's time for you to go to bed," I would coax.

"Not yet — there's a high tide and low coastal flooding advisory for Tallahassee — and a blizzard warning in the Rockies."

The real problem with easy access to information is the psychological damage it can do. Invariably, Mom would fall asleep in front of her TV, twitching as she dreamed of flood waters rising above roof tops in Bethlehem and the resulting spread of infectious disease.

I never needed to watch the Weather Channel to find out the degree of pending danger. I had simply to study Mother's features. Were an "alert" announced, my Mother's poor posture would change perceptively. She would sit up straight, attentive to her surroundings, similar to a rabbit in the back yard that has stopped munching at the sight of a weed whacker.

A "watch" required that Mom begin her vigil at the window, yet, of course, stay close enough to the television to remain in contact with command central.

An "advisory" would prompt my Mother to begin transmission of critical weather-related information to friends and loved ones. She often left telephone messages with my secretary.

"Please tell him there's a fog advisory until noon," she would solemnly pronounce. "Don't let anyone in the office leave for lunch until it's safe to drive."

A "warning" was a whole different ball game. An upgrade to this level of intensity required immediate action. She would slowly but deliberately shuffle off to the grocery store, joining a throng of other like-minded elderly, similar to a scene from the movie "Night of the Living Dead." Soon the store's shelves would be depleted of (besides the usual milk, bread, and eggs) every bottle of prune juice and roll of toilet paper in stock. Upon my arrival at her home, I would note the additional inventory.

"Mom, a 16th container of prune juice?"

"Better safe than sorry, son," she would respond as she admired her neatly stacked rolls of toilet paper against the living room wall. "That's how much you know. There's a transitional dew point warning issued for tonight."

An "emergency" gave rise to drastic measures. If you thought the bank was dangerous on social security check day, you ain't seen nothing until the Weather Channel has gone to Stage Five. I have known grocery store cashiers to quit in fearful anticipation of the approaching onslaught. The same gray horde again descends in slow motion upon the supermarket, this time body slamming one another in the aisles for anything from pea soup to toilet brushes.

Mom, upon her return, carefully stocked her shelves with her newly acquired bounty. I examined a package or two.

"Mom, sardines?"

"It was the only thing left in aisle eight!"

I wanted to ask her about the tampons and the jawbreakers, but decided the same answer probably applied. The next day, I made it into the office, despite the "wind shear" alert. Mrs. Doppler never did reschedule her appointment. I guess a bad storm must have knocked out her cable.

CHAPTER TWENTY: PATENT LAW

My father, God rest his soul, was an avid viola player. A viola is different from a violin. As Victor Borge once explained, a viola burns longer.

I am a pianist, and as such, am aware of the jealousy unjustifiably harbored against my musical lot by stringed instrument players. There are two reasons for the hostility: We have Chopin; and generally, we have a hand free in mid-measure to turn sheet music. Violists and other stringed instrument players don't, and as a result have, through the centuries, resorted to all kinds of unsuccessful schemes to assist with the turning of pages during crescendos and andante fortissimos.

My father's short-term solution was to marry my mother. And bless her heart, despite years of Dad's coaching, she proved to be, at best, a mediocre page-turner. Sometimes, as she stood by my father's side as he played chamber music quartets hour after hour, she would, in the selfish act of breathing, move slightly, thus altering the light rays reaching the sheet music, which further served to annoy him. Sometimes, she turned the page too soon — or too late — both mortal sins. And on one unforgettable occasion his bow got stuck in her sleeve. He would have looked for someone else to marry, but by then they already had children.

There was only one foolproof solution, and Dad knew it: He would have to design a self-activated page-turning mechanism.

Other members of my father's amateur musicians association, The Bow Benders' Acoustical Society, said it couldn't be done. But they didn't know my father.

Dad wasn't just a mild-mannered chemical engineer who worked days for Bethlehem Steel. At night, upon his return home, he would secret himself in his garage-laboratory and dedicate himself to but one goal — designing the perfect individual page turner. He began to eat his meals there. About three months after the undertaking, we heard a cry one night from the garage. "It's alive . . . It's alive!"

Indeed, it was. My father had invented the prototype for the perfect page-turner. But how? A rod attached to the musician's forehead with little mechanical suction cups designed to grab each page? Foot-activated springs, gently resting behind each score sheet? Or was it simply easier to marry someone like my mother, and teach her how to stand motionless, breathless, for several hours?

It turns out, as Dad would explain impatiently, the "rod attached to the head" design was too cumbersome. Imagine 50 violinists at a Boston Pops concert with rods and suction cups projecting from their foreheads. Same for a complicated foot device. There wasn't enough room on the stage for the music stands, much less additional paraphernalia.

The answer was so simple, and yet, it had escaped everyone for centuries.

"Ass cheeks!" he triumphantly declared after rejoining us for dinner one night.

"Ass cheeks?" Mom repeated.

"Ass cheeks," he confirmed. "It's as if the buttocks were specifically designed for this job alone."

I felt my fanny. "Are you sure?" I asked.

My father would not be denied. I hadn't seen him so excited since the recent discovery of a lost Haydn concerto (or, as my father more aptly explained, "it wasn't really lost, it was just 'haydn' ").

"This is going to revolutionize viola playing as we know it!"

He pushed aside the baked lasagne, and placed upon the dining room table a three-page diagram he had drawn. It depicted the back view of a man seated in a chair, playing a viola. The seat of the musician's pants had been artistically removed, exposing his derriere. I was momentarily whisked back in time to my grade-school years, when Mom insisted I still wear the pajamas with the big rear trap door. What if the guys had found out? In any case, the artist had inserted a small bellows or pump no bigger than a thimble in the unlucky musician's hiney crack.

Illustrations No. 2 and No. 3 reflected the meat of the design. When the left and right ass cheeks were momentarily squeezed together, a small but sufficient volume of pressurized air was created. The air then flowed through a clear plastic tube hidden in the underwear of the musician, and ultimately passed to a delicate spider-like mechanism attached to each page of the musical score. The slender "fingers" of this ingenious contraption would, in sequence, turn just one page of music per hiney squeeze.

I was amazed, but not entirely convinced. "What if you're experiencing irritable bowel syndrome?" I theorized. "You might unwittingly find yourself looking at the next movement."

"Oh, sure, there are little kinks to be worked out," my father conceded, "but the concept is stronger than Bethlehem Steel itself! I'm going to start the patent process tomorrow."

And so he did. The Patent Office in Washington, D.C., granted him the exclusive right to manufacture and/or sell the device, since, unbelievable as it may sound, no one had previously thought of the idea.

He lovingly named the mechanism "The Fox-o-Pager." At the time of his death, he had corrected most of the major design problems that initially had hindered mass production. Chaffing of the buttocks, as an example, appeared, for the most part, to be under control. Of course, finding a willing test market was the hardest part of all. I sure was glad I was the piano player in the family.

CHAPTER TWENTY ONE: THE REPO MAN

"I want you to repossess that dirt bike," the anemic little federal credit union examiner confirmed as he squinted through spectacles with the density of ice cubes. Not to make a snap judgment, but I had just met the guy and I already disliked him and his artificial alligator briefcase.

"The bike cost just $350.00 brand new," I reasoned, "and that was last year — it's probably only worth about 50 bucks now."

"Attorney Fox," Mr. Gelsinger smiled knowingly, "you don't seem to understand. Your client, the federally insured credit union, loaned the debtor, Harold Finkbone, $300.00 to buy the bike. In return, Finkbone promised if the loan were to become delinquent, your client, the credit union, could take it back as security for the loan . . ."

"Yes, but . . ."

". . . Now the loan is two months in arrears. Finkbone has failed to voluntarily return the bike, and so you, as legal counsel for the credit union, are cloaked with the mantel of authority — you alone possess the ethical obligation and sacred duty to pursue repossession of the dirt bike with all due haste and efficiency at your disposal. That is the unequivocal mandate of the federal law."

"Yes, but . . ."

"To do anything less places your client in a most precarious position," Gelsinger began to threaten. "You see, Mr. Fox, should you refuse to comply, I may be forced to issue a report to my superiors in Washington, reflecting that more than 3 percent of the loans issued by this credit union are delinquent, and therefore, that immediate governmental takeover of the credit union appears warranted. We intend, come hell or high water, to send a strong message to other potential delinquents."

Interestingly enough, my client could not have been in better financial shape. The Municipal Employees Federal Credit Union possessed approximately $800,000.00 in assets, with just 30 outstanding loans, totaling about $100,000.00. Finkbone's account was the only delinquent file we had — everyone else was current.

"Listen, Gelsinger," I boasted. "Out of $800,000.00 in assets, and $100,000.00 in outstanding loans, all that is delinquent is this one small $350.00 loan. Have you gone 'mental'?"

Gelsinger started to stretch a bony finger toward the office telephone. I was beaten, and I knew it.

"OK," I agreed. "I'll find the damn bike."

"That's more like it," Gelsinger smiled.

With those words, the examiner closed his briefcase, and left the office, without so much as offering me an invitation to lunch.

The next day, I reluctantly consulted the yellow pages under "R." The only ad proclaiming expertise in the rather unusual vocation I sought read: "The Repo Man — We Snatch 'Em." I dialed the number.

"Hello. Big Al here. What's your problem?" a gruff, but friendly voice answered.

"Hello," I replied. "This is Larry Fox."

I paused. There was that funny feeling again — like I was about to make a mistake, but it was too late to turn back.

"Talk to me, Big Larry."

"Do you repossess vehicles?"

"Well I sure as hell don't teach ballet!"

Pity.

"I represent a local credit union and . . ."

"Say no more, Bub. Uncle Sam wants you to snatch the collateral, right?"

"Why . . . yes," I said.

"Not a problem. What do we got? Luxury sedan? Sport utility vehicle? Yacht?"

"A dirt bike. A 1-year-old motorized banana yellow dirt bike."

"Ooh . . . big time" Big Al teased. "Even so, that makes things slightly more complex."

"It does?"

"Yup. A 10-ton garbage truck would be easier to grab. It's the lack of a recorded title: airplanes, boats, and motorized dirt bikes don't always have 'em."

"I didn't know that."

"Yup. When we grab something with a registered title, like a Mack truck, it's real simple. We just look to see that the VIN on the vehicle matches the VIN on the title. Piece of cake."

I was listening — but not entirely convinced.

"Now with dirt bikes, there ain't no title, so it's hard to tell if we're taking the right one. That's where you come in."

"Me?"

"Yup. You gotta come along. If we snatch the wrong thing, guess who's responsible?"

Oh great. If some irate teen-aged dirt-bike geek didn't seek revenge and blow me away, I'd wind up in jail on theft charges! I related my concerns.

"Not to worry, Big Lar. Most people are bad shots. Besides, you'll be safe in the truck while we make the grab."

Every voice of reason began screaming from deep within my legalistic soul urging me to hang up the phone and give Gelsinger the keys to the front door of the credit union. However, a naughty voice, its origin uncertain, urged me to throw caution to the wind.

"Go for it, you dork," the devilish voice taunted. "Take a chance! Do something exciting! All you ever do is sit on your ass in your cushy office and play lawyer. Just once, take a walk on the wild side. Who knows, maybe something exciting will happen? Maybe someday you might write a book!"

"Who said that?" I called out, as I spun around the room. But no one was there. Just Big Al calling my name through the receiver.

"Big Lar, you still there? Earth to Big Lar?"

"I'm no dork," I corrected him.

"Uh . . . yeah . . . whatever you say, friend," Al assured me.

"I'm coming with you," I announced. "When do we make 'the snatch'?"

Al seemed pleased.

"Tomorrow. It's Saturday — the best time to find vehicles. Folks ain't using 'em to drive to work."

That reasoning surprised me. Who would use a dirt bike to commute to work? But Al was the professional. I bowed to his expertise.

"You work Saturdays?" he inquired.

"Sure."

"OK, so I'll pick you up at your office at 9:00 a.m. sharp. It's on the way." With those words, he hung up.

How did he know where my office was located? I would soon learn that Al knew how to find people the way some dogs sniff out hard drugs at Miami International.

One thing you could say about Al: He was punctual. The next morning, at 9:00 a.m. on the dot, a gigantic tow truck with a dangling metal hook large enough to ensnare Godzilla pulled up to the front of my office. The truck had two parallel rows of passenger seats, and that was certainly convenient, since Al had brought along a portly female companion. I squeezed in the back.

"Big Larry!" the smiling driver announced as he stuck out an immense hand. "I'm Big Al. And this here is Big George . . ."

"Hi, Big Larry," the woman said. George was wearing a green Girl Scout den mother's dress with a sash of merit badges slung across her broad shoulders.

"Nice to make your acquaintance," she beamed, exposing a sizeable gap where her two front teeth once reposed. After I shook her meaty hand, she fiddled in her purse and pulled out an 8-inch cigar, which she set aflame by striking a match across one of her badges.

"Well, like I said on the phone," Al continued, "this is certainly convenient. Our other jobs are right on the way."

Other jobs? Who said anything about other jobs? I only agreed to get shot or arrested on credit union business.

Big Al and Bigger George were giddy. We were about to retake a dump truck whose owner was delinquent on his lease. Stealing someone's dump truck, however, didn't appeal to me, so I scoped out escape routes from the back seat of the lumbering tow truck. But I couldn't see a thing through all of George's cigar smoke. I was trapped.

"Tharr she blows!" Al sang out from his front seat vantage point.

About 100 yards ahead on the right side of the street sat a blue dump truck, backed onto the middle of a private lawn. As we approached, the truck's logo came into focus: "Richard's Roofing." A towering wooden ladder extended from the bed of the dump truck to the top of a roof three stories high. Two men were throwing old shingles from the roof into the bed of the truck.

"Now we've got him!" Al shouted in celebration. Without hesitation, he slammed on the brakes, and gingerly backed up his truck until it touched the front of Richard's debt-encumbered vehicle. With the skill of a surgeon, he gave the dump truck's bumper one little tap, the minute force of which dislodged the wooden ladder, leaving the two workers stranded on the rooftop. Al and George calmly affixed the hook of their tow truck to the bumper of Richard's dump truck while I crouched down in the rear seat, hoping there were no witnesses.

"What the hell is this, you son of a bitch?" said one of the rooftop prisoners as he glared down on us.

Al looked skyward. "Hey, you scumbag" he began. "Watch your mouth. Next time, be sure to make your loan payments, and you won't be up a tree without a ladder!"

Al, George and I drove away, dragging poor Richard's dump truck behind us. I could still see the roofers gesturing in the distance when my curiosity got the better of me. How did these guys know where to find the roofers? Was George with the razor stubble really a Girl Scout den mother? How would Richard get off

155

the roof? And where were we going now? Al was all ears.

"Roofing permits are always posted at city hall. Hit or miss, we just scout out job sites," Al explained. "Today was a hit."

He and George slapped a high five.

"And don't worry, Lar. The roofers'll monkey down the drain pipes."

"As for me," George chimed in, "believe it or not, I'm no Girl Scout. As you'll soon see, this get-up's a decoy."

"Knowing where to find the vehicle is the hard part," Al added. "It's what separates the pros from the amateurs. As an example, next we're gonna bag a Cadillac limousine. We think it's at St. Ursula's Church."

"How would you know?"

"Wedding announcements," George said between cigar puffs. "The bum who owns the limo service has a daughter who is getting married today. He'll spare no expense, right? A wedding calls for the Caddy."

This duo just stranded two roofers three stories in the air. Did I really have to ask this next one?

"Would you guys actually crash a wedding and haul away the happy couple's limo?"

"Oh pleeease," George snarled. "You ain't no different from us. You're going to break some kid's heart today when we grab his dirt bike."

George had a point, a point he intended to pursue. "Now take this limousine joker. Somehow he's got the cash for a fancy reception hall, but he don't have enough money to pay the bank? Send in the violins."

"Touché," I admitted.

George continued. "Do I criticize attorneys who evict tenants for nonpayment of rent? No. The truth is that ours is a noble profession bent on Justice. If it weren't for us guys, most people would fail to fork over their due, and the whole economic structure of this great country would collapse overnight!"

With those words, Al began to applaud. Seconds later, St. Ursula's Church came into view.

A line of unmanned polished town cars, led by a large black Cadillac limousine, stood at the ready in front of the church. Dozens of pink and white pompons, bows and ribbons decorated the sides of the car, and a "Just Married" sign hung from the back. "So sweet," Al sighed, as he reached under his seat and extracted a flat metal device similar to a shoehorn.

"What's *that?*"

"A popper. It pops the locks on cars," Al said matter-of-factly as he stepped from the truck, and calmly walked toward his prey.

Al positioned himself at the Cadillac's left front door. With the speed and skill of a sardine assembly-line worker slicing fish heads and packing slimy bodies in olive oil, Al worked his magic. With a quick thrusting motion, he opened the door, hot-wired the car, and drove away with pompons and bows in tow — all in about 30 seconds.

George couldn't help but admire Al's cunning. In solemn recognition, he scratched himself under his dress, then let out a belch. "We're outta here," he said.

"Won't the limo driver report the car stolen?" I questioned, waving the salami fumes away.

"Sure he will," George explained as he slid over into the driver's seat. "But we always give the cops a heads-up and, of course, a nice donation to the annual policeman's ball. They, in turn, advise the snatchee."

Now there was a legal term I had not previously heard. Organ music began to fill the air, as ushers in black tuxedos flung the stately wooden church doors open.

"Weddings always make me cry," George confided, as we drove away with Richard's dump truck still in tow.

"Dirt bike time," George said with a renewed spark in his eye. We proceeded past the city limits into the countryside. "I think the Finkbones live down the next road."

Al, driving ahead of us in the repo-Cadillac, had done his homework. He located the Finkbones without hesitation. The dwelling consisted of a small farmhouse and barn. Al parked the Caddy by the side of the road, and rejoined us in the truck.

"The bike's probably in the barn," Al surmised again with the voice of experience. "I'll get it. You keep 'em distracted."

George stepped out of the truck, carrying a Girl Scout cookie catalog and order form. He adjusted his long brunette wig, smoothed his green dress and walked to the front door. Meanwhile, Al disappeared into the barn.

George knocked and an unsuspecting Mrs. Finkbone answered. Within minutes, George was taking a cookie order. Meanwhile, Al emerged from behind the barn, and threw the dirt bike deftly into the back of the tow truck.

George returned in a few minutes. "She ordered four dozen of the chocolate mint," he confirmed. "My favorite, too!"

Maybe straight-laced federal examiner Gelsinger was right after all. About one week later, the credit union received payment-in-full from the Finkbones. I arranged to have Al return the dirt bike, along with four dozen chocolate mint cookies. As for Richard the roofer, and the limousine owner, Al advised me that they, too, brought their accounts current, and never again made a late payment. Oh, and the newlyweds hitched a ride in another car to the reception. But rumor has it the caterer has yet to be paid.

CHAPTER TWENTY TWO: THE SECURITY GUARD

Horace Thorndike owned a group of five department stores, appropriately known as "Thorndikes." The business had been in his family for generations, and now, as the last heir at age 82, he owned the company outright, lock, stock, and brazier department.

Horace was a crusty old bird whose word was law to the 300 employees who labored on his behalf selling clothing, household goods, sporting equipment, and jewelry. He knew just about everyone by name, most of whom had been with the organization for years. The employees were loyal, as was the small-town clientele.

Horace, a retailer his entire life, had grown eccentric over the years. Despite his significant wealth, he continued to work every blessed day and arrived in a beat-up Buick station wagon, which he would dutifully park in the chief executive's designated spot. Though he was in the clothing business, you wouldn't know it. He wore paint-splattered shoes, old, ill-fitting work pants and a clashing shirt. This was all topped off by a cloth hat from which dangled a dozen fishing lures. Thusly attired, he would conduct the business of the day from his Spartan corporate office, after which he would visit each of his satellite stores, to confirm that all was ship-shape in the retail world. Thorndike liked his work and enjoyed being in charge.

I did the company's legal work, which was voluminous enough for me to spend one day a week at the corporate office. I would review with management pending employment issues, credit card questions, contractual negotiations, shipping problems, etc. In this manner, I quickly became acquainted with most of the staff.

One day, the head of personnel decided to hire an additional security guard for the main store. I was asked to check at the local police station that the applicant — a 19-year-old — had a clean record. The information on his employment application seemed accurate, and the kid was hired. He reported to work the next morning at 8:00 a.m. sharp, and began patrolling the store.

Mr. Thorndike came to work, too. He reviewed the income and expense statements for the previous day, signed a new maintenance contract, and then decided to take his usual tour of the main store. He started his inspection as always in the men's clothing department, where he personally removed from the racks six new suits that had recently arrived. He inspected the fabric, silently approved, and replaced the suits on the racks. Then he made his way to the lady's department, where he examined several purses. Next came housewares, where he fidgeted with some cooking utensils, and turned on a blender. But it was his conduct in the jewelry department that caused the new security guard, who had been secretly tailing Thorndike, to leap into action.

Thorndike attempted to try on a lady's necklace, a portion of which got caught on a fishing lure. As he attempted to free himself, the security guard grabbed him, and ushered him out the front door. Thorndike walked around the back of the store, and returned to his office by way of the executive's private elevator. I was working in the next room when I heard him call out.

"Did somebody hire a new security guard?"

"Yes Sir," I responded as I came into view at his office door. "He started this morning."

"What are we paying him?"

"Minimum wage," I responded.

"Give him a raise," Thorndike barked. "And tell him not to throw me out of my store anymore."

160

CHAPTER TWENTY THREE: ASHES TO ASHES

My mother considered herself to be something of an environmentalist. She had been appointed by some divine authority known only to her to ensure that the local creek, the "Monocacy," remained in pristine, unpolluted condition. People like my mother can be helpful if you're a fish or tadpole, since these aquatic inhabitants often find it difficult to attend water quality meetings.

"Monocacy" is an ancient Indian word meaning "throw me back, I'm too small." Each year the creek was stocked with imported trout. Fishermen would, at the designated hour, show up, catch the trout, look at them, and throw them back into the creek in disgust. I always found this behavior to be bizarre, as I would imagine did most of the fish.

One day my mother learned through the environmental grapevine that third parties were about to build a house next to the creek, and that soil and sedimentation control required to protect the creek had allegedly been overlooked. Mom ran down to the Monocacy to inspect for herself, and was horrified to find that a tractor was moving earth near her precious tributary. Suspicious of the worst, she had, as usual, come prepared. When the workers took their coffee break, she did what had proven to be successful in the past — she handcuffed her left hand to the tractor, while brandishing a sign in her right hand, calling for her fellow citizens to rally to the aid of her fish friends. This tactic usually proved to be more successful than scheduling a court hearing for injunctive relief. "That takes too long," she once told me. "And lawyers cost money."

During this time, both my mother and father were dying from cancer. With unselfish dignity, they asked if I would bring them to the undertaker so they could plan their respective funerals. I picked them up at their house, then assisted them as they painstakingly entered the funeral director's office, which was similar to a gambling casino: There were no windows, and no clocks. The mortician was aware that Mom and Dad had lost their health. He was unaware that their sense of humor was still intact. After the usual mortician pleasantries, he began his solemn inquiry with my father.

"What type of funeral did you have in mind?"

"Do I need one?"

"I beg your pardon?"

"I'd just like to be cremated. Do I need a funeral for that?"

The mortician hesitated as he searched for an appropriate answer.

"Not necessarily. Will there be a gathering of friends and family?"

"Around me? I'll be gone. If they show up, they'll have to start without me. I'll be late. Get it? The late Mr. Fox?"

The funeral director struggled to keep his well-practiced composure — he loosened his tie and brushed non-existent lint from his left sleeve. "Do you desire a casket?"

"Do I need one? I'd like to be cremated."

"Not necessarily. You can be transported to the crematorium without one."

"Good. I'll leave my luggage at home."

"Do you wish to be embalmed?"

"Do I need to be? I just want to be cremated, you know."

In a twist of irony, the mortician sought to hide his mortification.

"Not necessarily. You can be cremated without being embalmed."

162

He scanned his list again. "Do you have a favorite suit in which you wish to be dressed?"

"Do I need one? I was planning to be cremated, you know. I'd hate to ruin a good suit."

"No, I suppose you don't need one." The funeral director was vanquished. Options weren't a big thing with my Dad. Had he been purchasing a car from the undertaker, it probably would have been ordered without a radio, heater, or steering wheel.

"How are the cremains to be disposed?"

"The what?"

"Your ashes."

"Do I need them?"

"Not necessarily." Without asking what should be done with them, the funeral director completed the first form, and turned to my mother. Her answers weren't much different, although she did have a favorite dress, and opted for a gathering of friends and family after she passed away. The mortician took careful notes. He had come to the last question.

"How are the cremains to be disposed?"

"That's a good question," she began. She turned to me. "Would you like them?"

"Mom, I'm honored," I began, "but don't you think your ashes should be placed at a location near and dear to your heart?"

"That's true," she mused. She turned back to the funeral director. She thought for a moment, and then made an announcement. "The Monocacy Creek," she proclaimed. "I've given my life to its preservation. That's where I'd like my ashes to be spread."

It was my mother's dying wish, and so it was honored. I never asked her if she intended such an irony — polluting the creek with her last act on earth, but somehow I think the humor of the situation had not escaped her.

CHAPTER TWENTY FOUR:
MILITARY JUSTICE

Recently I completed my enlistment in the United States Coast Guard Reserve. Most of my adult life had been spent as a small-town attorney toiling in a small law office. But one weekend a month and two weeks in the summer, I'd instinctively grab my sea bag, and head for the New Jersey shore. There, at places like Cape May, Sandy Hook, Atlantic City, and Barnegat Light, a transformation took place: I became Petty Officer Fox, Yeoman 3rd class. In other words, I was a clerk typist working on enlistment contracts, pay records, medical histories, and other mundane paper work that, of course, keeps the military running. It felt good to be part of a world-wide team that served the country and saved lives.

The other branches of the armed service just aren't the same. The Marines are an interesting lot. They think they're tough, but that's because those wimps never experienced Coast Guard Boot Camp. The Marines profess to be "looking for a few good men," and from my limited experience, the search goes on. Not long ago, my Coast Guard Unit and a neighboring Naval Reserve Unit decided to engage in joint-weapons practice. A couple of marines showed up as well. Soon I found myself standing in a pistol firing line next to a 6-foot 4-inch marine dressed in battle fatigues. This guy looked like he ate attorneys for breakfast.

"Load for your first string of rapid fire," the senior chief weapons specialist ordered.

Each of the 15 enlisted men on the firing line simultaneously rammed a clip of five rounds into his semi-automatic .45-caliber handgun.

"Is the firing line ready? . . . The firing line is ready . . . Ready on the right . . . Ready on the left . . . Ready on the firing line . . . Commence firing!" And with those words, the senior chief blew a whistle, signifying we had 10 seconds to hit our separate silhouette paper targets depicting a sinister criminal. A heart outlined upon the criminal's chest was our primary target. Smoke and deafening automatic-weapon fire filled the air as hot, spent brass casings flew in all directions. I squeezed off my first five rounds in quick succession, as did the other shooters.

"Cease firing . . . Cease firing," the senior chief called out at the conclusion of the 10-second exercise. The senior chief pressed another control button, and as if by magic, the paper silhouettes came racing up to our shooting line, so that each participant might inspect his marksmanship — or lack thereof.

I did OK. Two of my shots hit the villain's shoulder, and the other three rounds were within a 10-inch radius of his belly button. The target of the marine next to me told a much more impressive story. All five of his rounds existed within a 3-inch cluster about two inches above the center of the paper victim's heart. I hadn't seen such consistent shooting in some time. Apparently I was more impressed than was the marine.

"Damn!" I heard him scold himself. "All my shots was too high."

"Load for your second string of rapid fire," the senior chief barked. "Is the firing line ready? . . . The firing line is ready . . . Ready on the right . . . Ready on the left . . . Ready on the firing line."

"Wait!" my marine neighbor yelled back, as he struggled to take off his left combat boot and to throw it next to the right one he had already yanked off. He quickly joined the firing line, now standing only in his socks.

"Stand fast . . . Stand fast . . . the firing line is not ready," the senior chief confirmed.

166

"What the hell you doin?" the senior chief asked Corporal Stocking Feet in astonishment.

"My last group was two inches too high. My combat boots got two inch soles. So I took 'em off to lower my next group," the marine explained with the logic of a Rhodes scholar. The senior chief just shook his head and walked away.

"You're certifiable," I muttered in the direction of the marine.

"I'm what?" the giant protested.

"You're an idiot!" I reiterated, forgetting I was insulting a brainless crack shot holding a loaded .45 less than three feet from my own chest.

"We'll see about that, little sailor boy," the marine grunted.

"Is the firing line now ready?" the senior chief called out. "Ready on the right . . . Ready on the left . . . Ready on the firing line. . . Commence firing!"

Smoke, brass casings, and the deafening report of multiple automatic gunfire poured forth from the firing line once again.

"Cease fire . . . Cease fire . . ." came the familiar command. Soon the silhouette targets raced back to the firing line to meet us. I
didn't even bother to look at my paper victim — it was the bootless marine's target that I wanted to see. He had placed a 3-inch cluster of five rounds in the center of the target's heart, about two inches below his first volley.

"Told ya!" the sharpshooter exclaimed. "You sailor boys don't know shit!"

It's tough to argue with success.

My first duty assignment after graduating from boot camp was at Coast Guard Station Atlantic City, New Jersey, a Search and Rescue (SAR) unit. Its 58 enlisted personnel were supervised by one officer, a Lieutenant, commonly referred to by his subordinates as "The Old Man." He was 29. This was his first command since his graduation from the Coast Guard Academy. I was assigned as his new clerk typist. His previous yeoman had just received orders to report to an icebreaker patrolling waters near Anchorage, Alaska.

Station Atlantic City was similar in appearance to most of the other Coast Guard SAR stations built in the 1950s and '60s. The main building sat like a large barn next to a smaller boat house. A third building served as a combination gymnasium, classroom, storage area, and overflow dormitory. Each building had bright white exterior siding, topped with a red slate roof. The main building, constructed in Cape Cod style, boasted dormers jutting out every few feet. A working cupola stood above the roof, used occasionally as a central lookout tower from which one could scan the open sea for ships in distress. Basically, it looked like a nautical Howard Johnson's restaurant.

All hands on board stood at the ready to respond to any maritime emergency. Similar to a fire station with floating fire trucks, Station Atlantic City possessed diesel-powered surf boats capable of withstanding the most demanding of weather conditions and unruly seas. Our sailors routinely risked their lives at a moment's notice, venturing out upon the high seas in 30 knot gales in 20° temperatures, fighting 8-foot waves. Each "coastie" had a proven track record for courage under fire, an attribute upon which his other shipmates could rely. There was one exception, however — me. As the new boy on the block, I was an unknown commodity. For the safety of the other coasties, my capacity to react under stress would have to be tested, for even lowly clerk typists were sometimes needed to serve on the surf boats.

The first test of my resolve would come only hours after my arrival. At 2030 hours I headed for the berthing area and found a rack in which to sleep. No one had the luxury of an assigned individual rack. Alternating shifts of coasties slept when and where they could, waiting for the next emergency siren to signal their race to the waiting surf boats moored just 300 feet away at the dock on the bay.

I placed my sea bag under an open rack, and fell exhausted into the waiting mattress which was still warm from some recently departed body. Soon the laughter of two debating sea gulls dancing on the roof lulled me to sleep — but not for long. Into the darkness of the berthing area crept a large figure, perhaps twice my size.

"You asleep, Ace?" my unidentified companion whispered.

"No."

"This here upper rack above you is the only one left. If I take it, you won't be happy. You want to switch?"

I was too dog tired, and told him so.

"Your funeral, Pal," the dark figure announced, as he slung himself effortlessly into the upper rack.

The giant, now reposing above me, must have tipped the scales at 250 pounds. The interconnected coil support system responded to his weight by sagging like a basket, leaving the giant's derriere within inches of my face. He had already begun to snore. If just one of those hundreds of coils, all manufactured by the lowest governmental bidder, gave out under the strain, the best I could hope for would be a full military burial at sea with three gun salute.

The giant was right. There were no other available racks. The station mascot, Booter a German Shepherd, was stretched out in the rack to the right, wrapped up in a ratty Coast Guard survival blanket he always dragged around with him. His rear paws twitched as he dreamed a Coast Guard mascot dream. And if the giant wasn't snoring, Booter was. The combination of the sagging coils, and the medley of intermittent human-canine snoring, convinced me to seek out more hospitable sleeping quarters. I reached for my duffel bag, and journeyed to the boat dock area.

The summer moon shone upon countless waves bobbing across the bay, that ended their silent journey at the water line of our 44-foot surf boat. The lapping sounds against the hull were hypnotic. I climbed up the ladder to the boat, aware that three racks for the injured existed in the lower deck area. I had finally found serene peace and quiet, the movement of the gentle waves soothing me to sleep. Deep sleep.

"Who the hell are you?" the voice behind the rocking flashlight screamed at me. "Identify yourself, stowaway!" the voice demanded again.

I wasn't thinking very clearly at the moment, so I remained silent.

"Get up, idiot!" he said. "Nobody sleeps on my boat during a sortie. You'll work like the rest of the crew!"

Sortie? Crew? I soon learned that I was 15 nautical miles out to sea, now part of the crew on a mission to investigate a small downed airplane. I was quickly put to work collecting floating wreckage from the ocean with a grappling hook. We returned to base at daybreak. The boatswainsmate, Chief Santiago, the man with the flashlight, finally found time to approach me.

"Who gave you permission to vacation on my surf boat?"

"Well, you see, Booter was snoring, and this really big guy . . ."

"Grab him!" Santiago ordered his second in command, machinist's mate Honeywell. Honeywell did as directed, while Santiago took possession of my legs.

"You know what we do with stowaways? We throw them in the bay," Santiago, now judge and jury, proclaimed, as he and Honeywell carried me back to the dock area. The rest of the five-man crew began to gather around us.

"Can you swim?"

"Yes," I said regretfully.

"That's too bad," Santiago laughed, as he and Honeywell began swinging me back and forth. In mere moments, I was in free-flight above the bay, after which I became immersed in it, my sentence having been carried out. I emerged from the depths and climbed up the dock ladder, looking like a drenched cat and smelling like the bay.

The test had begun. Could I stand up to Santiago and the rest of my shipmates, who were holding their sides laughing?

"Why don't you go cry to the Old Man?" Santiago teased.

This was part of the test. If I complained to the officer in charge, I'd never gain the respect of my shipmates. I told Santiago

170

I didn't need some baby-faced Lieutenant to protect me, as I turned and sloshed back to the station house in wet boots, hopeful I was still in time for breakfast.

Morning reveille had already sounded. My first administrative duty was to conduct an audit of each shipmate's service file. There were 32 individual documents I needed to find in chronological order of priority, starting with the sailor's original enlistment contract, and ending with the current orders to report to Station Atlantic City. In between were such necessities as the service member's weapons qualification certification, pay scale computation, Coast Guard school and training history, annual medical examination, confirmation of drug testing, and designated level of security clearance. I began my audit with enthusiasm that comes with a full breakfast, and dry clothes.

The previous yeoman had done a good job. The files were, for the most part, in order. I'd be able to tackle the pay records in just a day or two. However, one file did catch my attention: Santiago's records were looking a little thin.

It was Thursday's mail call that caught Santiago's attention — specifically a letter addressed to him from the Coast Guard Infirmary at Cape May. The letter contained orders requiring Santiago to report for immediate immunization against a rather large battery of diseases.

Santiago didn't waste any time barging into my office.

"What stowaway trespasses here without my authority?" I inquired.

"Cut the crap, Fox! I just received orders that I report tomorrow for 12 inoculations. That was done when I enlisted eight years ago. The proof is in my service jacket. Now you had better send back confirmation and tell that lunatic doctor this is a mistake!"

"I'm not so sure it is, Santiago. In point of fact, I'm the one who brought this problem to the attention of the good doctor."

"What problem?"

"Yours is the only service record in the entire station missing Form DD2-403A!"

"Form what?"

"Certification of inoculation against typhus, diphtheria, beriberi, malaria, measles, chicken pox, and some weird malady a Coastie caught while serving in the Amazon rain forest."

"I ain't going to the damn Amazon!"

"Never say never. The previous yeoman was just reassigned to Alaska; which reminds me, he's the only one who can probably explain the whereabouts of your DD2-403A."

"It wasn't missing until you got here, Fox!"

"Actually, it wasn't missing until I was thrown in the bay."

"Why, you lousy son of a —!"

"Why don't you go cry to the Old Man?"

By Friday, the shore patrol had arrived to involuntarily remove Santiago to the Cape May Infirmary. He left in about the same posture in which I recall entering the bay.

They call it the *infirmary*, because if you survive the medical treatment administered there, you will, consequently, feel infirm. I recall my first "medical" there. I donned one of those government-issue paper gowns. I was nervous and began to perspire. The gown disintegrated before my eyes.

I managed to survive the eye, ear, nose, and throat doc. Dr. Reemer, the proctologist, was a different story. Some nurse with little regard for anyone's modesty, led what was left of me and my vanishing gown into the next room. What immediately caught my attention were the damaged ceiling tiles directly above the examination table.

Dr. Reemer, who wore his wrist watch around his elbow, had the coldest hands I have ever felt, though he never did offer a handshake. "This won't hurt a bit," was the last thing I heard before I passed out. Next thing I remember two nurses were picking out acoustical ceiling tile from my hair.

To this very same infirmary the unwilling Santiago now journeyed. Thanks to my review of his file and heart-felt concern for his health, he would soon be safe from the ravages of diseases found worldwide.

"You've looked better," I told him upon his return to Station Atlantic City. His wheelchair rolled to a stop near the mess deck dining table. He was rather bloated, and still had trouble talking. It was the reaction to the beriberi shot that had done him in.

"I'll get you, Fox," Santiago mumbled through swollen lips.

"I hope not," I confirmed, "I'd hate to loose your DD2-403A again, along with your pay voucher."

Chief Santiago thought for a moment, then he smiled a painful smile. We became friends after that and no one ever threw me overboard again.

"NOW HEAR THIS!" the station loudspeaker bellowed. "NOW HEAR THIS! Petty Officer Fox: Report to the Captain's quarters on the double."

The Coast Guard, and the other lesser nautical service that followed, namely the U.S. Navy (yes, the Coast Guard, established by Alexander Hamilton, is older than the Navy) have, over the centuries, developed their own distinctive language. Instructions in "Coastie" lingo generally convey an air of immediacy. One rarely hears the announcement: "LATER HEAR THIS."

The opposite is, of course, true in the civilian sector. As an example, whenever I dine at a Pennsylvania restaurant, invariably at the conclusion of the meal, the waitress will inquire of me: "Will that be all, then?" My Coast Guard training cries out to respond, "No, that will be all, *now*."

I was taught how to speak Coastie at boot camp. Soon I was referring to floors as *decks*, halls as *passageways,* ceilings as *overheads,* bathrooms as *heads,* kitchens as *galleys,* bedrooms as *berthing areas,* and windows as *portals*. The Lieutenant, the highest ranking officer *on board* was addressed as *Captain*. The Coasties serving under him were his *crew,* composed of individual *souls on board*. Sailors turned *port* or *starboard*, rather than left or right. There were literally hundreds of nautical terms and phrases, from *standing watch,* to being granted *liberty.* I liked speaking Coastie, and soon became fluent. To this language have been added several dialects. One visiting seaman apprentice from Wisconsin once asked me where he could find the station *bubbler* — a water fountain.

As instructed, I reported to the Captain's quarters *on the double. On the single* would have been unacceptable. I knocked on the Old Man's hatch.

"Acknowledge yourself," the voice from within called out.

"Petty Officer Fox," I confirmed.

"Enter," came the directive. I did so, coming to immediate attention.

"At ease, sailor," the Old Man, perhaps 15 years my junior, instructed.

It's funny. Every time some officer instructed me to be *at ease*, I could never quite do it. On the contrary, I was always slightly nervous. And never once did I hear the opposite command: *Now Be Nervous*, a natural trait with which I could easily have complied.

I now faced the Captain, who was the embodiment of the Coast Guard, as was the Coast Guard the embodiment of the Captain. Indistinguishable. One.

From his Coast Guard spit-shined shoes, to his impeccably pleated pants; from his freshly pressed powder-blue shirt, to his Coast Guard Academy ring; from his regulation haircut, to the gold bars on his jacket, he oozed Coast Guard. Pictures of ships and shipmates decorated his aseptic office. A framed picture of a butterfly sitting on a flower would have been blasphemy and grounds for immediate court-martial.

"Fox, I've got an assignment for you."

"Aye, aye, Sir!"

"Coast Guard Headquarters, Washington, D.C., has sent us a urine drug-testing kit. I want you to administer the test to all souls on board." The Old Man pushed a large FedEx box across his desk.

I was honored that the Captain trusted me to carry out this most delicate of tasks. After all, Coasties worldwide were periodically called upon to "piss in the bottle." Someone needed to be there to catch it, so to speak. Yet, at the same time, I was hesitant to accept my new designation as the official Collector of the Samples.

"Captain, I've never done this before," I said, trying in vain to weasel out of the assignment.

"Done what? Pissed in a bottle? It's easy, son. You just have to concentrate! Read the instructions and make sure everyone else concentrates, too. That's all, sailor — dismissed!"

I took the Captain's box, turned, rolled my eyes like a 15-year-old, and made my way back to the administrative office, about to embark upon yet another exciting Coast Guard adventure.

I had never administered a drug-screening test before, so I opened the package with both horror and curiosity. The inner box was marked "Coast Guard Uniform Urinalysis Test Packet," or the well-known "CGUUTP" for short. What a coincidence that "CGUUTP" was also the sound some of the sailors would make when giving their samples.

I quickly located the official instructions that had been drafted by Coast Guard Admiral Clarence Clearwater, the man who oversaw urination for the entire nation. Upon completion of the test, all of the sample bottles were to be returned by overnight mail to Coast Guard Headquarters, Washington, D.C. to the attention of Clearwater, himself. I began to sense that I was part of a phenomenon bigger than a bottle of piss. It dawned on me that my collection of urine, and scores of others from around the nation, would be winging their way back to Washington by day's end. Soon Clearwater would be awash in urine.

The instructions seemed disarmingly simple.

1. Place urine in bottle.

2. Secure cap.

3. Affix social security ID.

4. Return samples via overnight courier.

There were 58 Coasties on board Station Atlantic City. Some

were down at the boat shop repairing an engine. Some were on patrol or standing radio watch. Some were preparing lunch in the galley, and some, who had served on night duty, were asleep in the berthing area. Two were painting a boat, and one was down in the laundry. I had to locate each sailor, and give him or her a bottle in which to . . .

The term "bottle" might well have been an exaggeration. As usual, the government was on one of its cost-cutting crusades. What better way to save money, than to procure a urine-collection container smaller than a thimble. As a result, as each sailor handed the diminutive bottle back to me, it was usually filled up, and then some. Soon I knew enough to retrieve the microscopic bottlettes, armed with a sponge, rubber gloves, and a squeegee.

I ran each container back to my work area, then frantically attempted to locate more victims as they moved about the station or returned from ocean patrol.

There were three females on board. I found one standing radio watch. I handed her the diminutive container.

"What the hell is this?"

I explained. She didn't believe me. Apparently, from her anatomical perspective, this sailor required a bottle with a more user-friendly design. She shoved the bottle into my chest and told me to get lost. The other two females on board were equally offended. There was some talk of sexual harassment. I decided I better confer with the Lieutenant.

"Enter," the Captain said as I knocked on his office door. I advised him of my urine-collection road blocks.

"Fox," the Old Man exclaimed with a surprised look. "You're a law school grad! Just follow the directions some other Coast Guard lawyer drafted."

"But you see, Sir, the small size of the bottle apparently precludes a woman from . . ."

The Captain interrupted me. "Fox, you graduated from Coast Guard Boot Camp, too, right?"

"Yes Sir, I did."

176

"And as part of that Boot Camp training, you were taught to carry out orders as best you could, to the best of your ability, no matter what the obstacle, right?"

"Yes Sir, that's what I learned."

"Good. Then carry on, Sailor. That will be all."

"Aye Aye," I affirmed as I exited his office and shut the door. The discussion had been quite helpful.

I made my way to the galley, the domain of our "S.S." — the station subsistence specialist. In the civilian world, he would be called *the cook.*

With 20 years under his belt as a Coastie, SS1 Emmanuel "Cookie" Figuero had seen it all. He had prepared pork chops on ice breakers, chicken pot pie on buoy tenders, and hamburgers on ocean-going patrol vessels. He had weathered gales and 20-foot waves. His imminent retirement would be a profound loss to us all. I liked Figuero, and he liked me. He spoke in his thick native accent.

"Wha' you want, Fox?" he asked.

"May I borrow a small funnel?"

"Why you wanta de small funnel?"

Best to take the direct approach. After all, it was *his* funnel. "Remember when you filled that bottle for me this morning?"

"Oh, yes. I no forget."

"Well, female types on board need a funnel so they can . . . in the bottle, too."

Figuero thought for a moment, went to a drawer, and produced a small funnel that appeared to be, from my rather limited knowledge, custom-designed for the job. He handed it over.

"You washa good before you bringa back. I needa later for monkeypie dessert."

"It will be sterilized," I promised my friend, since I, too, intended to eat dessert that evening. I began to exit the galley, confident that I could now complete my duty assignment. But Figuero had one more question.

"Which enda de funnel dey use?"

I stopped dead in my tracks. I hadn't given it an ounce of thought. "I guess I'll leave it up to them," I said. That explanation seemed adequate. Figuero went back to peeling potatoes.

It took three hours, but I succeeded in collecting all the urine samples. The bottles now sat on my desk glistening in the afternoon sunlight. I read the next step of the instructions. *Fasten the caps on the bottles.*

Right. Caps on bottles. Caps. *Caps?* Headquarters had failed to enclose the damn caps in the FedEx package! It was useless to bother the Lieutenant again. I didn't need a second lecture on the ideals instilled at Coast Guard Boot Camp. I decided to return to the galley, with the aseptic funnel in hand.

"You clean real good?" Cookie questioned, as he examined it with one eye shut.

"Spotless," I confirmed.

"OK. Now I make dessert." He turned to his large oven, but I had another favor to ask.

"Cookie, do you have any clear plastic food wrap?"

Figuero pointed to a nearby drawer. "You bringa back whada you don't use," he instructed. "The Coast Guard don't have lotsa de money, you know."

I promised Figuero I'd return the unused wrap, and proceeded back to my waiting bottles. I carefully enveloped each sample bottle in clear plastic food wrap, placed a small rubber band tightly near the opening, and affixed each sailor's pre-printed social security tag as directed. I placed all 58 bottles in the return overnight mailing carton, and gazed with pride at a job — fraught with both adversity and excess urine — well done. The 58 little containers seemed to be standing in symmetrical rows, at parade rest, ready to march to Washington, awaiting my command. I called FedEx, and in less time than it takes an eight-cup-a-day boatswainsmate java head to fill a five-centimeter-by-volume urine sample bottle, the fruits of my labors were winging their way back to Headquarters in Washington — straight to Admiral Clearwater himself.

Each Coast Guard Station possesses, among its sophisticated communications equipment, a "land line," a special telephone that can immediately connect the caller, in emergency situations, to any other Coast Guard facility world-wide. Thankfully, I had never seen that telephone in operation, since its primary purpose was for wartime transmission of urgent directives.

The morning after I sent my FedEx packet to Headquarters, the land line rang for the first time in recent history. The Lieutenant answered it on the first ring, convinced the Japanese had just re-bombed Pearl Harbor. With a look of confused panic, he handed me the telephone.

"It's Headquarters. Some Admiral is looking for you."

I slowly extended my hand, wondering if the telephone, which was painted red, might now be hot to the touch.

"Hello," I began . . ."Yes, this is Yeoman Fox."

It was Clearwater — Admiral Clearwater. He had just received my overnight package, the package in which some of the samples, maybe a majority, had, as he put it "leaked in transit." I told him about the missing caps. He responded that the situation would be remedied in the morning, when I would receive another FedEx package, so that I might complete the testing procedure. I thanked him for his time, and the land line again grew silent.

The next morning, a FedEx box from Coast Guard Headquarters, Washington, D.C., arrived, addressed to me. I had forewarned all my shipmates that a second urine testing had been ordered. They were not pleased, nor was Cookie, who again reluctantly released his funnel into my care.

I opened the box, and quickly found an instruction sheet. The only other enclosure was 58 airtight caps — without the bottles.

Almost every adventure encountered in the Coast Guard was designed to test one's resolve. Boot Camp, shooting with the Marines, rescue operations off the New Jersey Coast, even the collection of urine, measured a sailor's ability to overcome

179

adversity. Ironically, the most difficult test I was ever to encounter actually occurred before I was sworn in as an enlisted man. To be considered as a candidate for enlistment, I first had to pass the Coast Guard Intelligence Test, a three-hour written multiple answer examination designed to ascertain my IQ and level of general knowledge.

I reported to the Philadelphia Armed Forces Induction Center as scheduled. The test started promptly at 0700 hours. I arrived 15 minutes early, as did about two hundred other aspiring recruits. Most were trying to gain entry into the Army or the Marines. These branches of the service required that just 50% of test answers be correct in order to gain admission. Entry into the Coast Guard, on the other hand, was contingent upon correctly answering 90% of the questions. Stupid people were not to be guarding the coast.

I played it cool, but was actually apprehensive. As a recent law school graduate, I was painfully aware that I didn't possess any useable "general knowledge." While I could answer questions on Latin derivations and recite the "Rule Against Perpetuities," in reality, I had very little knowledge of any importance to the military or to anyone else for that matter.

At 0700 the test proctor strode into the room. She stood at about 6 feet 2 inches, had a stripe on her uniform like a sergeant or general or something, and she was, without a doubt, the one in charge. Two hundred seats painted in camouflaged patterns were positioned in perfect military rows. Like lemmings, we all instinctively took our places.

"I'm Corporal Roberts," she barked. "You will find a test booklet under each seat. First, you are to complete the preliminary information. Print your last name in space No. 1, your first name in space No. 2, and your middle name in space No. 3. Print your social security number in space No. 4, your mother's maiden name in space No. 5, and your blood type in space No. 6. If you don't have a middle name, a social security number, a mother, a mother with a maiden name, or any blood, then stand up now, and enter the room to your left. They will give you whatever you're missing, and you'll come back later and take the test."

Thirty or 40 potential test-takers stood up and shuffled off through the door to the room at the left, some to be assigned social security numbers; others to receive mothers with maiden names. Our corporal returned to her gun-metal gray podium, and continued with the instructions.

"Put the number of years of schooling you have completed in space No. 7. Kindergarten don't count. So, if you only got through first grade, put down the number one and so on. If you didn't ever go to no school, then stand up and enter the room to your left. They'll rectify that, too."

About 15 future marines stood up and filed through the door to the left. At first, I was stunned, but then thought to myself: did not the Wizard of Oz give the scarecrow a brain?

I looked at question No. 7, and began to count on my fingers. Let's see . . . high school, college, law school. I wrote "19" on the form. The rest was easier to complete, although some other candidates also proceeded through the door to the left when it was determined they had no known address, birth date, or heart beat. The rest of us passed our completed questionnaires forward to the proctor. She quickly thumbed through each form. Then she stopped short.

"Where is this 'Fox' idiot?" she stammered.

This was not the first time I had been singled out for ridicule while seated in the midst of a large crowd of strangers. I still, to this day, turn red when I think back to the credit union league clam bake.

There were more than 1,000 league members under the open-air pavilion at the Leesport Grove. Because there was always a large turnout for this event, the food had to be ordered and reserved in advance. For $17.50, one could purchase either a clam bake with lobster, or a clam bake with chicken. I don't like lobster, so I ordered chicken.

"You know, you can get lobster for the same price," the nice credit union lady apprised me as she took my check.

"I don't like lobster," I confessed.

The clam bake was six weeks later. We played badminton, threw horse shoes, drank birch beer, played cards and swatted flies. Then it was time to eat.

I never saw so many clams. They hung in bunches of little white nets that sagged from the additional weight of potatoes, corncobs, and lobster or chicken. Hundreds of meals were being cooked in gigantic steamers, after which they were handed out to the enthusiastic crowd according to specific reservation number. The entire operation ran like a Swiss clock — except for one thing — everyone but I had received a meal. And then it happened. The announcement came over the loudspeaker system — the same system that had just bellowed the badminton schedules and horse shoe finals.

"Lawrence Fox: Please report to the cook. Your chicken dinner is ready!"

Everyone simultaneously stopped chewing and looked up. You could have heard a clam shell drop. Some at the back of the pavilion slowly rose from their seats to spy the alien. Credit union members nearby began to whisper as they pointed in my direction with butter-sauce soaked fingers.

"Didn't he know he could get lobster for the same price?" I heard one disbelieving soul whisper to a friend.

I slithered forward to claim my ill-begotten meal, two thousand eyeballs watching my every move.

My mind left Leesport, and returned to Philadelphia. One hundred eyeballs now turned in my direction as the proctor demanded an explanation for my insolence.

"Fox, is it that difficult to follow instructions? You put a '19' for question No. 7 instead of a '1' or a '9'! Now which is it?"

This could be trouble, and I knew it. Any answer perceived as insubordinate could banish me to the world behind the door at the left — a door from which no one had yet returned. I decided to err on the side of caution.

"My mistake, Ma'am. It should be a '9.' I made it through ninth grade."

182

The proctor shook her head as she acknowledged my error and erased the number one. I would be permitted to take the test.

"Now class," she instructed, "this is a three-hour general knowledge test. The first part consists of 50 questions on electronics, followed by another 50 on mechanical aptitude, then 50 on mathematics, 50 on the use of shop tools, followed by 50 on your overall knowledge of military science."

Electronics? Shop Tools? I didn't know which end of a battery to stick in a flashlight! I was dog dirt.

"Now class, let's look at the first sample question." I silently began to read to myself:

The eagle on a naval officer's hat faces:

(A) to the left;

(B) to the right.

Was that if you were looking at the hat, or wearing it? I dared not ask. The door on the left laid in wait.

"Now class, open your test booklets to the next page, the Electronics Test, and commence answering the questions."

I looked at the first question:

1. Birds that sit on high tension wires don't get electrocuted because:

(A) their toes are insulated;

(B) they know the difference between "live" and "dead" wires;

(C) they don't complete an electrical circuit;

(D) all of the above;

(E) none of the above.

I scanned the page for other more plausible answers, but found none. I began to panic, but decided to calmly, rationally, think things through. Answer (A) was probably wrong, because, if memory serves, birds don't have toes. Actually, the entire question was suspect. Birds don't "sit" on high tension wires either since very few of them have buttocks.

On to the next question in "Electronic General Knowledge." I studied it carefully as I had learned to do in law school.

2. Which topic is most closely associated with electricity:

(A) *lawn mower;*
(B) *bathtub;*
(C) *Benjamin Franklin;*
(D) *all of the above;*
(E) *none of the above.*

I quickly looked around the room. Everyone else was unhesitatingly jotting down answers, while I remained confused and alone in this crowd of strangers. Did "lawn mower" refer to a person or a machine, and if the reference were to a machine, was the machine equipped with a battery, or was it an old rotary push-mower that had no electrical source?

"Bath tub" was obviously a trick answer. Lots of people have been electrocuted while sitting in one of those. "Benjamin Franklin" was suspect, too. Just like birds, Ol' Ben probably knew instinctively which wires on a kite were "live" or "dead." Come to think of it, maybe the answer was "all of the above," or on second thought, was it "none of the above"?

The other sections of the test proved to be just as taxing. Who knows how many quarts of oil go into a car radiator, or which box wrench is used to fix a box. I left the testing room three hours later, deflated, having resigned myself to the fact that I just wasn't Coast Guard material.

Two weeks later I received the official notice that I had passed. My marks in the "Shop Tools" portion of the test were so high, my recruiter proposed sending me to Coast Guard diesel mechanics school. I declined, ultimately developing extensive hands-on experience in "urine gathering."

TWENTY FIVE: HOME FOR THE HOLIDAYS

Last week my law office staff celebrated *Secretary's Day*. Six months prior to that was *Boss's Day*. These are two of the newer greeting card industry-created national holidays. There may well be more on the way, like *Significant Other Day* or *Cable Repairman Appreciation Day*. It's just a matter of time.

Just like sheep led to slaughter, each year I dutifully proceed to the drugstore and stumble about with other well-intentioned bosses. I rummage desperately for a card for each secretary, paralegal, and receptionist. I know when it's Secretary's Day, because this important national holiday is conveniently pre-printed in my appointment book. How did it get there?

Well, one day a very bright greeting card company executive was having lunch with his equally imaginative floral-business friend. Struck with pity for all hardworking secretaries world-wide, the two decided it would be swell to set aside one special day out of the year to show how much we appreciate these people in our lives. Boy did that idea grab hold. Now, you must either produce appropriate cards, flowers, and expensive luncheons or suffer the consequences. When I'd forget my wedding anniversary, or the wife's birthday, the worst that would happen was her sullen stares until I'd apologize and take her out to dinner. But forget Secretary's Day, and kiss goodbye that Superior Court brief with the Tuesday morning deadline.

By the way, the card people are now trying to figure out a better way to celebrate *President's Day*, but there's that unsolved problem: both Washington and Lincoln are dead, so it's always awkward sending either one of them a birthday card.

Of course the most celebrated national holiday of all is also the most breathtaking, and I don't even have to buy a card. It's *Super Bowl Sunday*. I look forward to it each year with longing and anticipation.

I don't watch televised sports. Life is too short. I never actually sat through an entire football game. Once I tried watching for 10 excruciating minutes. Big men in helmets and tights slammed into each other, willingly, as loud whistles were blown, at which time, like well-trained pets, they'd stop the play. Some of the Neanderthal participants, clearly just learning to walk erect, were rumored to have been paid more in their three-month playing season than I could expect to earn in a lifetime. When priorities of remuneration are that unbalanced, I prefer not to add to them by tuning in — not as long as there are cardinals fluttering near a bird feeder and other priceless visions upon which to dwell. And if you're wondering, yes, I was beat up a lot in grade school.

Nonetheless, Super Bowl Sunday is my most favorite national holiday. It's the one and only day of the year when most of the bullies carelessly maneuvering 18-wheelers on the highways are suddenly absent from view. I can stroll in the mall without being jostled, for there are no crowds — just a few of us non-football types — quietly shopping. We smile knowingly at each other, aware of our unspoken common bond. On this one great day, the best seats in any restaurant or theater are available without waiting. Conversation is more subdued, more relaxed. All that inane jabber about "The Big Game" has finally ceased, for all those boorish people are home in team logo sweatshirts swilling beer and yelling at their television sets, as they teach a new generation of ill-fated children how to usher in this most significant of events.

It surprises me that most of these pigskin enthusiasts don't even understand how the term "Super Bowl" arose. Actually, the phrase was initially coined by the hydrogeologist who first described the phenomenon that occurs when 50 million couch potatoes simultaneously arise at half-time, and flush 50 million toilets. We're all just lucky the resulting torrent doesn't cause the earth to leave its assigned orbit.

To those of us laboring within the rarified atmosphere of a law office, the scheduling of staff "time off" is an inexact science and is therefore subject to yearly renegotiation. That's because there are three separate and distinct forms of holidays:
fixed, quasi-permanent, and floaters.

Fixed Holidays occur without exception on the same calendar date each year. Examples are the Fourth of July, Christmas, and New Year's Day. If every holiday fell into this category, there would be no scheduling confusion, since unalterable consistency would prevail.

Quasi-permanent Holidays always fall on the specific day of a specific week, but not necessarily on the same yearly calendar date. Thanksgiving always takes place on the last Thursday of November. Super Bowl Sunday is always celebrated on the last Sunday of January.

Easter is a *floater*. It is calculated by determining the first Sunday after the first full moon after the spring equinox, a date first promulgated by the Council at Nicaea, which always met on "Council of Nicaea Day" — a floater.

As an attorney, I am wary of so-called unwritten laws, like the unwritten "holiday scheduling law" to which my office staff continuously refers. I don't know who enacted this law, or how it came to be honored. The law mandates that if a paid holiday could conceivably fall on a weekday, but instead falls on a Saturday or Sunday, the support staff may elect to take off the following Monday, so that the holiday isn't "lost."

Those Mondays always prove to be interesting. Since I have neither receptionist nor secretary, I answer the phone myself. The conversation always begins the same way:

"Hello, law offices."

"Counselor, you're answering your own phone?"

"Yes. The receptionist and secretary have the day off."

"Wow — I wish I worked for you! I could use a long weekend."

Me, too. There's no Justice — just office overhead.

CHAPTER TWENTY SIX: DINNER TO GO

Old Man Marsh lived on the other side of Kreidersville, on a farm his family had cultivated for three generations. Similar to Marsh, the farmhouse, barn, chicken coop, and hog shed all leaned a little to one side.

Marsh was a man of limited means, and certainly looked it. His denim overalls and work shirt had holes in them where the patches had fallen off, similar to some of the slate shingles missing from his farmhouse roof. He was at least 70-years-old, and didn't have anyone to help him other than Jake, the farmhand. In order to alleviate some of his economic burden, I agreed to accept farm produce and portions of animals, as payment for legal services rendered. His Last Will and Testament cost him three chickens and a sack of potatoes. I reviewed his new septic system application in trade for some pork chops, and two jars of honey.

Each April 15, I reported my unusual income to the Internal Revenue Service on Form 8212(R), the "Non-pecuniary Direct Sources of Income" voucher. One year, a plucked turkey and some rhubarb inched me into the next tax bracket. For a while, I thought about paying the IRS its due with a bag of chestnuts and a pumpkin, but could find no literature to support the idea. Besides, the last thing I needed was to be audited over some jack-o'-lantern.

Marsh apparently couldn't afford to have his refuse hauled away. What he couldn't burn, he threw in a pile behind the barn, a practice begun by his grandfather and continued by his father. Over the years, this collection of interconnected and rusting bedsprings, car parts, farm machinery and paint cans had grown to the point that the local zoning officer began to take notice. The mess was beginning to imitate the great pyramids of Egypt. Marsh received a certified letter demanding that he remove the mess, so he called me for advice.

When I got to the farm about 5:00 p.m., Marsh was doing what he always did after a hard day of work — he was sitting in one of the rocking chairs on his front porch, chewing tobacco.

"Howdie," he called out as I stepped from my car. I took my usual seat in the rocking chair next to his. He produced a packet of tobacco from under what was left of his shirt and flashed it in my direction.

"Chew?"

"No, thanks," I confirmed, but I appreciated his neighborly attitude. He didn't have much, but what he had he willingly shared. I decided to get down to business.

"Marshy..."

"What?" (chew, chew, spit)

"You've got to get rid of that pile of junk out back, or you'll be fined."

"It ain't mine — (spit) — I inherited it from grandpa and dad. I just added a few little items."

"Marshy, it's 38 feet high! It's a hazard. And that's not the only problem."

"What else?" (chew, chew, spit)

"You can't burn your garbage anymore. That's against the law, too. You've got to pay a garbage man to haul it away."

"Why? I've been burning stuff out back all my life..." (chew, spit, chew)

Jake, the farmhand, came out of the house and took his place in the third rocking chair. He was chewing, too.

"Hi, Jake," I began.

"Hey," (spit, chew, spit). Jake was a man of few words — fewer with a wad of chew in his mouth.

Just then a FedEx truck pulled up in front of the porch.

"They're finally here," (chew, chew, spit) Jake observed matter-of-factly.

"About time," (chew, chew, spit) Old Man Marsh confirmed.
The FedEx man approached with a rectangular cardboard box, the likes of which I had never seen before. The box measured approximately 5 by 4 feet, but was just one and a half inches deep. It looked like a large table top, minus the legs.

"We'd better open her up out back so they don't get loose or nothin!" Marsh said, as he and Jake lifted the box.

Dumbfounded, I decided to follow my client, and paid close attention so as not to step in the spotty trail of tobacco juice left behind. Marsh produced a pocket knife, and carefully cut the seal. He then placed the box on the ground, and pried opened the 5-foot wide lid. I looked inside. There stood 500 baby ducklings, each one about an inch high. They all stood upright at attention. One of the fuzzy creatures, no bigger than a Ping-Pong ball, obviously the sergeant, gave a command, and everyone began to exit the box in an orderly fashion. Upon seeing the back yard farm cats, the battalion headed double-time to the scrap heap, and disappeared under some long forgotten pieces of aluminum siding.

No one — not Marsh, Jake, or the ducklings — appeared mystified by this display. It was as if the ducklings had booked their FedEx flight some time ago, and had made accompanying reservations to vacation under the trash heap.

"What are you going to do with 500 ducklings?"

"Feed 'em, and sell 'em," Marsh said. I've got to make a living somehow."

Did people actually purchase ducks?

"Who would buy a duck?" I inquired.

"Son, come back in a month, and you'll see."

About a month later, the township zoning code officer sent Marsh a criminal citation for maintaining an illegal junk heap. Marsh asked me to stop by the farm to discuss his options. It was early evening when I arrived. Marsh and Jake were already in their assigned seats on the porch. But there was something new — a handwritten sign stuck on a stake in the front yard near the road. Its message to passing motorists was simple: "Live Ducks — $5.00 each."

I climbed up the porch steps and sat in my designated spot, the third rocking chair.

"Chew?" Marsh offered.

"No thanks, Marshy," I confirmed. "Hi, Jake."

"Hey," (chew, chew, spit).

"Am I going to jail?" Old Man Marsh questioned.

My response was interrupted by the screech of automobile brakes. The vehicle's two occupants quickly exited the car, and approached us. I was the only person without a protruding wad of tobacco stuffed in my mouth, so the driver directed his questions to me.

"You have duck? I buy." This proposal came from a polite man, whose new Mercedes and hand-tailored Armani suit clashed with the backdrop of Marsh's junk pile and dented spittoons.

"It's them Chinese Restaurant guys, again," I heard Jake mutter to himself.

"Here are the rules," Marsh announced to his guests. "The duck is $5.00 if you catch him; $10.00 if Jake here has to go git him."

"OK. We catch." The driver motioned to his associate who pulled a pole with attached net from the rear of their car. Seasoned shoppers. Marsh noticed my curiosity was getting the better of me.

"Go ahead around back and watch if you want," Marsh said. "Jake and I'll be here when you return."

I started to think about the legal liability of permitting a third party to run around a farm trying to net a duck. I wondered if Marsh's homeowner's insurance policy had a rider for commercial duck hunting on the premises.

"Do you have a lot of customers?" I questioned as I stood up. Marsh deferred to his farmhand.

"There's maybe three hundred of them birds left, wouldn't you say, Jake?"

"Yup." (chew, chew, spit)

The number of sales astounded me. "But your farm is on the back road to Kreidersville."

"Word spreads pretty fast. The Chinese restaurant owners are like people from Maine," Marsh explained. "Those folks there got to have their live lobsters. These folks here got to have their live ducks. It would probably be a whole lot simpler if they just offered canned Peking."

I walked to the back of the farmhouse. There I witnessed a flock of agitated ducks, scrambling for cover as the two men darted about yelling instructions to each other in Cantonese. One of them looked like he was on a butterfly-collecting expedition as he dashed back and forth with his raised net. Once in a while, the other unarmed hunter would dive for a duck that then managed to scamper just out of harm's way. Some lucky ducks stood around on the side lines, quacking encouragement like cheerleaders at the big game.

I had seen enough. I returned to the calm of the porch. Soon the men reappeared, holding a worried duck by the neck. The thrill of the catch radiated from their sweaty faces. The duck was protesting its innocence to anyone willing to listen. One man's Armani suit was now torn at the knee. The other man's shirt sleeve was missing a gold cuff link. The driver handed Marsh a $5.00 bill.

"Quack...quack....quack..." was all I could hear.

"Bird make noise," one of the hunters noted.

"We can fix that," Marsh said dully. "Jake, get the duck tape."

CHAPTER TWENTY SEVEN:
SAFETY FIRST

"It's them OSHA guys again!" Mack Stearman blurted out from across my conference room table. He was even more agitated than the previous time his trucking company was cited by OSHA, the Occupational Safety and Health Administration.

"Those no good bureaucrats have charged me with another $1,000.00 violation, and this time it ain't my fault. I won't pay it."

I studied the crumpled "Notice of Violation" letter Stearman had produced from his back pants pocket. The document outlined the charges filed against his company. Some governmental accident investigator alleged that one of Stearman's dump truck drivers had backed his vehicle to within 10-feet of another employee, and then, without warning, had emptied enough gravel on the victim to bury him up to his knees.

I was confused. "Don't all your trucks have warning devices that sound an intermittent alarm when a truck backs up?"

"Of course they do. OSHA made us install them so our employees would know when a truck traveling in reverse gear was approaching."

"Then how come the employee who was covered with gravel didn't realize the truck was proceeding in his direction?"

"Because OSHA also makes everyone wear ear protectors. As a result, nobody can hear the truck warning signals."

The irony of conflicting safety regulations took me back momentarily to my days as a laborer at the Bethlehem Steel Plant.

195

I was lucky enough to have secured summer employment there while attending college. The money was good; the hours weren't. I worked the graveyard shift. To this day I have no concept of what the place actually looked like. I arrived after dark, and left before daybreak. The few small light bulbs dangling several hundred feet above were caked with iron dust, giving the illusion of distant stars illuminating the artificial foundry sky. I couldn't see a thing. I might as well have been working inside a cow.

"Here's your stuff, kid," the guy at the equipment locker told me my first night on the job. A hard hat, goggles, gloves, ear protectors, metatarsal shoes, and a respirator.

"You got to wear all of this stuff on the job, kid. That's the rules," he advised me. I struggled to position each piece of armor somewhere on my body.

"Hey kid, you with me?" the foreman asked as I continued to fiddle with my respirator. I had finally come to the conclusion that it wasn't a protective cup, and that it was actually designed to straddle my face.

"Pick up any steel rods you find over here, and dump 'em in the big pile over there. Got it?"

"Yes Sir," I confirmed, as I walked in all my new gear like Frankenstein's monster toward my wheelbarrow, which I could no longer see, since the foundry press had just emitted another huge cloud of smoke and fumes, most of which now coated my SAFETY goggles. It was no surprise that I had failed to see the small descending metal stairway directly in my path.

It must have been the steel toe of my SAFETY shoes that first became wedged in the corrugated SAFETY surface of the second step. As I began to career downward in the dark, I instinctively grabbed for the corrugated metal SAFETY handrail, but my heavy duty SAFETY gloves were too large to grip anything. It was at this time that my SAFETY hard hat fell over my eyes, causing my SAFETY goggles to smash into my nose, thereby dislodging my SAFETY respirator, which jammed into my mouth. If only I had put the respirator where first I thought it belonged. I

196

was about to remove the respirator, but the overriding pain of the SAFETY side shields wedged in my eye sockets rendered me motionless. To complicate matters, my SAFETY ear protectors had now slid sideways across my face. I fell into a heap at the bottom of the stairs.

"You OK, kid?" the foreman asked a few minutes later, after he tripped over my limp body in the dark. The sting of pain from his SAFETY shoe digging into the back of my neck returned me to a state of consciousness.

"Yes Sir," I sputtered as I struggled to my feet.

"Well thank God you were wearing your SAFETY equipment," he said.

I told Stearman he ought to pay the fine. Better safe than sorry.

CHAPTER TWENTY EIGHT: THE LAW OF THE JUNGLE

I owed him my life despite the fact the minor operation didn't even require overnight admission in the hospital. Nonetheless, because of his quick evaluation and surgical skill, a potentially fatal condition had been correctly diagnosed and successfully treated. I would forever be in his debt, and I so advised him. Dr. Frounfelker sensed my unconditional gratitude, and soon we became friends.

I made it clear to my office staff that if ever the doctor were to call, I was to be found and interrupted, no matter what. If, for example, I were participating in oral argument before the United States Supreme Court, the nine justices would just have to wait while I took the doctor's call. After all, he saved my life — they didn't.

"It's Dr. Frounfelker calling," my secretary advised me. I stopped dictating an agreement of sale, and reached for the phone.

"Norman, it's good to hear your voice," I began.

"Thank you, Larry. How are you feeling?"

"Just fine, doctor, thanks to you."

"Good. Well, since things are a little hectic around here, I better get right to the point. Do you remember helping me last year with the financing on my house?"

"Certainly. You got a mortgage through Federal Financial."

"Right...well, interest rates have dropped a quarter point since then, so I was thinking...hold on just a minute, will you, Larry?"

"Sure."

The doctor was now addressing someone in close proximity to himself.

"Look, that one's a bleeder. Pass the hemostats. We gotta go back in before we can close...Larry, you still there?"

"Yes."

"Good. So I was thinking maybe now is the time to refinance, if the bank charges aren't too...hold on a minute again..."

"OK."

"You're going to have to cauterize before you close. Then apply the pressure dressing...You still there, Larry?"

Despite our initial disjointed phone call, I ultimately was successful in securing more favorable financing for my friend. He thanked me for my timely assistance. It would be another three weeks before I would hear from him again.

It was four o'clock in the afternoon. I was looking forward to a quiet Tuesday evening at home.

"It's Dr. Frounfelker calling," my secretary advised me. I reached for the telephone, always glad to hear from the man who saved my life.

"How are you, doctor?"

"I'm OK, Larry. Look, I'm in sort of a bind, so I wouldn't ask this favor unless I really needed the help. Are you doing anything special tonight?"

In hindsight, it might have been more prudent to have asked "Why?" before admitting I had no prior plans. But the doctor sounded rather desperate, and I did owe him my life. I could never adequately repay him.

"Doc, I'm free this evening. What can I do for you?"

"Oh, thank God. You're a real lifesaver."

Doc sure sounded relieved. Here, finally, was the chance to partially repay in some small way my debt to this man, in the space of just one ordinary Tuesday evening.

"Three weeks ago, my 7-year-old son won three free tickets

from some local radio station to tonight's Flyers ice hockey game at the Spectrum. I've never seen him so excited. Anyway, I promised I'd take him and his little friend to the game. It's all he's talked about for weeks. But I just received a message from the hospital. A patient's condition has deteriorated, and it looks like I need to operate again tonight. My best guess is that I'll be tied up for five, possibly six-hours. Will you take the two boys to the game?"

The Spectrum is a sports complex located 60 miles from here in South Philadelphia. At one time there was some benefit to having that metropolis situated in relative proximity to my home town. Philadelphia had a classical radio station that played the masterworks 24 hours a day. Bethlehem was in its broadcasting area. Then one day, without warning, somebody changed the radio station to a country western format. This meant that as far as I was concerned, Philadelphia no longer possessed a single redeeming quality — not one. Sure, one could argue the city boasts an award-winning symphony and the Art Museum, but one must actually travel to Philly to enjoy them, and nothing is worth that.

Ice hockey is about as appealing to me as football. I watched a hockey game once on television for five minutes. Men with sticks slid around on some ice, and once in a while, they would try to kill each other. This happens in Philadelphia more often than you'd think — both inside the Spectrum and out.

The doctor had repaired my body. Would I now permit the two boys' hearts to be broken?

"I would be pleased to take your son and his friend to the game, Doc. When do I pick them up?"

"They'll be ready in an hour — and thanks, Larry."

The ride into the City of Brotherly Love was relatively uneventful: two car fires and a 6-mile back-up on the Schuylkill Expressway. I paid extra to park my jalopy in an upscale, secured lot where the guards appeared interested in stealing just the more expensive cars. The two boys couldn't contain themselves as we made our way with the masses toward the ticket collectors. I handed the man our three tickets. He handed back the stubs.

"Section M," he called out. As he did, several fellow spectators turned around and stared. A few pointed fingers in our direction and whispered.

"You know how to get there?" the ticket collector inquired.

"No, actually I don't," I confessed.

"Take them stairs over there, and keep following the M arrows."

"The M arrows?" I repeated.

"The M arrows."

I had unwittingly entered the Land Of Oz, from which there was no escape without the ruby slippers. I heard myself begin to hum the song "We're Off to See the Wizard" as we hiked up a flight of stairs. The two boys led the way.

We had been climbing for some time, when I chanced to recall a documentary film I once saw regarding Sir Edmond Hillarie's successful ascension of Mount Everest. Like him, I set up a temporary base camp at the twelfth plateau. It was then that an official Spectrum guide, perhaps a Sherpa, appeared from out of nowhere.

"Your tickets, Bub?" the Sherpa asked. I handed him our stubs.

"Oh," he snickered. "Keep movin'. Your seats are in M."

"Where am I now?" I panted.

"Between D and E."

I grabbed what was left of the three "free" tickets issued by that stinking radio station, and pressed on.

The Spectrum has a geometrically designed symmetrical roof, supported by exposed interconnected steel beams. Located above the steel beams, but just slightly below the roof is Section M. The boys helped me find our assigned location: M33, M34, and M35. I sat down exhausted. They were exhilarated as they gazed downward into the amphitheater's abyss. As I looked below, past the naked steel beams, I noticed what appeared to be cumulus clouds floating beneath us. As they drifted away, a white sugar cube came into view. Little ants were beginning to scurry about over its surface.

"They've come out on the ice!" one of the kids screamed.

"Don't the view just take your breath away," a portly man sitting in M36 suggested. "Hi, I'm Butch." He extended his sticky hand.

"Hi, I'm Larry," I tentatively replied as I wiped my hand on my pants.

"Gary, I don't recall seeing you guys here before, and I should know 'cause I got a season pass to this here seat!" He actually appeared to be rather proud of that fact.

As a season ticket holder, it seemed that Butch had come prepared. He was transporting three separate gargantuan paper tubs, each one containing substances intended perhaps for human consumption. Burdened by the limitation of but two hands, the ensuing balancing act at such a high altitude and low oxygen level took some skill on his part. He had wedged one container precariously between his thighs, as he gingerly positioned the other containers on the floor in front of his seat, carefully placing his large feet, graced with Flyer logo sneakers, between the food and drink-laden vessels.

"Them vendors won't climb up this far," he said knowingly, "so I get most of my snacks before game time. That way, I don't miss nothin'." He flashed a self-congratulatory smile as he leaned back in his seat, the seat to which he laid claim for an entire season. "Want some candy, Barry?"

"I'm Larry, and no thank you." My curiosity overcame me, so I peeked into the bucket, and saw a gazillion multi-colored, hard as a rock, stick-in-your-teeth sugar pellets. Butch scooped up a few hundred translucent bee-bees with a well-practiced hand, and successfully guided most of them into his waiting mouth, similar to a whale feeding on plankton.

He then took off his "Flyers" jacket, thereby exposing his "Flyers" shirt. He decided to leave his "Flyers" hat balanced on his head. The tattoo on the back of his hand, a "Flyers" insignia, didn't come as much of a surprise. The removal of the jacket exposed more than just a team shirt, though. Around his neck were draped a portable television set and a pair of high-powered binoculars. He activated the TV and adjusted its tiny antenna. A Flyers' ice hockey game instantly popped up on the screen that Butch now studied to the exclusion of everything around him.

The portable television fascinated me. "May I ask you a question, Butch?

"Sure, Harry!"

"Why would you buy a season pass, and climb up here to nose-bleed Section M, just to watch the same game on a portable TV?"

"Well, Perry," he said, "there's nothing quite like being here at the actual game, taking it all in from the best seats in the house!"

"These are the best seats in the Spectrum?"

"Yup! Ya see, up here I get to enjoy the game three different times, for the price of one! First, I watch the action on TV. Next, there's the three second time delay..."

"Time delay...?"

"Yeah. It takes about three seconds for the sound of the crowd's reaction to reach up here. So after the Flyers score a goal, or bash somebody's skull in, I get to hear the actual cheer. By then the instant replay comes on the tube, so I get to see it all over again. Get it?"

"Yeah, I get it," I heard myself say.

Butch was feeding one end of a 12-foot licorice strand into his mouth. His cheeks looked like those of a chipmunk preparing for winter. I could only imagine his diet at home. My guess is that tofu garden burgers and fresh vegetables didn't top the list.

"Shhh. Here's the face-off," he said as he stared in a trance at the mini-TV. I gazed at the screen, too. An errant puck had just been shot into the face of a lady spectator, dislodging most of her teeth. About three seconds later, I heard the barbaric scream of the crowd. The instant replay then gave a "close up" of the unfortunate victim, capturing the moment when she first began to swallow the puck. A few seconds later, the play resumed.

"Nobody ever gets hit by a puck up...," Butch began to lecture, but other events now interrupted his narrative.

"Goal!" he screamed, as he jumped from his seat. His enthusiasm inadvertently caused his bucket of translucent candies to catapult over the protective handrail. The container and its contents careened downward, disappearing into the abyss below. As it hurtled toward earth, sugar-coated pellets showered onto hundreds, perhaps thousands of unsuspecting fans.

Butch's snacks were now gone, but he took to this sudden loss rather well. "Like I said, best seats in the house. You never get pelted by sticky candy up here....Well, that's the end of the first period," he announced. "I guess I'll go take a leak."

"Me, too," both boys chimed in.

Super. I decided we better follow Butch, who surely knew his way around the Spectrum. We descended three flights and moved into one hallway and then another until we were part of a torrent of humanity, each individual with but one thought in mind.

"No toilets up at M," I overheard our guide explain. "The water lines can't go that high."

Not even in Coast Guard Boot Camp had I ever seen a toilet facility approaching the expansive magnitude of this one. There were about 50 toilets lining the far wall, and the same number of urinals on the opposite side. We each joined one of 50 separate lines of dozens of urination-bound sports enthusiasts, most of whom had sucked down countless beers or sodas. Patience and bladder control, at this point, were virtues.

There were about 100 shuffling fans ahead of me in my line, with similar counts in the other 49 formations. In other words, I now stood in a tile room with around 5,000 other males waiting to relieve themselves.

Murphy's Law, of course. All the lines were zipping along, while mine was close to a standstill. Chronic prostate problems I thought. There was, nonetheless, some slight forward progress — just enough to convince me to remain in place, rather than to seek my fortune at the end of another line.

There were now just seven or eight fans between me and the

Holy Grail. My eyes were pooling — but success was nearly in my grasp. One inch and then another. Ultimately, there was just one dawdler left, but like the others before him, he appeared to be taking an inordinate amount of time to accomplish a relatively simple task. Finally he turned to leave. It was then that I saw the reason for the hold-up.

The urinal I was about to use was rather large — large enough, in fact, for a man to recline in. Such a man, indeed, had. Despite the nearby flushing sounds, I could actually hear him snoring. There he was: quite drunk, drenched in urine from head to toe, however surprisingly content. Drinking beer from a bucket can do that. I stood there staring at him, momentarily oblivious to the 100 agitated men assembled behind me.

"You done yet, Ace?" a man breathing three inches from behind my left ear inquired.

In point of fact, I had not yet started. Contrary to conventional wisdom, even though I practiced law, I had never actually pissed on anyone before.

The gentleman behind me stuck his fat chin over my shoulder once again, an act I found to be disconcerting. This time he had some advice.

"He's asleep. Thousands of guys have already pissed on him without a second thought. It's decision time, Buddy."

The Law Of The Jungle. Know why you never see a tiger or a gorilla walking around in the rain forest wearing bifocals? Because animals with bad eyes, no matter how colorful or smart, get eaten by the other animals with 20-20 vision. I had this very evening witnessed two commuters' cars dissolve in balls of flame. I watched three times as some lady, once in slow motion, lost most of her teeth. I stood by as Butch inadvertently showered untold numbers of people with indigestible candy. Was I now going to add to this lack of decorum? This lack of conduct? Was I about to become just another uncaring pissing predator in the Spectrum Jungle?

"Finished, Pal?" the man now leaning against my back asked.

What should I do? What would Miss Manners do? On second thought, she may never have stood in a line slowed by a sleeping drunk reclining in a urinal. Time was of the essence. I had to decide. Needless to say, I haven't been to the Spectrum since.

The next day was Wednesday, and all hell had broken loose at the office. Mrs. Menkoff had called twice to inquire why her delinquent tenant with the eight mysterious live-in relatives hadn't yet been evicted, and, by the way, was it legal for them to cook every meal with garlic? Someone else claiming to be the Police Benevolent Association also called, seeking a $200.00 donation, in return for which my name would appear as a sponsor on their summer picnic napkins. And for the second day in a row, my law partner had activated the central air conditioning after the secretaries had taken yet another secret vote to turn up the heat.

I decided a break in the action was warranted. Time to visit the men's room.   Safe at last in the quiet solitude of my single-seater john.

"Larry? I'm so sorry to interrupt."

It was my secretary calling my name from the other side of the door. I hadn't even unzipped...

"What!"

"Again, I'm sorry to interrupt, but you told me if Dr. Frounfelker were ever to call that..."

It was Norman — the same one who had lured me into the Spectrum disaster last night. He was probably calling during an operation to see if he could lower his mortgage rate another goddamn quarter of a percent. I paused for a moment. After all, this man had saved my life...

"Piss on him," I shouted through the door.